PERSPECTIVES FROM SOCIAL ECONOMICS

Series Editor:
Mark D. White, Chair and Professor in the Department of Philosophy at the College of Staten Island/CUNY

The Perspectives from Social Economics series incorporates an explicit ethical component into contemporary economic discussion of important policy and social issues, drawing on the approaches used by social economists around the world. It also allows social economists to develop their own frameworks and paradigms by exploring the philosophy and methodology of social economics in relation to orthodox and other heterodox approaches to economics. By furthering these goals, this series will expose a wider readership to the scholarship produced by social economists, and thereby promote the more inclusive viewpoints, especially as they concern ethical analyses of economic issues and methods.

Published by Palgrave Macmillan

Accepting the Invisible Hand: Market-Based Approaches to Social-Economic Problems
  Edited by Mark D. White

Consequences of Economic Downturn: Beyond the Usual Economics
  Edited by Martha A. Starr

Alternative Perspectives of a Good Society
  Edited by John Marangos

Exchange Entitlement Mapping: Theory and Evidence
  By Aurélie Charles

Approximating Prudence: Aristotelian Practical Wisdom and Economic Models of Choice
  By Andrew M. Yuengert

Freedom of Contract and Paternalism: Prospects and Limits of an Economic Approach
  By Péter Cserne

Toward a Good Society in the Twenty-First Century: Principles and Policies
  Edited by Nikolaos Karagiannis and John Marangos

Law and Social Economics: Essays in Ethical Values for Theory, Practice, and Policy
  Edited by Mark D. White

Law and Social Economics

Essays in Ethical Values for Theory, Practice, and Policy

Edited by

Mark D. White

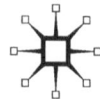

LAW AND SOCIAL ECONOMICS

Copyright © Mark D. White, 2015.

All rights reserved.

First published in 2015 by
PALGRAVE MACMILLAN®
in the United States—a division of St. Martin's Press LLC,
175 Fifth Avenue, New York, NY 10010.

Where this book is distributed in the UK, Europe and the rest of the world,
this is by Palgrave Macmillan, a division of Macmillan Publishers Limited,
registered in England, company number 785998, of Houndmills,
Basingstoke, Hampshire RG21 6XS.

Palgrave Macmillan is the global academic imprint of the above companies
and has companies and representatives throughout the world.

Palgrave® and Macmillan® are registered trademarks in the United States,
the United Kingdom, Europe and other countries.

ISBN: 978–1–137–44430–1

Library of Congress Cataloging-in-Publication Data

Law and social economics: essays in ethical values for theory,
practice, and policy / Edited by Mark D. White.
      p. cm.—(Perspectives from social economics)
      Includes bibliographical references and index.
      ISBN 978–1–137–44430–1 (hardback : alk. paper) 1. Law and
economics. 2. Economics—Sociological aspects. 3. Sociological
jurisprudence. I. White, Mark D., 1971– editor.

K487.E3L395 2015
340'.115—dc23   2014033001

A catalogue record of the book is available from the British Library.

Design by Newgen Knowledge Works (P) Ltd., Chennai, India.

First edition: March 2015

10 9 8 7 6 5 4 3 2 1

Contents

Contributors

Wayne Edwards is Associate Professor of Economics at the University of Nebraska Kearney. His research involves investigating the economic outcomes of rural populations, including issues of sovereignty, land rights, poverty, and service access.

Claire Finkelstein is the Algernon Biddle Professor of Law and Professor of Philosophy at the University of Pennsylvania. She writes at the intersection of moral and political philosophy and the law. She has published extensively in the areas of criminal law theory, moral and political philosophy as applied to legal questions, jurisprudence, and rational choice theory, and has recently begun writing on the law and ethics of war. One of her distinctive contributions is bringing philosophical rational choice theory to bear on legal theory. She has focused in recent years on the implications of Hobbes's political theory for substantive legal questions. She is currently finishing a book entitled *Contractarian Legal Theory* and is the editor (with Jens Ohlin and Andrew Altman) of a volume entitled *Targeted Killings: Law & Mortality in an Asymmetrical World* (Oxford University Press, 2012), and of *Hobbes on Law* (Ashgate, 2005). She is the Founder and Director of Penn's Center for Ethics and the Rule of Law and is currently the Chair of the Faculty Senate of the University of Pennsylvania.

Regina Gemignani is a PhD cultural anthropologist and a consultant with the World Bank. Her research interests include community development, gender and class inequities, public policy, and qualitative methodologies. She has conducted research in West and East Africa where she lived for extended periods of time, as well as in the United States. Her previous publications include *African Immigrant Religions in America* (coedited with Jacob K. Olupona) with New York University Press (2007).

David George is Emeritus Professor of Economics at La Salle University. He received a bachelor's degree in psychology from the

University of Michigan in 1969 and a PhD in Economics from Temple University in 1984. Professor George's main research interest has been the welfare implications of irrational choice that led to the publication of *Preference Pollution: How Markets Create the Desires We Dislike* (University of Michigan Press, 2001). A more recent interest has been changes in economic rhetoric in the popular press, which culminated *The Rhetoric of the Right: Language Change and the Spread of the Market*, published by Routledge Press in 2012. A longtime member of the Association for Social Economics, Professor George served as its president in 2005. He also serves on the boards of the *Review of Social Economy* and the *Journal of Socio-Economics*.

Robert M. LaJeunesse is Branch Chief of Expert Analysis at the Office of Federal Contact Compliance for the US Department of Labor. He provides expert analysis and testimony during the litigation of employment discrimination claims. After two years of service in the US Peace Corps, he obtained his PhD in economics from Colorado State University. His academic career included teaching appointments at SUNY-New Paltz and the University of Newcastle, Australia. His scholarly publications are primarily in the field of labor economics, including a monograph on the socioeconomic and ecological virtues of work time regulation, or what he calls the "social effort bargain."

Daniel MacDonald is Assistant Professor of Economics at California State University, San Bernardino. His research interests are in US economic history, labor economics, and law and economics. He is the recipient of the William Waters grant through the Association for Social Economics, and the Horvat-Vanek Prize through the International Association for the Economics of Participation. While completing his PhD at the University of Massachusetts Amherst (awarded in 2013), he was the Law and Society Graduate Fellow in the Department of Legal Studies.

Steven McMullen is Assistant Professor of Economics at Hope College. His research has focused on education and labor economics, environmental ethics, animal ethics, virtue ethics, and theology. His work has been published in *American Economic Journal: Economic Policy, Economics of Education Review, Journal of Animal Ethics*, and others. He is a fellow of the Oxford Centre for Animal Ethics and is currently working on a book on animals and economics.

Daniel Molling is a Research Associate at the Federal Reserve Bank of Kansas City, working in the macroeconomics department. His interests include macroeconomics, growth, development, urban economics, and education economics, as well as the intersection of ethics, theology, and economics. He graduated from Calvin College, where he worked at the Center for Social Research. His work with Steven McMullen was awarded the 2014 Warren Samuels Prize from the Association for Social Economics.

Osny da Silva Filho is a master's degree candidate in the University of São Paulo School of Law. He was Visiting Researcher in the University of California, Berkeley, and did part of his undergraduate studies in the Universities of Rome I and II. His current research concerns the role of legal scholarship in contract law, as well as the philosophical foundations of contemporary contract doctrine. He is currently a Researcher in the Fundação Getulio Vargas School of Law.

Stefano Solari is Associate Professor of Political Economy at the Department of Economics and Management of the University of Padua (Italy). His interests include the study of social economics with a particular focus on territoriality and social law from a broadly defined institutionalist perspective. Besides that, his research has concerned comparative capitalisms, with a particular focus on Southern Europe; the study of state-economy relationships; and the history and philosophy of political economy. His publications have appeared in *Review of Social Economy*, *International Journal of Social Economics*, *Journal of Economic Issues*, *European Journal of Public Policy*, and *European Journal of the History of Economic Thought*. He is book review editor of *History of Economic Thought and Policy* and scientific director of the Moressa Foundation (studies on migration).

Mark D. White is Professor and Chair of the Department of Philosophy at the College of Staten Island/CUNY, where he teaches courses in philosophy, law, and economics. He is the author of four books, including *Kantian Ethics and Economics: Autonomy, Dignity, and Character* (Stanford University Press, 2011) and *The Illusion of Well-Being: Economic Policymaking Based on Respect and Responsiveness* (Palgrave Macmillan, 2014), as well as over 40 journal articles and book chapters. He has also edited or coedited a number of books, including *The Thief of Time: Philosophical Essays on Procrastination* (with Chrisoula Andreou, Oxford University Press, 2010) and *Retributivism: Essays on Theory and Policy* (Oxford, 2011). He is the series editor of "Perspectives from Social Economics" for Palgrave Macmillan, and served as president of the Association for Social Economics in 2014.

Quentin Wodon is an Adviser in the Education Global Practice at the World Bank where he serves as cluster leader for equity, evaluation, resilience, and early childhood development. Previously, he managed the bank's unit working on faith and development, served as Lead Poverty Specialist for West and Central Africa, and as Economist/ Senior Economist in the Latin America region. Before joining the World Bank, he worked for Procter & Gamble, the International Movement ATD Fourth World, and the University of Namur, among others. He holds graduate degrees in business engineering, economics, and philosophy, and PhDs in economics and in theology and religious studies. He has published more than 350 books and articles, mostly on poverty and economic development.

Introduction

Mark D. White

Over the last half-century, the economic approach to law (or "law and economics") has become the most successful instance of "economic imperialism," the extension of the neoclassical economic paradigm to other fields of study. Given the shortcomings of that paradigm, however, law-and-economics misses much of the complexity of human choice and the ethical nature of the law that cannot be captured in terms of utility and efficiency alone. Social economics, on the other hand, emphasizes the importance of ethical values to economic theory, practice, and policy, but to date it has engaged very little with the law. Perhaps this is due to an antipathy to the economic imperialism of mainstream law-and-economics. After all, social economists tend to be methodological pluralists that respect the contributions and insights of other disciplines. But we do not have to "co-opt" the law in order to apply social economics thinking to problems involving the law or to incorporate legal aspects of the economy and society into our work. By its very nature, law is a social enterprise concerned with values such as justice, dignity, and equality, as well as efficiency—which is how social economists conceive of the economy itself. The economy and the law work together within a society to influence economic behavior and outcomes, and social economists need to acknowledge this interrelationship if we hope to understand the broader nature of the social economy we study.

In 1993, Steven Medema published his classic article "Is There Life beyond Efficiency? Elements of a Social Law and Economics" in the *Review of Social Economy,* in which he laid out various ways in which social economics could contribute to the economic analysis of law. In the 20 years since his article appeared, however, few have picked up his baton, much less run with it. This book is an attempt to rectify this situation and renew social economists' engagement with the law. Drawn from papers presented at meetings of the Association for Social Economics (at the Allied Social Science Association meetings) and the Law and Society Association, the essays contained in this volume explore several areas in which social economics and law can inform and enrich each other. Divided into theory and applications, the ten chapters in this volume, written by an international assortment of scholars from economics, philosophy, and law, employ a wide variety of approaches and methods to show how a more ethically nuanced approach to economics and the law can illuminate both and open up new avenues for studying social-economic behavior, policy, and outcomes in all their ethical *and* legal complexity.

On behalf on the contributors, I hope this volume inspires social economists to engage with the law in their work, introduces legal scholars to the unique advantages social economics can provide, and leads to greater cooperation between the two in the future.

*   *   *

I would like to thank the contributors to this volume, the rest of the presenters and attendants at the conference sessions at which they were presented, the Association for Social Economics and the Law and Society Association for hosting the sessions, and Leila Campoli and Sarah Lawrence at Palgrave Macmillan for their support and assistance in bringing this project together.

Part I

Foundations

Chapter 1

Toward a Contractarian Theory of Law

Claire Finkelstein

For roughly three decades, legal scholarship has been dominated by the application of mainstream economic theory to law.[1] The "law and economics" movement, as it is called, has had a substantial influence on nearly every domain of legal analysis. In addition to the financial subjects such as antitrust, bankruptcy, corporations, and tax law, economic analysis has become prevalent in basic fields such as contracts, torts, and property. It has even made inroads into subjects that have traditionally been noneconomic in nature, such as substantive criminal law.[2]

The infiltration of economic analysis into the traditional common law subjects is striking, in view of the fact that scholarship in these fields has long been characterized by philosophical and moral reasoning rather than economic. Legal philosophers schooled in ethics have historically found a natural field of application for their casuistical methods in the case-based, intuition-driven thinking in these fields. The so-called deontological approach to law, in contrast with the economic approach, does not represent a consistent set of theoretical commitments on the part of its proponents. Deontological theory includes, for example, both rights-based thinking about law, such as Ronald Dworkin's approach to legal interpretation, as well as "legal moralism," such as that associated with Lon Fuller or more recently by Michael S. Moore, and social practice theories such as that advanced by H. L. A. Hart.[3]

Painting with broad strokes, deontological accounts include most views that are non-consequentialist in nature. Despite the differences among such views, deontologists share a common approach to thinking about law, namely, a method known as "reflective equilibrium."[4] To approach a legal problem in reflective equilibrium means that intuitions drawn from particular cases in the fields under consideration

provide the raw data for the construction of ethical or jurispruden-
tial theories.[5] Reasoning from intuitions in reflective equilibrium is a
particularly good match for the style of reasoning in Anglo-American
adjudication, which is case-based, analogical reasoning. Yet this type
of reasoning has been unable to meet the demands of systematization
called for by legal doctrine, given the highly impressionistic and par-
ticularized nature of its approach. That, combined with the sense that
economic analysis can provide the rigor deontological theory lacks,
has drawn an increasing number of converts to economic analysis in
the legal academy. The split between the legal economists and the
moral theorists reflects the traditional division in moral philosophy
between utilitarians and deontologists. It is not surprising, therefore,
that this division has dominated legal theory as well.

In this chapter, I shall attempt to sketch the outlines of an alternative to both schools of thought, namely, a *contractarian* legal theory.
The appeal of a contractarian approach is that it holds out the promise
of an alternative to these two historic rivals and thus offers an end to
a long-standing stalemate in the legal literature. Furthermore, I shall
argue, the contractarian alternative allows legal theory to avoid the
major weaknesses of each of the traditional approaches while capturing the benefits of each. In this chapter, I hope to show that a
contractarian approach in the rationalistic tradition presents a viable
alternative to legal reasoning based on moral intuition, on the one
hand, and legal reasoning based on the idea of maximizing social
welfare, on the other.

The contractarian tradition takes as its starting point the same
assumption about the nature of human rationality as mainstream
economic analysis, namely that human beings are rational maximizers whose behavior is primarily determined by the payoffs to them.
Deontological reasoning starts from entirely different premises and
thus is difficult to see as a direct rival for the economic or the contractarian approaches to legal rules. My defense of the contractarian
approach is most naturally directed to those who share a commitment
to the rationalistic foundations that are common between mainstream
economic analysis and contractarianism, and it is primarily to these
scholars that the present defense of the contractarian approach will
be directed.

Economic Analysis and Rational Choice Analysis

The central assumptions of the law and economics movement can be
summed up with two theses, one descriptive and the other normative.

The descriptive thesis is that human beings are rational maximizers who reason instrumentally toward the attainment of their ends. This is the standard portrayal of rational agency in the economic tradition, one that is supposedly shared by contractarians as well, despite the differences between the economic and contractarian approaches. The normative thesis specifies the ultimate purpose of legal rules, namely, to maximize social utility, a view that law and economics inherits from the philosophical school of utilitarianism.

The use of economic methodology in legal analysis is not entirely new. Generic cost-benefit analysis has always occupied a place in American legal scholarship as well as in adjudication. In 1947, for example, Judge Learned Hand introduced the famous "Hand Formula" to American law in a case called *United States v. Carroll Towing*.[6] The Hand Formula is a test for determining whether the defendant has behaved negligently in a suit for civil damages, according to which the court is instructed to consider the following factors: the gravity of the resulting harm, discounted by the (ex ante) likelihood of the harm's occurring, which is weighed against the burden to the tortfeasor of taking adequate precautions against the occurrence of harm. If the burden of taking precautions is less costly than the discounted gravity of the evil caused by the failure to take precautions, the injurer should be deemed negligent for failing to take those precautions. The Hand Formula was thus an early foray into economic methodology as applied to law.[7]

But the great increase in popularity of economic analysis as applied to law is perhaps more accurately traced to two more recent scholarly breakthroughs. The first is Ronald Coase's famous article "The Problem of Social Cost."[8] In that article, Coase noticed what prior economists steeped in the Pigouvian model had not, namely that in the absence of transactions costs and adequate initial resources, it does not matter what allocation of rights and entitlements the law makes from the standpoint of efficiency: economic actors will buy and sell entitlements until the efficient allocation is reached. One implication of this observation is that efficiency is better served by the market than by legal regulation, as long as transactions costs can be kept sufficiently low. For this reason, it is preferable to regulate entitlements with a property rule than with a liability rule, as the former enables the market to reallocate entitlements in lieu of the legal system.

The second major publication is Richard Posner's *Economic Analysis of Law* in 1972. Prior to the release of this famous work, law and economics restricted its ambitions to demonstrating the utility of economic reasoning in a narrowly defined area of legal inquiry. Posner's book, however, expanded the ambition of modern law and economics to apply specific economic analysis to all areas of legal study, and also to the kind of meta-level analysis that provides the framework for legal debate. That ambition has in large part been fulfilled: in the past 30 years, most areas of study in law have been converted to explorations of economic concepts and models in an attempt to show that the central doctrinal puzzles in the law can be sensibly solved by the application of economic analysis. In this way, the systematicity of economic methodology has replaced intuition as the dominant mode of analysis in legal scholarship.

Along with this transformation has been the slow but steady change in judicial decision-making, by which judges now attend to arguments from efficiency to a much greater degree than they formerly did.[9] Cost-benefit analysis is often taken for granted as a sensible way to analyze competing considerations and values in just about any area of the law. In view of the impact of economic theory on the legal profession as a whole, it seems fair to say that non-economic theory has been largely relegated to the sidelines, both in academic writings and in potential impact on legal practice.

Several key features of mainstream economic reasoning as applied to law are worth noting: economic analysis is both reductionistic and revisionist. It is a reductionist philosophy in that it seeks to reduce the explanation for the development of legal doctrine to a single factor, namely the law's implicit attempt to create incentives for efficient behavior. As Posner has explained, legal economists see the common law as implicitly following the logic of efficiency, or what is treated as synonymous, the logic of social welfare maximization, even if judges, juries, and other legal actors do not consciously focus on maximizing social welfare as the goal of adjudication. As he writes, "Economics is the deep structure of the common law, and the doctrines of that law are the surface structure. The doctrines, understood in economic terms, form a coherent system for inducing people to behave efficiently, not only in explicit markets but across the whole range of social interactions."[10] Efficiency here is understood not as the idealized concept of Pareto efficiency, but rather in the more modest terms of Kaldor-Hicks efficiency.[11] The thought behind this descriptive claim is that the common law tends toward efficiency, regardless of its aims, because when judges and legislators focus on social welfare they will incidentally be promoting aggregate social wealth.[12] The reductionist tendency of law and economics, therefore, lies in the fact that it takes a purely descriptive stance toward existing law and finds nothing of normative interest in current or historical legal practice.

Paradoxically, however, law and economics is also radically revisionist: it seeks to reform existing legal institutions wholesale, based on its commitment to the view that the law should maximize social utility. Just as traditional utilitarian moral theory begins with the premise that there is only one item of value in the world, variously described as utility, pleasure, satisfaction, and so forth, economic analysis assumes that social welfare is the only item of value, and that the exclusive goal of any legal system ought therefore be to maximize it. Unlike the descriptive commitments of much writing on law and economics, this normative commitment is universally held among legal economists: the claim that legal systems ought to maximize social welfare is as fundamental to legal economists as the claim that individuals ought to maximize social utility is to utilitarians.

What is the explanation for the enthusiastic reception of economic reasoning in American jurisprudence? As George Fletcher writes,

> American law professors have been receptive to economic analysis…because the culture of American law has long had strong ties to utilitarian thought. The devotee of [law and economics] writes in a long line of theorists who think that all legal institutions should serve the interests of society…Any theory that can successfully obfuscate the difference between individual sovereignty in the market and the dominance of group interests in coercive decision making will surely gain a large number of followers.[13]

But the answer surely also lies in the drawbacks of deontological legal theory discussed earlier. First, unlike deontological approaches, economic methodology is often able to offer unambiguous recommendations on legal questions—recommendations that can be implemented and ultimately empirically evaluated according to the goals of economic theory. Noneconomic schools of thought have to date been unable to offer this kind of practical guidance. Economic approaches to substantive legal problems thus hold out the hope of removing legal reasoning and legal policymaking from the domain of moral intuition and placing it under the heading of *science*, where one might suppose one could have greater confidence in its dictates.[14]

Second, economic analysis relies on fairly sparse assumptions. The central theoretical commitment of law and economics is a widely accepted postulate about human nature, namely that human beings are rational maximizers who reason instrumentally toward the attainment of their ends. This is the standard portrayal of rational agency in the mainstream economic tradition, and one accepted by many different schools of thought in political and legal analysis.[15] When this assertion of psychological egoism is combined with the prescriptive thesis that the purpose of legal rules is to maximize social utility, a suggestion about the structure of legal rules emerges quite naturally: ideal legal rules alter payoffs to provide individuals with incentives to engage in actions that maximize social utility. This thesis is the point of intersection between economic analysis and utilitarianism. However, utilitarianism and law and economics have some significant differences, and understanding these differences will help to elucidate the challenges each faces. It will also help to highlight the advantages of a contractarian approach to law, given that it compares favorably to accounts that focus on social utility maximization.

Rational Agency and Normative Theory

Unlike legal economists, utilitarians are generally not committed to the economist's descriptive thesis about human nature. The early utilitarians, in particular, were clear about the fact that philosophical egoism, as it is sometimes called, does not provide a terribly good foundation for utilitarian moral theory. In his 1907 book *The Methods of Ethics,* for example, Henry Sidgwick wrote as follows:

> The difference...between the propositions (1) that each ought to seek his own happiness, and (2) that each ought to seek the happiness of all, is so obvious and glaring, that instead of dwelling upon it we seem rather called upon to explain how the two ever came to be confounded, or in any way included under one notion...Clearly, from the fact that every one actually does seek his own happiness we cannot conclude, as an immediate and obvious inference, that he ought to seek the happiness of other people.[16]

Bentham echoed the same theme when he suggested that the normative ideals of utilitarian theory could place considerable psychological strain on ordinary human beings, and that it might be difficult to cultivate an interest in actions that maximize social, as opposed to individual, welfare without a laborious education to prepare individuals for public life, an education the relevant government officials must direct. The education parents bestow on their children, for example, is only meant to assist government officials with their task of education. As he wrote:

> Indeed under a solicitous and attentive government, the ordinary preceptor, nay even the parent himself, is but a deputy, as it were, to the magistrate: whose controlling influence...dwells with a man to his

life's end. The effects of the peculiar power of the magistrate are seen more particularly in the influence it exerts over the quantum and bias of men's moral, religious, sympathetic, and antipathetic sensibilities. Under a well-constituted, or even under a well-administered though ill-constituted government, men's moral sensibility is commonly stronger, and their moral biases more conformable to the dictates of utility…their antipathetic biases more conformable to well-directed moral ones, more apt (in proportion) to be grounded on enlarged and sympathetic than on narrow and self-regarding affections, and accordingly, upon the whole, more conformable to the dictates of utility.[17]

But how to bring about this change in moral sensibilities? At the end of the day it is not necessary for individuals themselves to perceive the correctness of the principle of utility. The claim that utility is the highest, and indeed only, item of real value does not suggest anything about the psychological state of the bearer of that utility. Indeed, the utilitarian normative thesis does not require that subjects of a utilitarian regime even possess the *capacity* to reason in a maximizing way about their own utility. We could, for example, ask what the best life for cows would be and seek to maximize *their* utility by providing them with grassy fields and plenty of water. But we need not think cows capable of reasoning on their own behalf about what would maximize their own utility, much less of engaging in anything resembling instrumental reasoning. The only requirement that social utility theory imposes on the creatures to whom it applies is that they be capable of experiencing pleasure and pain, without which we could not meaningfully speak of their having any utility or well-being to maximize. Not coincidentally, therefore, utilitarian moral theory has long been preferred by those wishing to argue for the humane treatment of nonrational creatures. Peter Singer's arguments against factory farming and the meat industry is premised on a strict application of act-utilitarianism to animals.[18] Though the same conclusion is often argued for by way of extending the panoply of rights human beings are generally understood to have to our animal cousins, utilitarianism seems a more natural way of accomplishing the same end.

It follows, then, that the suggestion that human beings are rational maximizers with regard to their own welfare has nothing whatsoever to do with the normative claim that the right act or social plan is the one that most maximizes society's welfare. Indeed, individuals who are personal welfare maximizers are highly unlikely to care about whether their actions maximize *social* welfare. Personal welfare maximizers look out for themselves, and what serves the collective may or may not be consistent with the recommended course of action for the rational egoist. When this point is fully appreciated, rational egoism seems a particularly unlikely psychological foundation for philosophical utilitarianism as an ethical theory. For in order for the ideal of utilitarian moral theory to be met, human beings would most likely have to be *altruistic* in nature—the opposite of the narrowly conceived rational maximizers that mainstream economic theory standardly assumes.

The point can be made the other way round as well. When we make choices that maximize *social* utility, we usually end up sacrificing the welfare of some members of society for the sake of achieving greater gains for society overall. That is, maximizing social utility will usually result in some people faring worse while others—hopefully many others—fare better. Indeed, the most frequently heard criticisms of utilitarianism *depend* on this feature. First, it is often asserted that the central claim of utilitarianism, that the measure of right action is the one that maximizes society's welfare as a whole, makes utilitarianism *too demanding* as an ethical theory. It would not be ethical, for example, for me to brush my teeth or take a walk if there is another action I could perform that would increase social utility more than these self-serving actions would.

Second, utilitarianism does not seem able to account for a foundational concept of our legal and moral practices, namely, the idea that human beings have *rights*. This is for several reasons. An individual's assertion of a right he has may or may not serve to increase society's utility. There simply is no reason to suppose that the vindication of the rights of one person will have a positive effect on collective welfare even if it would have a positive effect on the welfare of the individual whose right it is. More complicated still, however, the notion of a right does not even appear to be strictly correlated with the concept of individual welfare. On some philosophical views, such as that of Immanuel Kant, a right is not fundamentally a welfare-based notion at all, but is instead a *claim* I may have that others do something or refrain from doing things, and any assertion of this claim may fail to realize what would be in my interest for them to do. Of course, the notion of a right is not entirely disconnected from the notion of individual welfare: individuals are generally thought of as the bearers of rights because these serve to protect the most essential elements of individual welfare. This does not mean, however, that any assertion of a right would serve to increase social utility. Finally, utilitarianism seems unable to explain why certain claims individuals have are not robust against considerations of social welfare. Rights must be respected, in other words, even if violating them would increase the overall calculation of social utility.

Implications for Legal Theory

What can we conclude from the disconnect between social utility and individual assertions of welfare? One implication is that the commitment of mainstream economists to psychological egoism stands in some tension with their simultaneous commitment to utilitarian normative theory, because individual maximizers would be unlikely to maximize their own personal welfare if social welfare maximization were the ultimate arbiter of desirable legal rules.

In the previous section we saw that following the normative theory of social maximization is unlikely to maximize the interests of the individual rational agents. But what about the converse? Might not rational maximizers be brought to care about the welfare of society as a whole, so that the individual theory of value and the social theory of value coincide? That is, might it be possible, as Bentham long ago suggested, to teach individuals, who are otherwise rational, that the best thing for their personal utility is to select their actions in a way that maximizes the welfare of society as a whole? The answer is that if it does not, in fact, maximize social utility for me to choose actions that are consistent with my maximizing my own welfare, I surely cannot be taught to care about social welfare against my better judgment. That is, I cannot be taught to care about social welfare unless I am just irrational enough to forsake my own maximizing (in the mainstream view).

It follows, then, that if agents are individually rational in this sense, it is highly unlikely they would be social welfare maximizers. This suggests that not only does rational actor psychology not entail the utilitarian theory of value, but that the two are actually in some tension with one another. The tension stems from the fact, as stated earlier, that when we maximize social utility, we usually end up sacrificing the welfare of some members of society for the sake of achieving greater gains in social welfare overall. That is, maximizing social utility will result in some people faring worse than they otherwise would, even though other people will fare better. This is another central reason why the normative theory of utilitarianism has been so controversial since its inception: in the process of maximizing social utility, we must often override considerations of individual welfare, including considerations moral philosophers think of as protected by the notion of a *right*. As has often been noted, traditional utilitarianism is indifferent to distributions of utility that do not affect total value.[19]

An important conclusion can be drawn from the foregoing discussion: the theory of individual rationality to which mainstream economists are committed is neither entailed by nor entails the theory of value that economists inherited from the early utilitarians. There is, in fact, no intrinsic relation between personal utility maximization and social utility maximization. And this suggests that a theory like law and economics that subscribes to psychological egoism at the same time that it assumes utilitarian normative theory has some explaining to do: it must explain why the normative theory it inherits from the utilitarian tradition is not fundamentally at odds with its assumption about individual human psychology.

To be sure, legal economists do have at least the rough outlines of an answer that reconciles the two, although they rarely (if ever) state the point explicitly. But if one were to press them hard they might say something like the following. The gap between the goal of social welfare maximization and individual instrumental rationality is admittedly real and is regrettable. The gap, however, can easily be closed with the judicious use of legal rules. When legal rules are correctly crafted, they will ensure that when individual actors maximize their own utility, they will be maximizing social utility as well. Legal rules are able to accomplish this convergence of personal and social utility by restricting individual maximizing within socially useful bounds. Thus, if wheat farming is more socially beneficial than gambling, laws should increase incentives to grow wheat and decrease incentives to gamble. Assuming that legal subjects are rational agents, they will respond to such incentives as intended, and the socially desirable balance between wheat farming and gambling can be achieved. Nevertheless, this thesis about the function of law leaves many questions unanswered, and as it turns out, it cannot supply an answer to our question about value without fuller elaboration.

For instance, what is the justification for imposing a legal system guided by the utilitarian theory of value on individuals who do not themselves perceive their own good as maximized in such a system? Does the legal economist suppose, for example, that individual agents would *select* welfare maximization as the overriding goal of the legal system? Given what we have just said, it seems unlikely that individuals *would* select this as the goal of the legal system. The question then urgently arises whether the legal economist has a way of justifying the imposition of a legal regime on rational individuals living under that regime that overrides the probable lack of consent. More in keeping with the economist's assumption of individual rationality is the suggestion that the best, most justified, most preferred legal regime for such agents would be the regime that *they themselves* would select, despite the fact that such a regime might have a lower level of total social utility than the one the economist might pick.

Legal economists do have at least the beginning of a response to this point. First, they maintain in effect that because there is no higher good than utility (or what they interchangeably call "welfare"), a regime with lower total welfare could *not* be intrinsically better than a regime with higher total welfare. It is thus a kind of definitional stop. As Louis Kaplow and Steven Shavell have recently put the point:

> Our central claim is that the welfare-based normative approach should be exclusively employed in evaluating legal rules. That is, legal rules should be selected entirely with respect to their effects on the well-being of individuals in society. This position implies that notions of fairness like corrective justice should receive no independent weight in the assessment of legal rules.[20]

Their argument for ignoring considerations of fairness is very simple, and it "derives from the fundamental characteristic of fairness-based assessment…As a consequence, satisfying notions of fairness can make individuals worse off, that is, reduce social welfare."[21] Kaplow and Shavell claim that a regime with greater total utility is *always* to be preferred over a regime with less total utility, since it is always possible to make some better off and none worse off in the regime with the higher total utility simply by having the winners compensate the losers. The system with the higher total utility is Kaldor-Hicks efficient, and in such a regime everyone is at least *potentially* better off than the alternative, contrasted with a regime that is a Pareto improvement, a more demanding standard by which no one can be made worse off by a change. For this reason, legal economists side with maximization over distribution, and will always prefer the regime with more, rather than less, total utility.

From the standpoint of individual rationality, however, these arguments beg the question. First, no single individual values welfare per se; each individual values only his or her welfare. And an increase in the welfare of any particular individual is precisely what maximizing social welfare does *not* guarantee. Second, there is a significant gap between *could compensate* and *would compensate* in the appeal to Kaldor-Hicks efficiency. Legal systems that produce high total utility and grossly unequal distributions for their subjects will not readily garner the assent of the winners to redistribute to the losers without having mechanisms of redistribution already firmly in place as part and parcel of the agreement. Because such mechanisms of redistribution may be costly, and therefore can also detract from the total social utility, it is clear that rational agents are willing to absorb some costs in utility for the sake of protecting their individual positions relative to others, despite an overall reduction in a possible scheme of social utility.

Contractarian Legal Theory

If rational agents would not, on balance, select the utility maximizing regime as their preferred legal system, what sort of legal system *would* they regard as most respectful of individual preferences? It is my contention that beginning with the same theory of individual rationality assumed by legal economists, the more compelling and natural form of legal justification would be contractarian rather than utilitarian. That is, *contractarianism*, not utilitarianism, is the political theory implied by the assumption that human beings are rational maximizers. Moreover, this thesis itself has a consensual justification, namely that contractarianism is the *normative* theory that rational maximizers would endorse to guide the adoption of legal rules. Contractarianism nevertheless remains almost wholly unexplored in legal theory, despite the popularity of rational actor theory in the law, and despite the prominence of contractarianism in political philosophy as well.[22]

Contractarian theories regard the major rules and institutions of civil society as legitimate insofar as they can be thought of as in some way based on, or justified by, an agreement among the individuals who must submit to their authority. There are roughly speaking two strains in the contractarian tradition: what we might call "normative contractarianism," on the one hand, and "rational choice contractarianism," on the other. Normative contractarianism descends from Immanuel Kant but it covers a variety of views, the most influential of which in recent years has been that of the late John Rawls. According to Rawls, we can best discern intuitions about justice in a liberal society by asking what principles of justice would be selected by individuals entering into a foundational political agreement with one another, prior to the existence of any actual social institutions. Rawls assumes that in this "original position," individuals would select basic principles behind a so-called veil of ignorance, meaning that they choose without any knowledge of the particular circumstances in which they will find themselves in society or what their personal characteristics will be.[23] Rational choice contractarianism, by contrast, descends from Thomas Hobbes and asks what form of social organization rational agents seeking to maximize their own welfare would choose to improve their positions relative to their presocial baselines.[24] To the extent the contractarian tradition has been brought into legal theory, it has been almost entirely of the former, normative variety.[25]

Legal theorists have tentatively explored the application of Rawlsian-style contractarianism to international law, punishment theory, contract law, and even to bankruptcy. The more straightforward project for the present work would have been the application of normative contractarianism to problems in legal theory, but it is quite deliberately my purpose to eschew this branch of contractarianism in favor of its rationalistic cousin, for the following crucial reason. What makes contractarianism a significant and potentially superior alternative to utilitarian and deontological legal theories is, at least in principle, that contractarian theories seek their justificatory force in the consent of legal subjects. What this implies is that the legal institutions that appear to be coercively organized are in fact the product of choice on the part of the governed. The more voluntary a legal organization, the easier it becomes to justify the imposition of the rules of that institution on presently unwilling subjects. Normative contractarian accounts, however, do not preserve the voluntariness of legal or other political arrangements. The notion of a contract plays a very different role in such accounts. Normative contractarian accounts seek to show legal or political institutions as *fair* rather than as consensual.

As Rawls writes, "Our social situation is just if it is such that by [a] sequence of hypothetical agreements we would have contracted into the general system of rules which defines it."[26] He continues:

> No society can, of course, be a scheme of cooperation which men enter voluntarily in a literal sense; each person finds himself placed at birth in some particular position in some particular society, and the nature of this position materially affects his life prospects. Yet a society satisfying the principles of justice as fairness comes as close as a society can to being a voluntary scheme, for it meets the principles which free and equal persons would assent to under circumstances that are fair. In this sense its members are autonomous *and the obligations they recognize self-imposed.*[27]

The sense in which obligations are "self-imposed" in Rawls's scheme is highly attenuated, because the original position involves neither actual agents nor actual agreement, and so a fortiori the individuals restrained by a system of justice have not in any sense agreed to be so restrained.[28] Rawls conceives of the members of the original position as the "representatives" of flesh and blood human beings, explaining why their "consent" could be binding for real legal subjects. As is often pointed out by critics of Rawls's original position, however, it is not clear why hypothetical creatures lacking in all human characteristics should be thought of as representing actual persons.[29] Rawls responds that actual representation of flesh and blood individuals is not what his theory seeks to articulate; it presents a political, not metaphysical conception of the person.[30] Each actual person should recognize the rules under which he is constrained as legitimate, not because he has literally given his proxy to a set of representatives, but because they correspond to his intuitions about the fairness of basic institutions, elicited through the thought experiment of the original position. But recognizing certain rules as *fair* does not, by itself, mean a person would consent to be governed by them. Fairness might ultimately justify *imposing* those rules on him, regardless of whether he accepts them. But that is a different story, and it is not, at any rate, a contractarian story.

Conclusion

One of the greatest attractions of the law and economics movement has been its assumption of rational agency and the possibility for systematization it provides. However I have suggested reasons to suppose that the assumption that human beings are rational maximizers does not necessitate a commitment to the normative thesis that human beings will favor maximizing *social* welfare. On the contrary, I have suggested that rational individual maximizers will choose *not* to maximize society's welfare, as that may compromise their own in the process. The traditional response from legal economists, that it is the function of legislation to bring individual incentives into line with the goal of social welfare maximization, avoids the need for altruism on the part of the individuals. This response, however, appears to miss the basic point, which is that given that political subjects have a hand in choosing their own mode of governance, and that they must endorse the principles on which their institutions are founded, they may well reject social welfare maximization as a legitimate goal of the political system.

Instead, I have argued, the assumption of rational agency quite naturally gives rise to what we might think of a contractarian, rather than utilitarian, principle of political governance. Instead of deriving principles from the abstract standpoint of society, we consider the standpoint of the individual maximizers instead, and ask what principles of governance individuals so situated would select. The relevant principle that rational agents would select, I have argued, is at the foundational level the principle of consent: individuals would not agree to give up their right to object to the terms of social interaction and to object precisely on the grounds utilitarians reject: namely that the chosen social interaction does not better their own individual case. The right of the individual to insist on participating in the terms of his own governance is thus the most plausible upshot of the assumption of rational agency. For those who favor law and economics, therefore, this provides an argument to prefer contractarian over utilitarian methodology.

Notes

1. By "mainstream," I mean to identify neoclassical economic theory as applied to the law. I am not considering applications of social economics or unorthodox behavioral economics, both of which may reach different conclusions than economists in the legal academy generally reach.
2. See Pennock and Chapman (eds), *Criminal Justice*.
3. See Hart, "Positivism and the Separation of Law and Morals"; Fuller, "Positivism and Fidelity to Law"; and Moore, *Placing Blame*. See also Dworkin, *Taking Rights Seriously* and *Law's Empire*. For an extreme statement of legal moralism, see Finnis, *Natural Law and Natural Rights*.
4. See Rawls, *A Theory of Justice*.
5. Hart, *The Concept of Law*, Chapter 9.
6. 159 F.2d 169 (2d Cir. 1947).
7. The Hand Formula has been formalized as follows: an act is in breach of the duty of care if B < PL, where B is the cost (burden) of taking precautions, and P is the probability of loss (L). L is the gravity of loss. The product of P and L must be a greater amount than B to create a duty of due care for the defendant.
8. Coase, "The Problem of Social Cost."
9. Richard Posner and William Landes have used "citation analysis" of cases to conclude that economic analysis is growing in influence compared to doctrinal analysis ("The Influence of Economics on Law").
10. Posner, *Economic Analysis of Law*, 249.
11. Ibid., p. 13. Kaldor-Hicks efficiency is a substantially weaker condition than Paretoism. A distribution of social goods is Pareto efficient if and only if it is not possible to alter that distribution to make someone better off without making another person worse off. A distribution is Kaldor-Hicks efficient if and only if it would be possible for the "winners" under that distribution to compensate the "losers." This is a concept of maximization, since a distribution that maximizes social welfare is Kaldor-Hicks efficient, but it may or may not be Pareto efficient. For an excellent analysis of the different concepts of efficiency employed in the economic analysis of law, see Coleman, "Efficiency, Utility, and Wealth Maximization."

12. Legal economists have some disagreement on this point. In *Fairness Versus Welfare*, for example, Kaplow and Shavell restrict their attention to the normative ambitions of law and economics. Part of their reason for this is that they reject Posner's claim that the logic of doctrinal development has been largely that of welfare maximization. As they say, their thesis is "entirely normative" (4) and that they "do not assert that the law fully reflects the prescriptions of welfare economics," and further rue the fact that "the law is influenced by notions of fairness" (92).

13. Fletcher, *Basic Concepts of Legal Thought*, 162.

14. This was the ambition of John Austin, who was a determined defender of a "science of jurisprudence." See *The Province of Jurisprudence Determined*, 112.

15. Posner, *Economic Analysis of Law*, 3 ("The task of economics, so defined, is to explore the implications of assuming that man is a rational maximizer of his ends in life ... "). Contemporary examples of this portrayal in contractarian political philosophy include David Gauthier, *Morals by Agreement*, and James Buchanan, *The Limits of Liberty*. The economic account of rational agency also can be found in standard accounts of game theory; see, for example, Ken Binmore, *Game Theory*, and Douglas G. Baird, Robert H. Gertner, and Randal C. Picker, *Game Theory and the Law*, 11.

16. Sidgwick, *The Methods of Ethics*, 411–412.

17. Bentham, *An Introduction to the Principles of Morals and Legislation*, chap. VI, para. 42.

18. See Singer, *Animal Liberation*.

19. See, for example, Anthony Kronman, "Wealth Maximization as a Normative Principle," 232.

20. Kaplow and Shavell, *Fairness Versus Welfare*, 3–4.

21. Ibid., 52. See also Claire Finkelstein, "Legal Theory and the Rational Actor."

22. The most discussed modern contractarian theory is, of course, John Rawls's "justice as fairness" from his book *A Theory of Justice*.

23. Ibid.

24. For a comparison of legal contractarianism and law and economics, see Finkelstein, "Legal Theory and the Rational Actor," 404–11.

25. See Treanor, "Rawls and the Law," introducing the symposium in *Fordham Law Review*, vol. 72 no. 5 (2004), that discusses the impact of Rawls's scholarship on legal world.

26. Rawls, *A Theory of Justice*, 13.

27. Ibid. (emphasis added).

28. See Sharon Dolovich, "Legitimate Punishment in Liberal Democracy," which presents a Rawlsian account of punishment based on hypothetical consent.

29. Michael J. Sandel, *Liberalism and the Limits of Justice*.

30. See Rawls, "Justice as Fairness" and *Political Liberalism*, 27.

Bibliography

Austin, John. *The Province of Jurisprudence Determined.* Ed. Wilfrid E. Rumble. Cambridge: Cambridge University Press, 1995 [1832].

Baird, Douglas G., Robert H. Gertner, and Randal C. Picker. *Game Theory and the Law.* Cambridge, MA: Harvard University Press, 1994.

Bentham, Jeremy. *An Introduction to the Principles of Morals and Legislation.* Oxford: Oxford University Press, 1907 [1789].

Binmore, Ken G. *Game Theory: A Very Short Introduction.* New York: Oxford University Press, 2007.

Buchanan, James M. *The Limits of Liberty: Between Anarchy and Leviathan.* Chicago: University of Chicago Press, 1975.

Coase, Ronald H. "The Problem of Social Cost." *Journal of Law and Economics* 3 (1960): 1–44.

Coleman, Jules L. "Efficiency, Utility, and Wealth Maximization." In *Markets, Morals, and the Law,* 95–132. Cambridge: Cambridge University Press, 1988.

Dolovich, Sharon. "Legitimate Punishment in Liberal Democracy." *Buffalo Criminal Law Review* 7 (2004): 314–329.

Dworkin, Ronald. *Law's Empire.* Cambridge, MA: Harvard University Press, 1986.

———. *Taking Rights Seriously.* Cambridge, MA: Harvard University Press, 1977.

Finkelstein, Claire. "Legal Theory and the Rational Actor." In *The Oxford Handbook of Rationality,* edited by Alfred R. Mele and Piers Rawling, 399–416. New York: Oxford University Press, 2004.

Finnis, John. *Natural Law and Natural Rights.* Oxford: Clarendon Press, 1980.

Fletcher, George. *Basic Concepts of Legal Thought.* Oxford: Oxford University Press, 1996.

Fuller, Lon L. "Positivism and Fidelity to Law: A Reply to Professor Hart." *Harvard Law Review* 71 (1958): 630–672.

Gauthier, David P. *Morals by Agreement.* Oxford: Clarendon Press, 1986.

Hart, H. L. A. *The Concept of Law.* 2nd ed. Oxford: Clarendon Press, 1994 [1961].

———. "Positivism and the Separation of Law and Morals." *Harvard Law Review* 71 (1958): 593–629.

Kaplow, Louis, and Steven Shavell. *Fairness versus Welfare.* Cambridge, MA: Harvard University Press, 2002.

Kronman, Anthony T. "Wealth Maximization as a Normative Principle." *Journal of Legal Studies* 9 (1980): 227–242.

Moore, Michael S. *Placing Blame: A General Theory of the Criminal Law.* Oxford: Oxford University Press, 1997.

Pennock, J. Roland, and John W. Chapman (eds). *Criminal Justice: NOMOS XXVII.* New York: New York University Press, 1985.

Posner, Richard A. *Economic Analysis of Law.* 7th ed. New York, NY: Aspen Publishers, 2007.

Posner, Richard A., and William M. Landes. "The Influence of Economics on Law: A Quantitative Study." *Journal of Law and Economics* 36 (1993): 385–424.

Rawls, John. "Justice as Fairness: Political not Metaphysical." *Philosophy and Public Affairs* 14 (1985): 223–251.

———. *Political Liberalism.* New York: Columbia University Press, 1993.

———. *A Theory of Justice.* Cambridge, MA: Belknap Press, 1971.

Sandel, Michael J. *Liberalism and the Limits of Justice.* Cambridge: Cambridge University Press, 1982.

Sidgwick, Henry. *The Methods of Ethics.* 7th ed. London: Macmillan, 1907 [1874].

Singer, Peter. *Animal Liberation: A New Ethics for Our Treatment of Animals.* New York: Random House, 1975.

Treanor, William M. "Rawls and the Law." *Fordham Law Review* 72 (2004): 1385–1386.

Chapter 2

Environmental Ethics, Economics, and Property Law

Steven McMullen and Daniel Molling

Conflicts between economic and environmental concerns are numerous, occurring at the highest level of academic methods and in many specific policy applications. Sometimes these conflicts are the inevitable result of trade-offs and differing priorities. Often, though, the conflicts run deeper, to the differences between the worldview of economists and public policy practitioners on the one hand and environmental scholars and activists on the other. To overcome these policy-related conflicts, we must work to bridge the conceptual gap between these schools of thought by identifying the roots of the conflicts and rethinking the institutions that shape our economic life.

One of the pivotal institutions at the center of many economic-environmental debates is the legal, economic, and ethical conception of property and ownership. Property rights are usually conceived as a bundle of rights to control part of the material world by a human, with corresponding duties to noninterference on the part of other humans.[1] The owner, in turn, has well-defined sets of use-limits designed to protect the rights of other humans. Though there are some critics of the "bundle of rights" analogy, this view remains the dominant paradigm.[2] Moreover, this view undergirds economic analysis, which usually places weight only the preference-based welfare of humans and assumes that exchanges and actions by humans take place in the context of a particular, anthropocentric, property rights framework. The assumed property regime determines which goods are exchanged, the type of exchange that occurs, and the resulting economic values that are placed on things.

We argue here that an alternate property regime would be more consistent with the inherent value of environmental goods and the ecological context of those goods. Such a regime creates an alternate legal context for more ecologically friendly economic analysis. Specifically, we argue that economic thinking has (unnecessarily) adopted an anthropocentric, simplistic view of the environment, which inevitably places the discipline at odds with other environmental scholars. Moreover, property rights play an important role in economic thought about the environment. The alternate property regime that we propose would retain this importance while also bringing economic thought in line with the philosophical literature on environmental ethics. They key requirement of this alternative property regime is that ownership of environmental goods must include a duty to make decisions about the property in such a way that the interests of creatures (in the case of animals) and ecosystems (in the case of land and plants) are pursued.[3] The result is a property concept that has the stewardship of the owned environment at its foundation.

The Environmental Ethics Critique

The field of environmental ethics is young but is sufficiently well established that scholars in other fields can draw upon major themes in its literature. Two such themes animate our discussion of property and economics: (a) that environmental "goods," variously defined, have some intrinsic value apart from the preferences of humans; and (b) that environmental goods ought to be conceived of as uniquely situated in a particular ecological context and are thus often not substitutable or separable. Both of these ethical claims conflict with dominant property conceptions in law, economics, and policy, and therefore present a challenge to practitioners in these fields.

To understand the first part of this critique, it is helpful to categorize the different types of value that can be attributed to a part of the environment. First, there is an anthropocentric instrumental value, which is the use value that humans are willing to ascribe and is measured well by the market price. Second, there is an anthropocentric non-use value, which is the value that humans attribute to the mere existence of the element of the environment. There is a real debate about the best way to measure and include nonuse values in environmental policymaking, or even whether existence value should be considered at all when making policy.[4] Third, there is nonanthropocentric instrumental value, which includes the value of an element of the environment to all other parts of the environment, human and nonhuman. Finally, there is nonanthropocentric nonuse value, which we refer to as "intrinsic value." The consensus in the environmental ethics literature is that most human ethical obligations toward the nonhuman natural world stem from some intrinsic value, which is variously described at the level of an organism (biocentric) or ecosystem (ecocentric).[5] This intrinsic value need not be infinite, as some claim,[6] or even equal to the intrinsic value of a human life, in order to motivate a substantive critique of many social-scientific approaches to environmental valuation. If one recognizes the existence of environmental intrinsic value, it becomes clear why current conceptions of property rights and standard methods of environmental valuation have frequently been criticized. Property rights, as they are normally understood by policymakers, lawyers, and economists, are by nature anthropocentric and may cause the well-being of the natural nonhuman environment to be undervalued or ignored completely.

The anthropocentric criticism is typically given voice by environmental ethicists, although some, following Bryan Norton, have argued that anthropocentrism is not inconsistent with strong environmental protection.[7] His argument relies on the idea that a diverse and well-preserved natural environment is beneficial to human beings and that these benefits will be more widely recognized in the future. Norton has suggested that there are two main varieties of anthropocentrism: strong and weak. Strong anthropocentrism suggests that all value lies in the felt preferences of human beings, whereas weak anthropocentrism is the view that value lies in the considered preferences of human beings. The difference is that considered preferences can only be expressed after careful deliberation and rational thought, while felt preferences can simply be a momentary whim or unreasonable desire. Norton argues that after careful thought and with good information, people would make choices that would preserve the natural environment and the result would be little different from operating under a nonanthropocentric ethic that attempts to assign intrinsic value to nonhuman creatures. As indicated previously, other environmental ethicists disagree with these claims.[8] Critics argue that economic thought and policy based on anthropocentric principles will lead to environmental decay regardless of how enlightened the policymakers are because there will always be situations in which human interests and the well-being of the natural environment may be directly opposed.

A common critique of anthropocentric approaches is that they rely on the preferences of humans, which are subject to change and not consistent across all people, and thus are insufficient for environmental protection. For example, Laurence Tribe speculates that it could be possible to replace trees with plastic trees, serving a human desire for shade just as well as their natural counterparts.[9] A clever marketing campaign could even be sufficient to convince people in the area that the plastic trees are just as good and have a similar aesthetic appeal. Even so, Tribe argues, fleeting human preferences should not be placed above more important values like respect for nature and respect for life. Mark Sagoff echoes Tribe's argument, again emphasizing that protection of the environment should not be contingent on human preferences and that nature should be preserved "for its own sake."[10]

A nonanthropocentric ethic that recognizes intrinsic value in the environment need not assert equality between the value of human well-being and the value of environmental goods. It is still possible to hold that human well-being is more valuable but that intrinsic value should be counted and weighed in any environmental cost-benefit analysis. One example of an economic study that exemplifies this approach is Charles Blackorby and David Donaldson's study of the valuation of animal well-being, which uses a "critical-level" utilitarian approach that gives some weight to animal welfare.[11] Similarly, as we will argue here, nonanthropocentric policy regimes need not assert a political equality between human well-being and environmental goals.

Another major theme from environmental ethics comes from the observation that every organism is ecologically embedded and interconnected to a high degree.[12] As a result, it is difficult to do any analysis well if we assume that different parts of the environment are substitutable or separable, as economists often do. This has been a criticism of standard environmental valuation as well from within the economics profession. Ecological economists in particular have argued that many economists implicitly or explicitly assume that natural capital can be easily substituted for manufactured and human capital, leading them to undervalue the former.[13] As a result, ecological economists argue for pursuing "strong sustainability," which includes a preservation of natural capital in addition to human and manufactured capital, as opposed to "weak sustainability" that only requires that economic output be nondecreasing over time.

However, even strong sustainability, which works as a rule for policy, does not exhaust the concerns of environmental ethicists. What is needed is a recognition of the connections between different parts of the natural world and a corresponding respect for those connections, which sustain communities of organisms. This, in fact, is the main reason why an "animal rights" perspective is incomplete: one can recognize the individual dignity of nonhuman animals but ignore the embeddedness of those animals in a particular ecosystem.[14] The reverse is also true in that recognizing the embeddedness of organisms in an ecosystem is not enough to prevent some of the abuses of animals that the "animal rights" perspective is concerned with.

The Economic Approach

The two major themes outlined here constitute a dual critique of economic and public policy analysis that researchers in economics and public policy have yet to take into account. It is not always recognized how fundamental these criticisms of the standard economic tool set really are. Taking the two elements of this critique in turn, we will argue here that these elements constitute an ethical critique of standard economic models, economic valuations, and current models of exchange, all of which lie at the core of the discipline.

First, the discipline of economics, and much of the resulting public policy analysis, is decidedly anthropocentric. Standard models assign values to environmental goods based on the revealed preferences of human actors; that is, values are assigned based on the trade-offs that humans are willing to make, on the margin, in favor of particular environmental goods. The preferences and welfare of nonhuman creatures are given weight only indirectly when humans gain utility from their welfare. Similarly, the value attached to ecosystems and species is conceived only in terms of their long-term value to humans. If one accepts that nonhuman creatures, species, and ecosystems have some inherent value, this anthropocentric approach leads to some ethically unacceptable outcomes. For example, there are cases in which nonhuman animals have relatively well-defined, known preferences, but because human preferences are at odds with nonhuman animal preferences, these nonhuman preferences are ignored in economic analysis.

With some notable exceptions, nonhuman animal preferences are ignored, even when modeling the value of environmental goods or the animals themselves.[15] Moreover, assigning market values to environmental goods is an ethically problematic process. For example, it is not uncommon to assign zero or near zero value to ecosystems or species, either because they have little use value to humans or because of a relative abundance. This is not because market actors are taking a particular ethical position regarding the inherent worth of these animals or ecosystems, but because we have established a set of theory and a set of practices that cannot easily account for these types of value.

Economic approaches to valuing environmental goods are often lauded for this very reason: they do not attempt to delve into the world of nonuse value, and thus avoid the ethical dilemmas that might accompany such an effort. This is done by limiting the set of environmental concerns that are considered to those about which people have preferences. In doing so, this approach defines all environmental concerns as preferences that people hold about the environment, thus staking out a supposedly value-free approach to adjudicating environmental conflict.

Such an approach works well for goods that function well as commodities: those goods about which different people have different values and which have little or no nonuse intrinsic value. Unfortunately, these same methods are problematic when used to make decisions about the fate and welfare of creatures and ecosystems that have intrinsic value outside of human preferences.[16] The exchange value is well defined by these methods, but to use an anthropocentric exchange value as a decision rule for whether a creature should be allowed to continue to exist can be problematic. In these cases, the supposedly neutral economist is actually taking a very strong ethical position when he or she makes decisions about environmental goods by assigning market values to them. Market valuation is only ethically defensible if (a) the entirely of the intrinsic value of the environmental good is accurately reflected in human preferences for the good, which is unlikely; or (b) the environmental good does not have any intrinsic value. When these conditions are not satisfied, the exchange value is only measuring a small part of the ethically relevant values needed to make a good decision.

The second conflict between economics and environmental ethics rests on the observation that environmental goods are ecologically embedded and connected in ways that are rarely reflected in economic analysis. When a plot of land is sold, the market price will depend on the value placed on the land by the seller and the marginal buyer. This price accurately reflects the value of the land, inherent value aside, only if the sale or use of the land has no positive or negative impact on the surrounding ecosystem. Ecological economists and ecologists have convincingly argued that this no-externality case is the exception to the rule. In order to do economics well, then, we have to understand the underlying natural relationships that characterize the environment we inhabit. Without this knowledge, economic valuation, by assuming that environmental goods are separable and substitutable, will generally understate the environmental externalities imposed on surrounding landowners. Moreover, market values will systematically ignore externalities imposed on the surrounding ecosystem, which do not impact other landowners.

The Dominant Conception of Property and the Environment

In legal scholarship, the dominant conception of a property right stems from the work of Wesley Hohfeld, who lays out the idea that any right also has a corresponding duty or duties on the part of other people and differentiates rights from privileges or mere powers.[17] For example, a person's right to life includes the duty of all other people not to commit any action that would take that life. A property right to a piece of land could include a duty for all other people not to trespass on that land. In law, these rights are always stated as being between people, with any subsequent duties relating to people or groups of people only.

Moreover, in economics as in law, ownership consists of a bundle of rights, where the owner usually has the right to use, sell, modify, and exclude others from the property in question.[18] Each of these individual "rights" in the bundle can, in theory, be restricted or limited separately, though there are those who argue that the rights in a "bundle" are actually more unified than the bundle of rights theory suggests and should be preserved as a unit.[19] Environmental restrictions that restrict the use of property in some way, then, generally will limit one or more of these property rights. It is for this reason that some have argued that these restrictions constitute a "taking" of value by the government, requiring compensation and justification.[20]

In fact, property rights have long been at the center of debates about environmental protection, which usually center around conflicts between owners' economic interests and the economic and ecological interests of other owners or the local ecosystem. Resolutions to these conflicts can take a couple of forms, depending on the nature of the conflict. In some cases, the conflict takes the form of a "commons problem" where multiple agents have the right to use an environmental resource and each user has an incentive to overuse the resource.[21] In these and other more general situations of negative externality, assigning exclusive property rights over the resource can provide people with the proper incentive to conserve the resource.[22]

This is the primary contribution of the "Free Market Environmentalist" movement, which has argued, building on the work of Ronald Coase, that "there are no environmental problems if property rights are fully private and transaction costs are zero. Of course, some people might still wish for more pristine streams or cleaner air, but then people always want more of all things."[23] By paying attention only to the exchange value of environmental goods based on the preferences of individual humans, the free-market environmentalists, as well as many environmental economists, maintain that markets, assuming properly defined property rights and the necessary conditions for Coasean bargaining, will protect the environment properly.

If environmental goods are understood to have intrinsic value, however, then there will be cases in which assigning anthropocentric property rights will not be enough. In fact, there are a number of cases where property arrangements that give a person the right to the long-run market value of the property can even be the impetus for its destruction. Douglas McCauley gives the example of a native bee population that was estimated to provide $60,000 in "pollination services" to the surrounding coffee farms; after those coffee farms were converted to other crops that did not need pollination, the economic use value of the local bees was effectively eliminated.[24] Even more dramatically, John Terborgh argues that in many cases, tropical rain forests really are more valuable dead than alive, and that even responsible cost-benefit analysis can conclude that the forests should be destroyed.[25] Finally, Edward O. Wilson documents how the stocking of commercially valuable fish in Lake Victoria has been commercially successful but devastating for the native species in the lake.[26] It is not necessarily the case that stocking a lake with fish or cutting down part of a rainforest is unethical, but each of these examples shows how the limited type of value taken into account by commercial incentives will often result in undervaluing parts of the natural world.

As John M. Meyer has argued, a legal and ethical conception of property that places the environment under the absolute control of individual property owners will not be able to adequately preserve the environment.[27] It is possible for the government to protect the environment under such a property regime, but only by repeatedly violating owners' property rights or compensating owners for any lost exchange value. Moreover, the practice of environmental economics is so thoroughly dependent on anthropocentric assumptions that even a reformed economic theory would conflict with a property concept that gives owners complete economic control of the environment. It is for this reason that reforming the economic approach to the environment must start with altering the legal and moral conception of property that underlies these conflicts.

Alternative Property Concepts

In recognition of the many property disputes that arise in debates about the environmental protection, a number of scholars have proposed alternative property concepts that might be more environmentally friendly. Because our current property regime inhabits both ethical and legal space, rethinking property and ownership is no simple task. A suitably nonanthropocentric property concept must accomplish three tasks. First, it must recognize the intrinsic value of nonhuman elements of the environment. Second, it should preserve, in a nonarbitrary way, the moral content of human ownership. This means that theft should remain a moral as well as a legal wrong that even the government must respect. Finally, the new property regime must fit practically into a set of social institutions in which humans are in a position of authority. In this section we will consider a pair of such proposals, arguing that neither meets these criteria for an environmentally friendly property ethic, and in the following section we will propose a preferable solution.

Given the argument for elements of the environment having intrinsic value, it is first worth justifying human ownership of the environment at all. Animal rights scholars have made sophisticated arguments for abolition of human ownership.[28] They argue that in light of human abuse of animals and key ecosystems, the best way forward is to abolish ownership and pursue a policy of minimal human intervention. Though these arguments may not apply to plants or ecosystems, this position is a common one among animal advocates.

While it is possible to make some headway by transitioning some animals from being property to being free-living, there are two reasons that this solution only sidesteps the problem. First, and more important, abolishing the ownership of some animals or ecosystems can only be a solution on the margin. It is likely not feasible to limit human ownership to only human artifacts without also significantly worsening the overall human treatment of the environment. Abolition without a strong policy of human nonintervention will only result in creating a large number of "commons" problems, where human interaction with the environment is plagued with incentives to exploit rather than to preserve. Moreover, the number of species and ecosystems that could plausibly flourish without human intervention is quite small given the current distribution of humans on the planet.

Second, abolition avoids the problem rather than solving it is because abolition, in our legal tradition, is really just a transfer of ownership from individuals to the state.[29] The government is the de facto protector and manager of all environmental goods and has ultimate ownership authority where individual ownership does not apply. For example, white-tailed deer populations in the United States are thus mostly free-living, but in many ways their population is tightly controlled by state governments. The same is true of any land that is not privately owned in the United States, which by default is under the control of the federal or state government. Government ownership of this type, then, is only preferable to private ownership if the government is more likely to place an appropriate value on environmental goods and protect the functioning of ecosystems. In practice, however, according to the "public trust doctrine" government bodies are mandated to use a "natural resource management" approach, which is based on the same anthropocentric economic logic that drives private ownership decision-making.[30] Moreover, adding more ecosystems and species to de facto government control would likely only decrease the quality of government protection.

Another alternative property concept, proposed by Meyer, is to redefine property as a "discovered" social consensus that is responsive to ecological constraints.[31] This revision contains two key points. First, he argues that property cannot be defined prior to realization of a particular social consensus about ownership. That is, social organization, conventions, and government come prior to property, and these need not answer to some prior moral law. The language of property "rights" can be problematic for this formulation. Second, Meyer argues that property must be reconceived as a social consensus that manages a web of relations between people and between people and ecosystems. This, he argues, is much more consistent with actual property law and prevents total commodification of the environment.

While Meyer's redefinition of ownership could improve the standing of the environment in property law and policy, it does so at a high cost. By defining a weaker property concept, Meyer frees policymakers from the obligations of an absolutist individual property "rights" framework but creates very little in its place. There is no moral content defining the obligations of individuals to the environment or the obligations of the government to individuals in this framework; that is, the social consensus that results is arbitrary in nature, constrained only by ecological necessity and political forces. It is just this fact about government action to protect the environment—that it can appear arbitrary and politically motivated—that undermines the moral obligations that individuals and governments do have to the environment.

An Environmentally Conscious Property Ethic

In order to shape an economic theory and practice that is not subject to the dual environmental ethics critique, it is important to frame a property concept that incorporates both intrinsic value and ecological interconnection. Once such a moral and legal property regime is established, economic practice can proceed in a way that is consistent with real respect for the environment. The shape of the resulting economics, however, depends heavily on the redefinition of property. A weak property concept that leaves individuals with little political or moral claim to the natural world might free up the state to regulate environmental exploitation more heavily, but it could also undermine the moral and legal obligations individuals have to protect the environment under their control. Consequently, one key element of property law ought to be to locate the responsibilities associated with ownership clearly in the hands of the owners and not with the state.

Additionally, since the failings of modern environmental economics are primarily ethical in nature, we argue that the best way to alleviate this harm is to more firmly establish moral obligations in the economic relations and analysis that we criticize. This, however requires a stronger, not weaker, property concept, in which the human-environmental relationships characterized by "ownership" include real rights on the part of humans as well as duties that humans have toward their property. These rights and duties, then, would provide the moral framework from which government action could proceed in a principled fashion.

The best metaphor for this revised conception of property is to think about ownership as an "office" that the owner holds. This office grants the owner real power, but also contains a well-defined set of responsibilities and a built-in accountability to other actors in society.[32] Included among these responsibilities is the duty to maintain the care and order of the property itself, so a concept of ownership as an office has, built-in, the possibility of duties on the part of the owner, not merely rights over and against other owners.

The duties that human owners should have toward their property should depend heavily on the nature of the thing that is owned (its intrinsic value) and the ecological relationships that the property participates in. For example, there are different duties associated with the ownership of a toaster compared to owning a dog, and dog owners are typically understood (at least in the United States) to have a duty to provide some minimal level of care for the animal that they own. Indeed, there are in many cases formal laws protecting many kinds of companion animals and (less often) farmed animals from poor treatment. The existence of this type of law may be an indication of a perceived moral obligation of animal owners to avoid causing unnecessary harm to animals. These laws hold the owner of the animal responsible for harm done, reflecting the fact that ownership creates unique responsibilities to living creatures that are owned even if an owner's mistreatment of an animal has no effect on other humans.

Furthermore, even if a person stops enjoying his or her ownership of a dog, their moral obligation to care for their dog does not disappear, as long as they retain the office of owner, suggesting that it is not only human utility that is a primary concern. This widely recognized moral obligation often seems to be premised (implicitly if not explicitly) on a concept of intrinsic value of certain types of animals. Importantly, these obligations are not exceptions to or restrictions on property rights; they are central to the concept of ownership itself. What we argue for, then, in this chapter is for more widespread and less arbitrary recognition of moral responsibility to living creatures that is created when one takes on ownership of living creatures, land, or other natural capital important to an ecosystem.

The duties that attend ownership also might originate from ecological relationships. Both John Meyer and Robert Goldstein argue that we can use lessons from the science of ecology to better understand connections between living creatures and the impact of property use.[33] For example, there may be uses of property upstream that do not directly harm the property but do harm ecosystems downstream, as with fertilizer use in suburban or agricultural areas. In these cases, recognition of the connections between different parts of the environment is essential for ethical action.

This type of concern is easily modeled as an economic externality where an action by one party has a positive or negative impact on another party not directly involved in that action. The recognition of environmental intrinsic value, however, expands the set of ecological externalities that are ethically significant. In normal property law and standard environmental economics, persons are responsible for the market value of damages that they cause to other persons. A consistent environmental ethic demands that we also consider the impacts of property use on the well-being and functioning of the larger ecosystem even if it does not change the market value of anyone's property.

One helpful way for this kind of property ethic to be integrated into property law is to apply the concept of "equitable self-ownership" to animals and possibly to land.[34] In this framework, the equitable owner takes on the role of a trustee, in which their legal power must be exercised for the benefit of the property (animal or land). The equitable owner does not have the same legal agency or power as a "normal" owner, but does have some recognized rights regarding the property arrangement. A movement toward redefining ownership of the natural world to reflect this arrangement would open the door for obligations to be defined, on the part of owners, toward the state, fellow humans, and property itself.

The Role of Government and Environmental Regulation

At first glance, this way of thinking about ownership might seem to leave a large role for government regulation and a relatively small role for traditional environmental economic analysis, but these impressions are mistaken. Despite the fact that the duties that attend ownership do constrain the owners of property in some significant ways, our proposal is still a "strong" individual property concept, for a few reasons. First, property owners, in our view, still have a unique claim on the use of, and fruits of, the environmental goods that they own. As a moral claim, we are articulating property rights that the government and other people have a duty to respect. In fact, the moral basis for a person's claim to the fruits of their property is more easily defensible if those owners also have duties to maintain the well-being of the environment that they own. Second, outside of broad abuses that must be regulated by government, specific decisions about environmental stewardship ought to be subject primarily to the prudential judgment of the owner. It is possible to envision a property regime based on strong respect for the environment that still leaves considerable room for the aims and vision of the owner of property.

How, then, would government policy be affected by this vision of property? The idea of having duties to one's property might imply that the state should formalize these duties into law. In many cases, such regulations could be improvements over the status quo. Moreover, despite the strong moral claim that it establishes for owners, this formulation also establishes a particular type of regulation as legitimate and necessary. Currently, it is often argued that environmental regulation infringes on property rights.[35] This conflict is accepted even by ardent environmental advocates. In this mode of thinking, the "taking" of property must be justified by the human benefits from environmental protection.[36]

However, both these arguments implicitly deny a person's duties to their property. In our formulation, government regulation that protects living creatures could be seen as upholding property rights *and* the responsibilities that come with property rights, and thus do not constitute a violation of owners' rights or a "taking" that requires compensation. This is not to say that government regulation should never be seen as a taking, as there are significant costs to many types of regulations including environmental regulation. When the government is simply upholding a property owner's moral responsibilities to their property, however, the label of "taking" can be misleading.[37]

A second way in which government policy might change as a result of this property concept is in the underlying criteria used to justify policy. Current utilitarian justifications for environmental law depend on the long-term and short-term well-being of humans that is affected by the environment as measured by current estimates of human preferences. Human economic interests, however, can be both arbitrary and variable, and our knowledge of the ecosystem is too limited to forecast long-run ecological outcomes from policy changes. Property law that establishes some basic legal rights for the natural world, predicated on real intrinsic value, provide a more stable and predictable metric for environmental protection.

A New Environmentalist Economics?

To address the dual environmental ethics critique, economists will need to develop ways to account for the interests of nonhuman animals and ecosystems apart from their anthropocentric use or nonuse value. Including consideration of the welfare of the environment in cost-benefit analysis, in addition to the human welfare considerations, will only make economic analysis more useful, effective, and ethical. While there are significant theoretical barriers that need to be overcome before we can integrate nonhuman interests with any precision, there are likely a number of places where even an imprecise consideration of the interests of animals or ecosystems will yield obvious and significant changes in policy. For example, animal agriculture is one area in which animals' interests could significantly sway cost-benefit analyses.[38]

The primary difficulty that arises when doing cost-benefit analysis in the presence of intrinsic value, however, is that such comparisons inevitably lead to situations in which different and incommensurable values need to be weighed against each other. For example, when deciding how to control water drainage from a suburban neighborhood, the low-cost option for the human residents might involve a traditional storm sewer system. Such a setup can often overwhelm local watersheds during periods of high precipitation, however, and wreak havoc on local water ecosystems. The ecologically friendly option is to include many natural areas that will absorb water runoff from buildings and yards rather than channeling it all to local rivers and streams. Even in this small-scale policy decision, however, incommensurable value comparisons arise. The ecologically friendly option requires significant restrictions on land use by humans as well as the creation and care of local wetland areas. A standard anthropocentric cost-benefit analysis could be used to compare the ecological benefits to humans of a healthy watershed to the costs associated with more sustainable development. Such an approach, however, might ignore the well-being of the animals that depend on the ecosystems in the local rivers and streams, and focus instead on public health concerns and the impact on local fishing industries.

Moreover, recognizing the interests of other animals and ecosystems, even if they could be converted into comparable units, does not solve the dilemma, unless a strong assumption is made about the relative weight of different types of concerns. Any utilitarian calculation of this sort depends on some deontological propositions that dictate who is in the community of beings that deserve moral consideration. While these questions are not easily answered, some decisions need to be made in the policymaking framework regarding which beings have interests that will be considered and weighed (and how this can be done).

One way to approach this type of conceptual problem is to set some rules outlining clear bounds within which policies can be formulated on prudential grounds, even if precise comparisons of value are difficult. Our argument is that property rights play a key role in delineating some of these foundational rules within which policy analysis and exchange can proceed. In fact there are at least three different functions of this type served by property law. First, the holder of property rights will be able to extract the fruits of their property and any rents from Coasean bargaining; therefore, property laws define the distribution of benefits from economic exchange. Second, property law dictates the types of goods and the types of uses for goods that can be exchanged and thus valued. Currently, for example, in most places humans are not the sort of beings that can be owned, exchanged, or easily valued in the marketplace. Third, property law dictates the obligations that accompany ownership, especially regarding the proper use or care of the property. For each of these functions, a small change in property law can dramatically alter the nature of exchange in markets for these types of goods.

By altering the property status of environmental goods, then, we are not committing ourselves to a final positional ranking of values between these goods, nor claiming that all creatures have some moral status. Instead, such a move redefines the limits within which the utilitarian logic of the market and public policy can proceed, while at the same time acknowledging the ethical value of environmental goods and their interconnections.

Conclusion

We have argued in this chapter that two fundamental insights of environmental ethics are largely at odds with modern environmental economic practice. Moreover, the conflict between economic and environmental thought often rests in the underlying concept of property that grants power and obligations only to humans and the state. We propose a change in the concept of property and property laws so that animals and other parts of the natural environment can be granted legal recognition. This would clarify the moral and legal obligations that humans have as a result of claiming political and economic control (ownership) over the natural world. This legal and moral change in the concept of ownership, in turn, sets the stage for the field of economics to develop analysis that recognizes necessary ecological relationships and the inherent value of animals and ecosystems.

The changes we suggest are not trivial. There would be real changes in wealth that would result from such a legal move. Some people would be significantly worse off economically if the law required some basic recognition of the interests of ecosystems and animals. This alone is enough to warrant a thoughtful, deliberate, and gradual change that different actors can predict and plan for. That said, after the adjustment costs have been borne, changes in economic practice will probably yield a new equilibrium that more accurately reflects the true value of the natural world.

It is worth noting that only a subset of environmental concerns can be addressed using this approach. In the case of global environmental problems, such as climate change, our approach would help by establishing individual moral obligations for the care of ecosystems. This approach would not resolve the global commons problems, however, or significantly alter our energy technologies. As such, a distinction should be made between micro-environmental and macro-environmental issues, and our approach is explicitly meant to address only the former.

Finally, the fundamental conflict between environmental ethics and economic thought is an important one. Unless a resolution is attempted, we will never move past the political adjudication of two very different ways of thinking about the environment. The result of using the political system to resolve this conflict is that the solution will be inevitably inconsistent, arbitrary, and unacceptable to both sides. An intellectually consistent approach that takes cost-benefit analysis seriously and also recognizes a broader set of environmental values might be the only way to make real environmental progress.[39]

Notes

1. Hohfeld, "Fundamental Legal Conceptions as Applied in Judicial Reasoning."
2. Merrill and Smith, "Making Coasean Property More Coasean."
3. It is common for an environmental animal ethicists to refer to the "interests" of nonhuman animals and ecosystems, often following Singer, *Animal Liberation*. Such interests are often thought to be biologically identifiable, however, their moral standing is the subject of much disagreement.
4. Boudreaux and Meiners, "Existence Value and Other of Life's Ills."
5. Nash, *The Rights of Nature*.
6. McCauley, "Selling out on Nature."
7. Norton, "Environmental Ethics and Weak Anthropocentrism."
8. Callicott, "Non-anthropocentric Value Theory and Environmental Ethics"; McCauley, "Selling out on Nature"; Westra, "Why Norton's Approach Is Insufficient for Environmental Ethics."
9. Tribe, "Ways Not to Think about Plastic Trees."
10. Sagoff, "On Preserving the Natural Environment."
11. Blackorby and Donaldson, "Pigs and Guinea Pigs."
12. For a collection of these arguments, see Norton (ed.), *The Preservation of Species*.
13. Gowdy, "Terms and Concepts in Ecological Economics."
14. Holmes, *A New Environmental Ethics*.
15. Blackorby and Donaldson, "Pigs and Guinea Pigs."
16. Sagoff, "Economic Theory and Environmental Law."
17. Hohfeld, "Some Fundamental Legal Conceptions as Applied in Judicial Reasoning" and "Fundamental Legal Conceptions as Applied in Judicial Reasoning."
18. Coase, "The Problem of Social Cost"; Demsetz, "Toward a Theory of Property Rights."
19. Merrill and Smith, "Making Coasean Property More Coasean."
20. Epstein, "Holdouts, Externalities, and the Single Owner"; Meyer, "The Concept of Private Property and the Limits of the Environmental Imagination."

21. Hardin, "The Tragedy of the Commons."
22. Hill and Meiners (eds), *Who Owns the Environment?*
23. De Allessi, "Property Rights as the Basis for Free-Market Environmentalism," drawing upon Coase, "The Problem of Social Cost."
24. McCauley, "Selling out on Nature."
25. Terborgh, *Requiem for Nature.*
26. Wilson, *The Diversity of Life.*
27. Meyer, "Concept of Private Property."
28. Francione, "Animals—Property or Persons?"; Regan, *Empty Cages.*
29. Goldstein, "Green Wood in the Bundle of Sticks."
30. Ibid.
31. Meyer, "Concept of Private Property."
32. Katz, "The Regulative Function of Property Rights"; Essert, "The Office of Ownership."
33. Meyer, "Concept of Private Property"; Goldstein, "Green Wood in the Bundle of Sticks."
34. Favre, "A New Property Status for Animals."
35. Meyer, "Concept of Private Property"; Hill and Meiners (eds), *Who Owns the Environment?*
36. Meyer, "Concept of Private Property."
37. Joshi, Krishnan, and Lave, "Estimating the Hidden Costs of Environmental Regulation."
38. Norwood and Lusk, *Compassion, by the Pound.*
39. The views expressed herein are those of the authors and do not necessarily reflect the position of the Federal Reserve Bank of Kansas City or the Federal Reserve System.

References

Blackorby, Charles, and David Donaldson. "Pigs and Guinea Pigs: A Note on the Ethics of Animal Exploitation." *Economic Journal* 102 (1992): 1345–1369.

Boudreaux, Donald J., and Roger E. Meiners. "Existence Value and Other of Life's Ills." In *Who Owns the Environment?*, edited by Peter J. Hill and Roger E. Meiners, 153–285. Lanham, MD: Rowman & Littlefield, 1998.

Callicott, J. Baird. "Non-anthropocentric Value Theory and Environmental Ethics." *American Philosophical Quarterly* 21 (1984): 299–309.

Coase, Ronald H. "The Problem of Social Cost." *Journal of Law and Economics* 3 (1960): 1–44.

De Allessi, Louis. "Property Rights as the Basis for Free-Market Environmentalism." In *Who Owns the Environment?*, edited by Peter J. Hill and Roger E. Meiners. Lanham, MD: Rowman & Littlefield, 1998.

Demsetz, Harold. "Toward a Theory of Property Rights." *American Economic Review* 57(2) (1967): 347–359.

Epstein, Richard A. "Holdouts, Externalities, and the Single Owner: One More Salute to Ronald Coase." *Journal of Law and Economics* 36 (1993): 553–586.

Essert, Christopher. "The Office of Ownership." *University of Toronto Law Journal* 63 (2013): 418–461.

Favre, David. "A New Property Status for Animals: Equitable Self-Ownership." In *Animal Rights: Current Debates and New Directions*, edited by Cass R. Sunstein and Martha C. Nussbaum, 234–50. New York: Oxford University Press, 2006.

Francione, Gary L. "Animals—Property or Persons?" In *Animal Rights: Current Debates and New Directions*, edited by Cass R. Sunstein and Martha C. Nussbaum, 108–142. New York: Oxford University Press, 2006.

Goldstein, Robert. "Green Wood in the Bundle of Sticks: Fitting Environmental Ethics and Ecology into Real Property Law." *Boston College Environmental Affairs Law Review* 25 (1998): 347–430.

Gowdy, John M. "Terms and Concepts in Ecological Economics." *Wildlife Society Bulletin* 28 (2000): 26–33.

Hardin, Garrett. "The Tragedy of the Commons." *Science* 162 (1968): 1243–1248.

Hill, Peter J., and Roger E. Meiners (eds). *Who Owns the Environment?* Lanham, MD: Rowman & Littlefield Publishers, 1998.

Hohfeld, Wesley Newcomb. "Fundamental Legal Conceptions as Applied in Judicial Reasoning." *Yale Law Journal* 26 (1917): 710–770.

———. "Some Fundamental Legal Conceptions as Applied in Judicial Reasoning." *Yale Law Journal* 23 (1913): 16–59.

Holmes, Rolston. *A New Environmental Ethics: The Next Millennium for Life on Earth*. Abington, UK: Routledge, 2011.

Joshi, Satish, Ranjani Krishnan, and Lester Lave. "Estimating the Hidden Costs of Environmental Regulation." *Accounting Review* 76 (2001): 171–198.

Katz, Larissa. "The Regulative Function of Property Rights." *Econ Journal Watch* 8 (2011): 236–246.

McCauley, Douglas J. "Selling out on Nature." *Nature* 443 (2006): 27–28.

Merrill, Thomas W., and Henry E. Smith. "Making Coasean Property More Coasean." *Journal of Law and Economics* 54 (2011): S77–S104.

Meyer, John M. "The Concept of Private Property and the Limits of the Environmental Imagination." *Political Theory* 37 (2009): 99–127.

Nash, Roderick Frazier. *The Rights of Nature: A History of Environmental Ethics*. Madison, WI: University of Wisconsin Press, 1989.

Norton, Bryan G. "Environmental Ethics and Weak Anthropocentrism." *Environmental Ethics* 6 (1984): 131–148.

——— (ed.). *The Preservation of Species: The Value of Biological Diversity.* Princeton, NJ: Princeton University Press, 1988.

Norwood, F. Bailey, and Jayson L. Lusk. *Compassion, by the Pound: The Economics of Farm Animal Welfare*. Oxford: Oxford University Press, 2011.

Regan, Tom. *Empty Cages: Facing the Challenge of Animal Rights*. Lanham, MD: Rowman & Littlefield Publishers, 2005.

Sagoff, Mark. "Economic Theory and Environmental Law." *Michigan Law Review* 79 (1981): 1393–1419.

———. "On Preserving the Natural Environment." *Yale Law Journal* 84 (1974): 205–267.

Singer, Peter. *Animal Liberation: The Definitive Classic of the Animal Movement.* New York: Harper Perennial, 2009.

Terborgh, John. *Requiem for Nature.* Washington, DC: Island Press, 2004.

Tribe, Laurence H. "Ways Not to Think about Plastic Trees: New Foundations for Environmental Law." *Yale Law Journal* 83 (1974): 1315–1348.

Westra, Laura. "Why Norton's Approach Is Insufficient for Environmental Ethics." *Environmental Ethics* 19 (2008): 279–297.

Wilson, Edward O. *The Diversity of Life.* Cambridge, MA: Belknap, 2010.

Chapter 3

Individual Rights, Economic Transactions, and Recognition: A Legal Approach to Social Economics

Stefano Solari

Although markets are based on legal foundations and judiciary problems often concern economic issues, the twentieth century saw a progressive methodological divide between legal and economic studies. In particular, economic theory stands on quite simplistic legal concepts that contribute to hide some important issues at stake. This divide has not been reduced much by the development of the field of law and economics, which simply applies the economics method to legal issues. A necessarily more fruitful field of interaction between these perspectives is promised by social economics, which, since its beginning, has adopted a more integrated and interdisciplinary approach, including the study of property rights and institutions. In particular, among the many issues debated in social economics, the theme of justice in economic exchanges over the course of history has stimulated much fruitful research that still deserves to be further developed. In this field of research, the study of the legal variables comes into direct interaction with economic reasoning. Consequently, categories used in the economic analysis should be harmonized with the legal framework. On the other hand, the choice of the legal theory on which we develop social economy studies is crucial in determining what can and what cannot be seen in terms of pathologies in human interaction.

Modernity brought the idea of individual property rights as a complex phenomenon. However, economics adopted a simplistic view of property as a fundamental institution, understating the complex interaction of different rights and obligations that frame the legal environment of economic processes with an insufficiently elaborated tool. Here, a more elaborate view of legal elements will be proposed in order to analyze the interactions constituting exchanges. The legal perspective will be inspired by classical natural law, without necessarily following the Aristotelian or Thomistic frameworks. The classical idea of objective good and of moral law as inspiration to human interaction through practical reasonableness is here read through the lens of more contemporary philosophical work.[1] This allows us to use ideal principles as an ethical reference while adopting a practical approach to social-economic concrete action according to the typical ideal-realist perspective. This approach draws special attention to social law (in the sense of norms developed and accepted by a community) and opposes legal positivism. The organic view of society typical of classical natural law will be fitted to the contemporary idea of individual rights by simply accepting the latter as a partial analysis of legal relationships. On the other hand, the connection with social economics is made through the institutionalist framework, which maintains many aspects of the ancient organic view of the social fabric.[2] Therefore, concepts of the classical tradition, including the ideal-realist approach, are fitted into a transaction approach to be able to study the fairness of economic processes from a different perspective compared to the proceduralist one.

The starting point for my analysis is that "the members of a human society are bounded together by a network of rights and duties" determining a relational space.[3] In order to understand the role of the law in economic processes, a comparable relational approach to economic intercourses is needed. John Commons's concept of transactions is an appropriate framework by which we can study economic and legal elements in a unitary view of human action.[4] Commons's transaction approach is able to frame the often cited relationships of conflict, mutuality, and order, and it can also include law and rights as part of the interrelationship.

Property Rights and the Law

The idea of individual rights was not part of classical political philosophy and gradually emerged only from canonist studies in the late Middle Ages.[5] The individualism of modern political and economic thought isolated individuals from social relationships and endowed them with property rights, which were defined as "natural" in the sense of having priority over any other claim or law and thereby constituting a defensive sphere of private autonomy. In the classical world, we could find concepts such as the law, the just thing, the right order of society, and right behavior, but no notion pointing to a "defensive" relationship of the individual to political authority based on an individual legal endowment.[6] Any right was defined to some obligation through a juridical relationship—which was part of a relational and organic view of the law.

The social philosophy of political liberalism shaped a political economy that incorporated the idea of individual right as individual endowment or a kind of stock. Property rights were conceived as a defensive principle to protect the individual sphere of liberty from the authority of the state. As a consequence, the relational principle that shaped ancient theories of the law and that led to the idea of *Ordo* was lost to the advantage of a claim of individual autonomy and freedom.[7] Unfortunately, after modern natural law achieved the acknowledgment of individual control over property (to defend the individual from the claims of the sovereign), this idea of individual rights evolved in a view of society where property rights came before any other duty and, above all, neglected any obligation that the individual has in relation to his community.

Moreover, property rights, which originally were intended to be an all-inclusive concept that in the view of Hobbes concerned our own life, body, family affections, and wealth, became a simple "stock-package" pointing to the specific relationship between the individual and the property.[8] It came to consist in a right of exclusion that had to be defended by the state, functional to a conflict-ridden view of society. This perspective is still dominant in both libertarian views of society as well as liberal-progressive conceptions of the economy. Even those who argue in favor of the extension of individual rights into social and economic rights often conceive them as an individual stock and not as an organic interdependence of claims in society.

An example of this fact is the definition of basic rights by Henry Shue as "the minimum reasonable demands that everyone can place on the rest of humanity."[9] Here the right is conceived as an open claim and not as a relationship between individuals.[10] The usual critique to this kind of conception is that, finding no specific obliged individual as a counterpart, it leaves to the state all charges of assuring its minimal fulfillment. Therefore, due to the way rights are conceived, they are not easily transformed in "justiciable rights" and therefore the government has to assume the costs of fostering them. That, in turn, makes society very vertical and bureaucratic because the interaction between the claimants and those who actually supply the service is mediated by the state through public administration.

The problem in contemporary economics is that property rights are simply taken as objects of transactions and seen as an invariant stock.

Exchanges are not shaping or affecting rights; instead, they are simply transferring their ownership to other individuals. This theorization is in many cases perfectly suited to economic studies. Therefore, these rights concern property and consist of a relationship between the individual A and the good G. That right-stock can be transferred from individual A to individual B and be subject to evaluation. The evaluation of a right-stock depends on subjective use value determining reservation prices and on the social evaluation given by relative scarcity determining the market price. But the nature and form of the right itself is not seen as changeable by economists. Moreover, individual or social rights or any moral obligations are presumed neutral to the process of market evaluation, and similarly, wealth effects and externalities are excluded or regarded as "incidental." Properties of the good as well as the good itself are therefore associated and seen as objective and simple in their unity, not affected by the context and by the personality of traders. The result is that we tend not to question the fairness of market prices.

This theoretical architecture may seem appropriate to describe exchanges involving relatively homogeneous commodities. But most transactions do not involve simple commodities but rather "services" of a heterogeneous nature. Most transactions in a service society involve the creation of value out of interpersonal relationships and activities in which the quality of the persons involved is crucial, such as labor relations or the consultancy of a tax advisor. In other cases, rights are sold that allow the access to some performance or information, such as getting on the train or reading an e-book. In all these cases the coincidence of the good G and the property right connecting A to G is a misleading way of explaining how transactions work.

The problems that a legal approach to social economics has to deal with are, first, the genesis and nature of individual property rights. Then, it has to deal with the relationship between property rights and other human and social rights as well as obligations and liberties. Finally, it must study the criterion to evaluate justice in exchanges— that is to say, criteria for fair evaluation in relation to the nature of legal relationships.

Contemporary Conceptions of Rights and Justice

The theory of justice proposed by John Rawls had a major impact on economics and has become an important reference for liberal thought.[11] It interprets justice as a distributive problem and it justifies government reallocation of resources by a procedural logic.

However, this theory does not question the outcome of markets based on an intrinsically fair process, but looks at only the resulting distribution of income. It assumes that fostering free markets assures efficiency with a side effect of bad distribution of income. That implies an external ethical point of view that is theorized as the "original position." This theory totally neglects any problem connected to commutative justice and the genesis of rights. Its critics have pointed out its contradictory materialism, but this is not our concern here.[12]

The position of Ronald Dworkin's work is relevant here. He is not a positivist and therefore he acknowledges the fundamental role of moral obligations in line with the classical approach, but at the same time he adopts an individualist perspective.[13] The interesting aspect of Dworkin's approach is his idea of the *unity of value*, that is to say, unity of moral and ethical values.[14] He argues that a well-working theory of justice is based on morals: in this view the law is not competing with morals, but can be seen as a branch of political morals, which is a specific branch of the wider concept of personal morals. The latter, in turn, is a part of the conception of how to live well, or the ethics of dignity.

In this way, Dworkin interprets personal interest as framed by an ethical ideal. He admits that, today, the Greek view of unity of the two spheres of value (morals and interest) has survived in a degraded form. Greek ideals affirmed that the good life is something beyond the satisfaction of desires because it also involves caring for others. Modern political and economic philosophy abandoned the integrity of morals and ethics, instead conceiving interest and ethics as conflicting: morals in this case means subordination of personal interest to ethics. As a consequence, in Dworkin there is both a superior point of reference given by ethics and an ideal logic of derivation of law from morals.

Dworkin defines individual rights as something residual from collective ends of society related to ethics.[15] Individual rights are therefore subordinated to collective ends; the definition of individual legal positions is not derived directly from interindividual relationships, but it is mediated by general ethical and political principles. He distinguishes *background rights*, relative to society in general, from *institutional rights*, relative to the effect of specific institutions. Moreover, he also distinguishes between arguments of principles and policy: a policy standard is an objective to be reached, such as an economic improvement, whereas a principle is a standard to be observed as fundamental requisite of justice and equity. Principles are not hard and fast rules, but a general orienting device affecting the culture of a community.

Dworkin's aim to rejoin rights with classic principles is partially successful because it allows us to interpret his theoretical work as a reinterpretation of the political community (*polis*) in present times. Nonetheless, it represents still an open-ended and vertical conception of rights as they are defined relative to the state, and they are not discussed in their genesis. Dworkin therefore bases his reasoning on a priority assigned to public law compared to private or social law. However, the idea of principles as field organizers and elements able to align behavior can have interesting application in a social-economic theory of economic transactions inspired to the classic tradition.

A Horizontal View of Rights: Recognition

The individualization and the verticalization of the idea of right, originating from a preferential relationship between the individual and the state, does not contribute much to the social-economic analysis.[16] In fact, since the beginning of social economics, a critique of this conceptual architecture was conducted by those who—from Sismondi to the Jesuits—focused on the problem of social justice. The emphasis on the social economy inspired by the classical approach privileges social law and concrete legal relationships. Therefore, rights are justified not by abstract philosophical principles but by their actual acceptance by the involved individuals. On the one hand, we need abstract ideas of the good and of genuine humanity, and on the other, rights are concrete positions in actual relationships.[17] The justification of rights requires understanding the logical thread that connects the juridical elements framing economic interactions.

There are many precedents for this line of thinking in modern philosophy. Thomas Scanlon expressed a similar concern, although from a contractualist perspective, pointing out the need of requirements of *justifiability* to others.[18] Oswald Hanfling similarly argues that rights belong to a language game that includes the exchange of reasons.[19] Contemporary contractualists as Alan Gewirth found justification of rights in purposeful human action, which is to say, in specific deliberations.[20] Historically, this has led to constitutionalism, but formal laws can be empty of practices; the problem is to explain actual rights operating in social relationships. Amartya Sen, from his applied perspective, affirmed that rights can be functional to positive freedoms.[21] But he could not explain the source of rights and, actually, rights and capabilities are two competing concepts in Sen's "a-juridical" system, which is based on the pragmatic idea of assuring human capabilities in a nonrelational setting (a good theoretical system in itself but not related to our problem).[22]

The approach followed here is classical in the sense that priority is given to moral law guiding effective individual action, framed by social customs and institutions. The basic idea is that, in social economics, we should understand how actual, observed economic behavior is affected by the social fabric. Therefore, priority is given to rules and rights as effectively perceived by acting people and not from an abstract general theoretical perspective. On the other hand, human behavior has to be studied in its social dimension, that is to say, from a relational perspective.

A similar approach characterized the ethical thought of Edmund Burke: the true law comes from moral customs diffused in a community.[23] He argued that the rules more apt to foster the well-being of a society emerge from the experience of that community; therefore, rights derive from actual customs and precede formal law. The approach presented here does not take this view as normative but as an applied theorizing perspective. Justification for rights can be shaped inside a practical view of social-economic interactions.

More specifically, this chapter contributes to a rediscovery of Hegel's *Philosophy of Right* and Rosmini's ideas on the law for aspects affecting economics.[24] The main idea that these authors stressed is the fundamental act of *recognition* on which any community is based. Recognition is the cognitive act by which each person acknowledges the human identity of another person, and is also the ground of the respect due to the other's identity, including her specific living sphere ("property" in classical terms) that is at the ground of any juridical relationship. Rights are not valid by themselves or by metaphysical reasons, but because others have felt a natural obligation to recognize them. A right, according to Rosmini, is in itself a moral entity that emerges in the relationship between personal freedom and moral law.[25] Therefore, in this view, the idea of duty logically precedes that of right (while remaining independent).[26] The rights of others that we recognize are obviously obligations that we are, directly or indirectly, willing to fulfill.[27] This aspect makes the juridical relationship fundamentally reciprocal and grounded in history.[28]

In Hegel's thought, reciprocal recognition, mediated by ideal juridical forms, is the foundation of property rights.[29] Property is generated in exchange by reciprocal agreements which include the recognition of property. The foundation of individual autonomy is the intersubjective recognition that our needs, beliefs, and capabilities deserve to be fulfilled. It is based on a common moral principle that becomes embedded in practices, beliefs, and institutions. Exchange therefore includes two lines of communication, one concerning the reciprocal recognition of rights and the other based on prices.

This perspective is at the same time cognitive and behavioral. It asserts that rights are what we recognize to each other, and this recognition has an ethical aspect because we attach a dimension of "ought to be" on what we recognize to each other. At the same time, however, we do not have an ideal result to achieve: morals are based on abstract principles that we have to adapt to actual situations and not on ideal states to reach. The content of a right includes what history presents as actualizations of these relationships as mediated by (perhaps imperfectly) shared ideal values. So, there is a realist dimension in this framework of analysis that allows to understand exactly what are effective rights and obligations, and there is a moral dimension concerning the rights that we ought recognize to others according to the ethical vision of the society that we would like to live in. This does not mean that we cannot define universal, natural, or fundamental rights, but this is an issue beyond this chapter.

Once we accept the factual-ethical dimension of rights, we can work out some specification on the exact architecture of juridical relationships involving individuals and the political authority. Here, many classifications of rights can be described, as that between positive rights (or entitlements) and negative rights (or freedoms), similar to Kantian perfect and imperfect duties.[30] In the case of positive rights, we should recognize (and be ready to pay for) the specific forms of collective action that are assigned to fulfill such rights.

Economic Transactions and the Legal Framework

According to Gianfranco Tusset, writing about Gustavo Del Vecchio (an Italian economist who developed a relational approach to economic exchanges), the relational approach to economic interactions can be traced back to the work of Friedrich von Hermann and to Henry Dunning Macleod.[31] Apparently, Hermann influenced the work of Eugen Böhm-Bawerk, which directly inspired John Commons's conception of transactions.[32] The characteristic of the relational approach to exchanges is that it fundamentally involves legal variables, that is to say, rights, obligations, and rules.

Starting with his first work, Commons attempted to systematically connect juridical elements with economics.[33] In his *Legal Foundations of Capitalism*, Commons elaborated a legal framework to study transactions under the hypothesis that economic outcomes are fundamentally shaped by the institutional framework, and he adopted and slightly modified the legal theory of Wesley Hohfeld.[34] In this perspective, the allocation of goods takes place in a juridical environment, where individuals act in a space defined by rights, duties, and working rules. Hohfeld's framework is based on a three-term relation (two persons and an act-description) giving birth to the following rights:

> *Right* of A, corresponding to *duty* of B
> *Privilege* of A, corresponding to *no-right* of B
> *Power* of A, corresponding to *liability* of B
> *Immunity* of A, corresponding to *no-power* of B

This relational scheme of legal elements was modified by Commons to shape his model of transactions. Actually, in Commons's model, transactions always involve at least five actors: the two interacting individuals A and B, two nontransacting individuals C and D representing the opportunities not taken (or opportunity costs) and the administrative authority in charge of regulating economic processes.[35]

Commons did not use the notion of preferences but rather the simple classical difference between *use value* and *exchange value*, which determines the opportunities of a transaction. Compared to Hohfeld, Commons's aim was also to emphasize transactions taking place within organizations (managerial transactions) and the role of the political administrative authority in allocating resources (rationing transactions). His end was to describe property as a social creation, a legal construct that can be adapted and modified, so property is embedded in social and legal relations in which power and authority are also relevant. In this way, Commons includes some element of administrative control in his legal positions.[36] The resulting framework is basically conflict-ridden and based on imperfect opposites that never coincide perfectly, such as right-duty, exposure-liberty, power-liability, and immunity-disability.

To each legal attribute of A, some corresponding position of B determines a relationship of limits and reciprocation. To this reciprocal interaction, Commons adds the state and the two respective "opportunity costs" of supply and demand of respectively individual C and D (the next best alternatives to A and B). Therefore, a transaction is a multilateral form of relationship. It involves the decision to reciprocally modify rights, often compensated by money (which is itself a specific right on a symbolic accounting unit), and consists of a consensual modification of the juridical spheres of the parts under the framework of customs, rules, and institutions.

Laws and working rules, constituted by practices and customs, integrate this framework. Actually, rules and institutions contribute to define the legal position and, at the same time, govern the dynamics of the transaction: rules affect rights. Therefore, rules and rights are complementary in defining the legal environment. Commons particularly focuses on institutions and laws that are under the control of the government because he is interested in how society is steered politically by modifying the legal positions of actors.[37] However, he includes working rules resulting from social interactions, such as customs and habits, among the institutions affecting exchange, leaving room for our analysis (specifically, Commons talks of legal, moral, and economic sanctions).

The transaction is also the framework in which the process of *evaluation* takes place, a process "oriented" by institutions, specifically the working rules defining the respective entitlements.[38] Institutionalism stresses the role of *social* evaluation instead of evaluation based on the simple market process of neoclassical economics. Social evaluation is affected by the complexity of relationships and by the specific arrangement of institutions and also underlines the role of individual positions, particularly wealth, in affecting outcomes. Therefore, this view supports our double channel including recognition of rights and prices.

Commons in this way reaffirms the distinction between *freedom* and *liberty*: the latter presupposes a legal framework and a legal capacity of the subject to be able to hold rights and duties. Therefore, liberty cannot be defined without considering the respect of each right.

Rights, the Law, and Evaluation: Giving Priority to Social Law

Commons's transaction framework can be expanded to highlight the development of effective rights through reciprocal recognition and their effect on the distributional outcome in exchanges. The specific act of reciprocal recognition among individuals is the fundamental and effective foundation of their interactions. Therefore, a right is an issue of reciprocal communication and agreement in a structured legal environment, and not a simple static tradable element. In this way, rights emerge and are defined in a transactional process and not a simple input to it. The element underlined here is that the cognitive process of recognition underlies any economic and social interaction; it affects the legal positions of players and, as such, has an impact on the economic outcomes of the transaction.

On the other hand, there are different kinds of rights and rules that enter transactions. This perspective of the right as a moral power in a relationship implies a further theoretical aspect: it is not possible to sharply separate the property right from other kind of rights and liberties (as in the classical idea of property). This fact is evident in a service economy where the willingness to pay of buyers depends on a variety of qualitative factors. The literature normally distinguishes human rights from social rights and economic rights. Human rights tend to be generally acknowledged by international institutions, and many constitutions state a variety of social rights for their citizens. Economic rights are more controversial, with the notable exception of property.[39] However, the approach taken here is that constitutions and formal laws are relevant, but effective rights, obligations, and liberties depend on the specific recognition between individuals.

Property is (part of) the set of entitlements of a person. The fact that property is tradable does not make it completely autonomous from other obligations attached to it or to the whole personality of the holder. Property can be complex and involve specific duties (such as maintenance, safety, externalities, and common benefits). Therefore, the personality of a trader, the set of her entitlements, and even the quantity of her endowments, all affect the outcome of the evaluation process concerning the specific right traded (property of a good or the labor of the individual). It is not only relative scarcity that affects prices, but also the status of the interacting persons as well as specific context variables.

Economic rights are not limited to property, but involve all entitlements of the exchanging parties, including the effective competences of the individuals, their reputation, formal certification of competences, and so forth. They can involve immunities (such as from externalities), freedoms, powers, and responsibilities. There are also entitlements arising as an effect of the working rules, such as the way of granting the performance, incentives to comply with agreed performance, or the penalties applied in case of unsatisfactory performance—briefly, all points normally included in contracts.

What is relevant here is that social and human rights can also factor into the interaction, especially when engaging low-pay work. Human and social rights can interact with the economic, such as in the case of slavery, which reduces also the economic rights of the slaves. Ethnic minorities are discriminated against in many ways including the economic point of view, and women often get wages or salaries that are significantly lower than that of men. This kind of interaction is often analyzed under the label of "discrimination." The fact is that very strong rights of one part opposed to the weakness of the other in a transaction can reinforce the former's power and create a sort of liability in the counterpart, making the transaction less "horizontal." That can have monetary implications, in particular when prejudices and the consequent distortion of recognition becomes shared in a community.

A specific problem that can be studied is how the insufficient recognition of the juridical position of the counterpart leads to downplay her assets in the process of evaluation. This means that the process of evaluation—fixing individual reservation prices—is affected by the underlying process of recognition of the counterpart. Buyers faced with weak counterparts tend to define lower reservation prices, and sellers, when they are not recognized for what they are and deserve, also tend to feel compelled to fix lower reservation prices. Independently of the relative scarcity on the market (if the market exists), the emerging price would be lower than that coming out a situation of equal partners. If we consider our partner an inferior being, our reservation price for anything she can sell us is lower than the standard; the opposite when we deal with somebody we consider a prestigious person.

This process can worsen into a backward feedback when the expected lack of recognition leads to expected low evaluation inducing individuals to adopt low-profile strategies. For example, people may not study because they expect that the eventual title would not assure them proportional recognition, which can entrap people in lower qualifications. The reverse can also take place: the act of evaluating a specific property in a transaction can indirectly affect the respect for other rights of the individual, including human rights. The typical example is that of a salary that is too low to ensure a decent life for the worker. Even if that kind of labor is abundant, the pay should not be so low as to harm the worker's human rights. From this perspective, low pay is equivalent to insulting the person. Therefore, recognition affects the distribution of income (and perhaps also redistribution through the political recognition of social groups).[40]

The consequence is that, in order to increase the fairness of exchanges, we need a policy able to foster the juridical position as well as the social position of people in weak positions or with weak entitlements. Moreover, some counterbalancing intervention can also help in equalizing the situation. The most typical example is the diffusion of education and literacy at the end of the nineteenth century that had the effect of reducing poverty. Today, we can single out the problem of migrants, whose situation requires an active policy to ensure a balanced position in transactions.

Rights can be defined and enforced by the constitution and by formal laws, but their origin and their effective definition and respect are the result of social interaction. Classic natural law sees natural rights as the product of a universal moral law that induces individuals to respect other people's positions in a reciprocal dimension. But reality shows the existence of relevant discrimination, and as a consequence, universal moral law does not necessarily grant equality. It remains useful to analyze actual situations as well, because they can be a point of reference for government policies.

Commons shaped the concept of transactions to include state authority as an essential condition of exchanges. At this point, some insights supplied by Dworkin are particularly useful. The state and other institutions are responsible for defining background rights, which constitute the standard that should be respected and define the respect that individuals deserve and are obliged to observe. Such rights should be derived from an idea of progress and improvement of civil society guided by shared ideal principles that can also be derived from philosophy, ideology, or religion. Education is the main policy that can be enacted in this regard. As a consequence, the definition of rights is not given by a static reciprocity, but rather is part of an evolving juridical framework in which the law has both to acknowledge people's values and assure a shared direction. The state should therefore assume an ethical role because it assumes the task of impressing a direction to the juridical evolution through democratic processes.[41]

The second kind of intervention inspired by Dworkin is designed to balance specific institutional rights. Similarly to what nineteenth-century Jesuit Luigi Taparelli argued, there is some need to counterbalance the different weight of persons in order to obtain balanced transactions.[42] This intervention can be performed by institutions that, affecting transactions, are able to reinforce the rights of weak categories of people (such as workers, women, or migrants). This is the case in favor of labor legislation that helps reinforce the position of laborers relative to employers. Consequently, contrary to the liberal argument that liberalization increases efficiency, labor protection legislation can display positive results in economic systems suffering from insufficient respect of labor rights.

Conclusion: Commutative Justice
in Economic Interactions

The problem of social justice cannot be fully adequately tackled by state-centered theories that frame this problem as a purely distributive problem. The consequence of such theoretical frame is to surrender to any commutative injustice in the name of presumed market efficiency and to charge the state and other institutions of solving the insurmountable problems of increasing inequality. This is the theoretical limit of the perspective of Léon Walras, John Stuart Mill, and, more recently, John Rawls. As argued by Axel Honneth, the procedural perspective cannot help much avoiding this underevaluation.[43] He therefore adds a "justice of needs" and a "justice of performance" (in connection with labor remuneration) to the "procedural" to achieve an effective social justice.

In this chapter, I have used the concept of recognition to argue that the problem of social injustice primarily arises in the market from some unavoidable processes of unfair evaluation in which weak people are progressively set apart. Therefore, there is a serious problem of social evaluation in the market that is not purely economic but that social economists cannot avoid analyzing. The spontaneous emergence of norms, habits, and opinions is a fundamental aspect of human interaction. It acquires an important role in economic interactions in which it represents the most effective legal element. However, it can also have shortcomings and some negative impact by preserving or increasing inequalities that certainly are not functional to a fair functioning of the market.

In this framework, we can see that the historical role of social and labor legislation was not to reduce inequalities by redistributing wealth (that was theorized mostly by the current liberal-progressive trend in economics). Rather, the primary role of this legislation was to reinforce the juridical position of contracting parties in the market, ensuring in this way a result closer to commutative justice. Contemporary reformers, busy in dismantling past institutions, apparently disregard this fundamental aspect.[44]

Notes

1. Practical here means "with a view to decision and action"; see Finnis, *Natural Law and Natural Rights*, 12.
2. The pragmatic background of institutionalism also shares some epistemological aspects of the classic practical approach.
3. Hanfling, "Rights and Human Rights," 63.

4. We refer in particular to John Commons's early study, *The Distribution of Wealth*, and to the paper "Institutional Economics."

5. See the studies of Tuck, *Natural Rights Theories*; Reid, "The Canonistic Contribution to the Western Rights Tradition"; and Tierney, *The Idea of Natural Rights*.

6. The *Magna Carta Libertatum* of 1215 had an explicit defensive character and in part some individualist dimension. It had an important impact on the conception of eventual theorization of law. In the feudal world, any autonomy in the use of property was achieved thanks to "privileges" assured by the emperor or king.

7. The idea of *Ordo* survived in the German economic studies up to *Ordo-Liberalism*.

8. See Schlatter, *Private Property*.

9. See Shue, *Basic Rights*.

10. This idea has also shaped the form of twentieth-century welfare states developed out of the universalist principles theorized in the Beveridge Report in 1942. Universalism is achieved by state's supply of adequate public services and, in particular, by the *decommodification* of some service. In fact, some social rights (such as the right to health) have found some implementation following the same path that property rights took for implementation: by letting the state provide a specific service or guarantee.

11. Here, I refer to Rawls's *Political Liberalism* that updates his book *A Theory of Justice*.

12. See, in particular, Habermas, "Politischer Liberalismus"; and Honneth, "Das Gewerbe der Gerechtigkeit."

13. Legal positivism presumes that the law is the result of explicit social practices and institutional decisions.

14. The *unity of value* argument is particularly developed in Dworkin, *Justice for Hedgehogs*. Dworkin defines "ethics" as the study of how to live well and "morals" as the study of how we should treat the others.

15. In *Taking Rights Seriously*, Dworkin discussed rights to equal consideration and respect and argued that there is no trade-off between liberty rights and equality rights; in other words, there is no general right to freedom.

16. Those who start the theorization of rights from the individual have difficulties proceeding to an operational political-economic theorization, and they tend to crowd out social law in favor of top-down reforms. Joseph Raz, in *The Morality of Freedom*, also tends to follow this direction.

17. Many scholars found the idea of rights in the principle of human dignity or human needs. The latter principles are certainly useful in theory but they remain vague in practice.

18. See Scanlon, *What We Owe to Each Other*.

19. Hanfling, "Rights and Human Rights," 62.
20. See Gewirth, "Human Dignity as the Basis of Rights" and *The Community of Rights.*
21. See Sen, "Elements of a Theory of Human Rights."
22. Sen affirms that while rights involve claims, freedoms are primarily descriptive characteristics of the conditions of persons (ibid., 328). Martha Nussbaum, in "Capabilities as Fundamental Entitlements," on the other hand, tends to see the freedom perspective as too vague. Moreover, some freedoms limit others. Therefore, she sees the capability perspective as complementing the approach based on rights.
23. On Burke's philosophy, see Harris, "Edmund Burke."
24. Concerning Hegel, we follow the path of Honneth in *The Struggle for Recognition* and *Suffering from Indeterminacy,* as well as the insights of Ver Eecke, *Ethical Dimensions of the Economy.* On Rosmini, see Hoevel, *The Economy of Recognition.* In the theory of Honneth, recognition is something we should struggle for; in Rosmini it is a natural attitude that does not lead to a transcendent "we" as in Hegel. In this way, to Rosmini, the right to property is at the same time personal, interpersonal, and social. (The first modern philosopher of recognition was Rousseau, but there is no specific revival of him; see Neuhouser, *Rousseau's Theory of Self-Love.*)
25. See Rosmini, *Principles of Ethics.*
26. See Hoevel, *The Economy of Recognition,* 103.
27. See Rosmini, *The Philosophy of Right* (both volumes).
28. We see this in the Kantian scheme as well; for instance, see White, *Kantian Ethics and Economics.*
29. See Hegel, *Philosophy of Right.*
30. Hertel and Minkler's edited volume *Economic Rights* provides various categories that can be used in the analysis.
31. See Tusset, *Money as Organisation*; refer also to Hermann, *Staatswirtschaftliche Untersuchungen*; and Macleod, *Principles of Economical Philosophy.* For the work of Del Vecchio, see *Ricchezze immateriali e capitali immateriali.*
32. See Böhm-Bawerk, *Rechte und Verhältnisse vom Standpunkte der volkswirthschaftlichen Güterlehre.* The influence of Böhm-Bawerk on Commons is presented in Fiorito, "John R. Commons, Wesley N. Hohfeld, and the Origins of Transactional Economics." It is not clear how much inspiration Commons received from the work of Macleod. Consequently, the idea of basing the study of economic processes on transactions owes to the German economy both the use of ideal-types and the relational approach.
33. See Commons, *The Distribution of Wealth.*
34. See Hohfeld, *Fundamental Legal Conceptions.*
35. In particular, see Commons, "Law and Economics." For what concerns the legal elements entering production, Commons (in

The Distribution of Wealth) singles out personal abilities, capital, monopoly privileges, and legal rights.

36. See Fiorito, "John R. Commons, Wesley N. Hohfeld, and the Origins of Transactional Economics."
37. See Commons, "Law and Economics" and "Institutional Economics."
38. On the process of social evaluation, see Tool, "A Social Value Theory in Neoinstitutional Economics."
39. See Hertel and Minkler, *Economic Rights.*
40. See the exchange between Honneth and Margalit in "Recognition."
41. The problem of stating what is the just thing in the classical tradition is solved by assuming an external point of view to be able to study the balance of positions.
42. His thought on the point is resumed in Mastromatteo and Solari, "Jesuits and Italian Unification."
43. See Honneth, "Das Gewerbe der Gerechtigkeit."
44. I am indebted to Daniel Finn, Kevin McCarron, and Robert E. Prasch for comments on the first draft of this work.

Bibliography

Böhm-Bawerk, Eugen von. *Rechte und Verhältnisse vom Standpunkte der volkswirthschaftlichen Güterlehre.* Innsbruck: Wagner, 1881.

Commons, John R. *The Distribution of Wealth.* New York: Macmillan, 1893.

———. "Institutional Economics." *American Economic Review* 21 (1931): 648–657.

———. "Law and Economics." *Yale Law Journal* 34 (1925): 37–82.

———. *Legal Foundations of Capitalism.* New York: MacMillan, 1924.

Del Vecchio, Gustavo. *Ricchezze immateriali e capitali immateriali.* Alessandria: Società poligrafica Alessandrina, 1908.

Dworkin, Ronald. *Justice for Hedgehogs.* Cambridge, MA: Harvard University Press, 2011.

———. *Taking Rights Seriously.* Cambridge, MA: Harvard University Press, 1977.

Finnis, John. *Natural Law and Natural Rights.* Oxford: Clarendon Press, 1980.

Fiorito, Luca. "John R. Commons, Wesley N. Hohfeld and the Origins of Transactional Economics." *History of Political Economy* 42 (2010): 267–295.

Gewirth, Alan R. *The Community of Rights.* Berlin: Springer, 1998.

———. "Human Dignity as the Basis of Rights." In *The Constitution of Rights: Human Dignity and American Values,* edited by Michael J. Meyer and William A. Parent, 10–28. Ithaca, NY: Cornell University Press, 1992.

Habermas, Jürgen. "Politischer Liberalismus—Eine Auseinandersetzung mit John Rawls." In *Die Einbeziehung des Anderen,* 65–127. Frankfurt: Suhrkamp, 1996.

Hanfling, Oswald. "Rights and Human Rights." *Royal Institute of Philosophy Supplement* 58 (2006): 57–94.

Harris, Ian. "Edmund Burke." *Stanford Encyclopedia of Philosophy* (2010), http://plato.stanford.edu/entries/burke/.

Hegel, Georg W. F. *Philosophy of Right*. Kitchener, Ontario: Batoche, 2001 [1820].

Hermann, Friedrich B. W. von. *Staatswirtschaftliche Untersuchungen*. München: Werber, 1932 [1870].

Hertel, Shareen, and Lanse Minkler (eds). *Economic Rights: Conceptual, Measurement, and Policy Issues*. New York: Cambridge University Press, 2007.

Hoevel, Carlos. *The Economy of Recognition. Person, Market and Society in Antonio Rosmini*. Dordrecht: Springer, 2013.

Hohfeld, Wesley N. *Fundamental Legal Conceptions as Applied in Judicial Reasoning, and Other Legal Essays*. Edited by D. Campbell and Ph. Thomas. Aldershot, UK: Ashgate, 2001 [1919].

Honneth, Axel. "Das Gewerbe der Gerechtigkeit. Über der Grenzen des zeitgenössischen Prozeduralismus." ("The Trade of Justice: The Limits of Contemporary Proceduralism.") *Zeitschrift für Sozialforschung* 6 (2009): 3–22.

———. *The Struggle for Recognition: The Moral Grammar of Social Conflicts*. Cambridge: Polity Press, 1995.

———. *Suffering from Indeterminacy. An Attempt to Reactualization of Hegel's Philosophy of Right*. Amsterdam: Van Gorcum, 2000.

Honneth, Axel, and Avishai Margalit. "Recognition." *Supplement to the Proceedings of the Aristotelian Society* 75 (2001): 111–139.

Macleod, Henry D. *Principles of Economical Philosophy*. London: Longmans, 1872.

Mastromatteo, Giuseppe, and Stefano Solari. "Jesuits and Italian Unification: The Form and Economic Role of the State in the Writings of Taparelli." *Il Pensiero Economico Italiano* 1 (2014): in press.

Neuhouser, Frederick. *Rousseau's Theory of Self-Love. Evil, Rationality and Drive for Recognition*. New York: Oxford University Press, 2008.

Nussbaum, Martha. "Capabilities as Fundamental Entitlements: Sen and Social Justice." *Feminist Economics* 9 (2–3) (2003): 33–59.

Rawls, John. *Political Liberalism*. New York: Columbia University Press, 1993.

———. *A Theory of Justice*. Oxford: Oxford University Press, 1971.

Raz, Joseph. *The Morality of Freedom*. Oxford, Oxford University Press, 1986.

Reid, Charles J., Jr. "The Canonistic Contribution to the Western Rights Tradition: A Historical Inquiry." *Boston College Law Review* 33 (1991): 37–92.

Rosmini, Antonio. *The Philosophy of Right, Vol. 1: The Essence of Right*. Translated by Denis Cleary and Terence Watson. Durham, UK: Rosmini House, 1993 [1865].

————. *The Philosophy of Right, Vol. 2: Rights of the Individual.* Translated by Denis Cleary and Terence Watson. Durham, UK: Rosmini House, 1993 [1865].

————. *Principles of Ethics.* Translated by Denis Cleary and Terence Watson. Durham, UK: Rosmini House, 1988 [1845].

Scanlon, Thomas. *What We Owe to Each Other.* Cambridge, MA: Harvard University Press, 1998.

Schlatter, Richard. *Private Property: The History of an Idea.* London: Allen & Unwin, 1951.

Sen, Amartya. "Elements of a Theory of Human Rights." *Philosophy and Public Affairs* 32 (2004): 315–356.

————. "What Do We Want from a Theory of Justice?" *Journal of Philosophy* 103 (2006): 215–238.

Shue, Henry. *Basic Rights: Subsistence, Affluence, and U.S. Foreign Policy.* Princeton, NJ: Princeton University Press, 1996.

Tierney, Brian. *The Idea of Natural Rights: Studies on Natural Rights, Natural Law and Church Law 1150–1625.* Atlanta, GA: Scholars Press of Emory University, 1997.

Tool, Marc R. "A Social Value Theory in Neoinstitutional Economics." *Journal of Economic Issues* 11 (1977): 823–845.

Tuck, Richard. *Natural Rights Theories: Their Origin and Development.* Cambridge: Cambridge University Press, 1979.

Tusset, Gianfranco. *Money as Organisation: Gustavo Del Vecchio's Theory.* London: Pickering & Chatto, 2014.

Ver Eecke, Wilfried. *Ethical Dimensions of the Economy.* Berlin: Springer, 2008.

White, Mark D. *Kantian Ethics and Economics: Autonomy, Dignity, and Character.* Stanford, CA: Stanford University Press, 2011.

Chapter 4

Institutionalist Method and Forensic Proof

Robert M. LaJeunesse

With the sophistication of empirical methods, social science experts have expanded their influence in many forms of litigation. This chapter suggests that forensic economic analysis, when conducted properly, is more closely aligned with the holistic method of economic inquiry followed by institutionalists and other heterodox schools than the formalism of the neoclassical paradigm. It draws upon the methodological differences delineated by Charles Wilbur and Robert Harrison to show that a method of "pattern modeling, storytelling, and holism" provides a better description of reality and truth than relying on a formal model that is more prescriptive than descriptive.[1] A deductive method that serves as a parable to achieve an abstract ideal is of little use in the legal setting. Probative forensic analysis requires a holistic melding of anecdotal evidence (storytelling) and empirical validation. As the US Supreme Court acknowledged in the context of employment discrimination (in *Int'l. Brotherhood of Teamsters v. United States*), stories give context to the statistics.[2]

Formalism versus Holism

Formalism is a method of inquiry consisting of a formal system of logical relationships abstracted from any empirical content it might have in the real world. The theory of the firm, for example, is intended to apply to the behavior of any firm in any production process, using any inputs, at any set of relative prices with any prevailing technology. Formalism relies heavily on mathematics, axioms, and deductive methods derived by separating an empirical process into its obvious divisions. Marshall Sahlins points out the difficulty that formalist models have when applied to nonmarket settings with uncomfortable anthropological facts:

> "Formalism versus substantivism" amounts to the following theoretical option: between the readymade models of orthodox Economics, especially the "microeconomics," taken as universally valid and applicable *grosso modo* to the primitive societies; and the necessity—supposing this formalist position unfounded—of developing a new analysis more appropriate to the historical societies in question and to the intellectual history of Anthropology.[3]

Formal models are perceived as capable of yielding axioms or formal laws. These law-like statements are not empirical generalizations but are logical deductions that make a priori statements about necessary connections between abstract entities. The theory of utility maximization, for instance, does not describe how actual consumers behave, but how an ideally rational consumer *should* behave, which is determined from logical deduction rather than from observation. The axiomatic statements that emerge from formalist models are difficult to falsify empirically because of changing ceteris paribus conditions. In much of mainstream theory, truth about reality lies in the logic of the theory. Realizing the limitations of formalism, institutionalists such as Thorstein Veblen, John Commons, and Wesley Mitchell dissented from this view of economic theory and method.

Beginning in the 1940s, economists began revamping economic theory in an effort to make it empirically testable.[4] Mimicking the practice of physicists, logical positivism attempted to show that empirically falsifiable propositions could be derived from formal models. According to one of its most clarion proponents, Milton Friedman, the goal of positive economics "is to provide a system of generalizations that can be used to make correct predictions about the consequences of any change in circumstances. Its performance is to be judged by the precision, scope, and conformity with experience of the predictions it yields."[5]

With the development of computerized metrics, many economists have become positivists, viewing empirical verification as the sublime task of social science. Many believe that the sciences are differentiated only by subject matter, and not methodology. An event or behavior to be explained is viewed as a prediction of a correlational relationship. The activity is then subjected to empirical testing in the form of statistical inference or direct observation in order to assess the truth of the observation. Positivist scientists aver that the pursuit of scientific truth proceeds by accumulating potentially falsifiable but ultimately confirmed propositions about the subject matter.

With the emphasis on predictive ability, concerns for the realism of assumptions or the versatility of the structure of positive economics are minimized. Assumptions facilitate abstraction and allow positivist economists to offer explanations of economic behavior without capturing the entire patchwork of reality. One reason why discredited theories, such as the "natural rate of unemployment" and the NAIRU, are not abandoned in mainstream economics is because the subject matter of economics is not amenable to generalizations that form a useful basis for prediction. Positivists often attempt to rationalize the failure of models by blaming the ceteris paribus clauses, the data, or the specific testing procedures. As Wilbur and Harrison contend:

> Positive economics thus becomes perfectly insulated from refutation. It cannot be harmed by demonstrating that the assumptions and laws of the formal model are abstract and unrealistic, and the model is not rejected when its predictions fail to fit the facts...When a theory is able to obtain such a high level of insulation that its substantive hypotheses are, in practice, nonfalsifiable, we contend that the theory collapses into an *a priori* formal model that compels assent by its logic, not by its conformity with empirical reality. As such, economic theory functions more as a prescriptive than descriptive device. That is, theory functions as a parable to elucidate the ideal toward which we should strive.[6]

When formal methods fail to generate the anticipated outcome, mainstream economists resort to "storytelling."[7] They are forced to depart from logical deductions and tell stories about imperfect competition, frictions, externalities, irrationalities, and a variety of social limitations to utility and profit maximization. The term "storytelling" is not offered pejoratively, but as an accurate description of most work in the social sciences. Indeed such storytelling is compatible with legal inquiry, which embraces a fact pattern specific to the case at hand. Any use of positivist analysis in the legal setting must be subsumed within the facts of the case.

Forensic evidence generally relates to any material such as facts, objects, documents, analysis, and opinions suitable for submission to a jurist (either judge or jury) during litigation of a legal dispute. For the social scientist, forensic testimony typically entails an analysis of the facts revealed during the discovery process. Trial judges perform a gatekeeper role to ensure that the expert testimony meets the relevancy, rigor, and reliability standards of jurisprudence. In federal courts, the admissibly of testimony by a qualified expert is governed by Federal Rule of Evidence 702, which provides that (1) the testimony is based on sufficient facts or data; (2) the testimony is the product of reliable principles and methods; and (3) the witness has applied the principles and methods reliably to the facts of the case.[8] The role of the forensic witness is to apply reliable analytic methods to case-specific evidence to provide some clarity to the trier of fact. Given these restrictions, expert testimony requires a holistic analytic approach.

Institutionalists have adopted methods that emphasize holism over formalism, which are well-suited to forensic inquiry. Wilbur and Harrison argue that institutionalists have engaged in a twofold task of both critiquing the standard theory and developing their explanations of social phenomena.[9] The holistic nature of institutionalism minimizes the use of formal models and results in a process of storytelling, which Abraham Kaplan has referred to as a "pattern model."[10] Socioeconomic behavior is explained by identifying its place in a pattern that characterizes the ongoing processes of change in the entire system. Akin to the legal setting, empirical or statistical proof of economic behavior requires the repetition of competing models against evolving data sets for the holistic analyst. In contrast to the replication of results that has eluded mainstream economic research of late, the federal rules of evidence mandate that data sets and other foundation evidence be provided to opposing experts so that result can be replicated and validated.[11] The case study (or pattern-modeling) approach is absent from the formalist approach that abstracts from reality and insulates itself from validation of the theory itself.

The methods practiced by institutionalists can be described as holistic, systemic, and evolutionary. Economic behavior is viewed as a process of change embedded in a set of social institutions or relationships. Whereas the unit of investigation for the classical or hedonic schools of thought is the relation of man to nature, institutionalists focus on the relation of man to man. The smallest unit of activity for institutional economics is a transaction between participants, not the production of a commodity or the utility derived from it.[12] At its methodological core, institutionalism is more social in nature and better-suited to examine the legal disputes of social participants.

The institutionalist method is evolutionary because social reality changes in response to changing patterns of relations. American institutionalists such as Veblen, Commons, and John Kenneth Galbraith have stressed the role of conflict, power, and coercion in their analysis of vested interests, absentee ownership, collective and political bargaining, and public utility regulation. The work of contemporary institutionalists continues to feature the conflict that emerges from changes in technology, social institutions, and distributions of power. Positivist models simply cannot incorporate the diversity of variables, the specificity of institutions, and the minutiae of behavior that is required to fully comprehend an evolving society.

When an economic method overemphasizes precision and rigor, it will tend to fall into theoretical stagnation.[13] Under a preoccupation with logical and empirical detail, it will be difficult for theories to stay abreast of societal and technological change. On the other hand, the vagueness and suggestiveness of holism can lead to creeping speculation. Wilbur and Harrison illustrate the need for balance: "A central problem of any methodology is how to strike a balance between precision and rigor, on the one hand, and vagueness and suggestiveness, on the other, and how to relate the two so that they synergize rather than cancel each other."[14] Since the legal system is case-driven, it is constantly forced to consider evolving social norms. It is imperative, therefore, that forensic analysis features the evolutionary aspects of the holistic approach.

Holistic Methods and the Legal System

Since the legal system evolves through case-specific examinations, it has little use for logical generalizations regarding anticipated behavior. Articulating how agents "should have behaved" does not inform the fact finder when considering a limited set of evidence. Indeed, even suggesting how individuals or organizations tend to behave as a reflection of social norms (social framework analysis) has been severely restricted by the Supreme Court in the recent *Dukes v. Wal-Mart* decision.[15] In that case, plaintiffs alleged that as many as 1.5 million female workers were treated less favorably than men by Wal-Mart's decisions regarding pay and promotion. Expert testimony by a sociologist attempted to show that Wal-Mart possessed a corporate culture that made its decisions "vulnerable" to gender bias. In denying certification of the class, the majority was convinced that the social framework analysis could not specifically determine how often stereotypes played a role in Wal-Mart's decisions. The Supreme Court majority held that

> whether 0.5 percent or 95 percent of the employment decisions at Wal-Mart might be determined by stereotyped thinking is the essential

question on which respondents' theory of commonality depends...If [the expert] admittedly has no answer to that question, we can safely disregard what he has to say. It is worlds away from "significant proof" that Wal-Mart operated under a general policy of discrimination.[16]

Analysis of the social influence on economic behavior may still be admissible after the *Dukes* ruling, but it must make some attempt to incorporate the facts of the case at hand. Gregory Mitchell, Laurens Walker, and John Monahan conclude that "if experts go beyond providing context for a case through a description of general social science research to make claims about the meaning of social science principles for a particular case, then those case-specific claims should be the product of reliable case-specific research."[17] Indeed the Supreme Court's repudiation of deductive reasoning detached from the facts of the case is analogous to heterodox critiques of formalist economic methodology. Both stem from the realization that overly broad generalizations, suppositions, and conclusions provide little insight to the specifics of a particular matter.

The Supreme Court has not ruled that objective, quantifiable evidence is the only avenue of forensic proof; a holistic assessment is still required. Empirical conclusions alone are rarely enough to sway judges and juries. The Supreme Court has not reversed its belief that the standard of proof should go beyond logical and positivist statements: "Statistics are not irrefutable; they come in infinite variety and, like any other kind of evidence, they may be rebutted," and their usefulness "depends on all of the surrounding facts and circumstances."[18] The probative weight of the evidence is not only dependent on the accuracy of the empirical data, but to the relevance of the economic model and statistical methods applied to the issues in dispute. In fact, by requiring more case-specific evidence from sociological testimony, the *Dukes* ruling validates the holistic approach to socioeconomic inquiry because it states that experts must work harder to tell a story that fits a pattern. To prove a "pattern or practice" case, the forensic analyst needs to fashion a credible pattern model from the relevant evidence.

The "pattern model" of investigation is better-suited to a case-specific discipline such as the law because it is not the sheer scale of the system that is important, but that the particular system under investigation constitutes a unified whole. In the pattern model method, the analyst tests hypotheses about recurrent themes by consulting a wide variety of data, including case studies, survey data, personal observation, and empirical studies. Similar to the task of the jury and judge, the institutionalist economist engages in a process of cross-checking different kinds of sources and evidence to evaluate the plausibility of one's initial interpretations. The process of contextual validation can never produce the rigorous certainty espoused by logical positivists; it can only indicate varying degrees of plausibility. Similarly, the law has established varying burdens of proof with differing degrees of plausibility required at various stages of litigation. The various standards of proof such as reasonable doubt, preponderance of the evidence, and pretext all recognize that the degree of plausibility will differ as the legal settings and stages vary.[19]

Just as a litigator needs to build a holistic argument to prevail in court, the institutionalist method attempts to link validated hypotheses or themes in a network or pattern that captures the multitude of connections between that part and the whole system. The researcher is reasonably certain that an explanation is correct if new data and different kinds of evidence fit the pattern; a similar burden is placed on the trier of fact in a legal setting. The jurist must serve as an impartial arbiter of the reasonableness of the proposition or explanation. Empirical analysis is one piece of a puzzle that, when considered in conjunction with the other evidence in this case, reveals whether discrimination played a part in the decision-making.[20]

Brockway illustrates how the law focuses on the details that positivist economists would ignore as ancillary, if not superfluous, information:

> Economics and the law are both divisions of ethics. An important distinction between them is that motive or intention is central in the law but is insignificant in economics. A man is discovered with a smoking gun in his hand, standing over a bleeding corpse. It may be quickly proved that homicide has been committed by the man with the gun. But what did the man intend? If the killing was done with malice aforethought, it was murder. If it was done in a sudden rage, it was manslaughter. If the gun happened to go off when the man tripped, it was accidental death. If the killer shot to defend himself, the homicide is justifiable. And if the killer is unable to distinguish right from wrong, he is not a criminal, but may be, as they say, institutionalized. That a man has been killed is the beginning, not the end, of the law's concern.
>
> With economics, it is the other way entirely. The intentions of economic agents matter only to them or to those entitled to pass judgment on them, but not to the economy—and not at all, as far as economic consequences are concerned, even to the agents themselves. Entrepreneurs may, with the best intention in the world, set the price

for their products too high (or too low) and thus ruin their companies, their investors, their employees, and themselves. Their good intentions do not mitigate their companies' losses or the consequent diminishing of the GDP.[21]

Since the law acknowledges context, motivations, and intentions, a major challenge for the forensic economist is grasping the parameters placed on the application of theory and technique by legislation and case law. For instance, the option of which comparators to choose in an employment discrimination case is governed by the statute cited in the initial pleadings and the case law that has developed around that statute. The appropriate analysis may not necessarily accord with labor market theory or the expert's own opinion of the "correct" comparative analysis. In a recent case involving a claim of discrimination against mothers, the court held that the proper comparison under the Americans with Disabilities Act (ADA) was not between women who took maternity leave and similarly situated male workers, but rather the treatment of those women upon their return to work compared to the treatment of all leave-takers upon their return.[22] The forensic expert has to be aware of the social context in which legislatures and jurists have drafted and interpreted laws in an effort to achieve a balance between competing social interests. Failure to appreciate this balance often results in analyses that amount to thinly veiled advocacy.

Although the positivist approach may appear to be more objective on the surface, David Greiner points out that normative issues arise even when conducting the putatively objective task of regression analysis.[23] In defining a regression model, the forensic analyst is tempted to see the litigation answer before assessing the model's goodness of fit. As mentioned earlier, deciding whether the model adequately addresses the data and the litigation question requires a value assessment. Finally, manipulating the regression by adding, subtracting, or modifying variables can result in wholesale changes to the results. Greiner argues that "at each stage of the [model-building] process of exploration and assessment, the substantive result, the litigation answer, stares the analyst in the face. Only the superhuman can completely disregard the temptation to lean towards a result favorable to a chosen side, consciously or not."[24] The facts of the case, legislative statutes, and case law, all determine the parameters of a relevant analysis. Forensic examinations conducted by social scientists are not likely to rely on the objective application of empirical methods alone as the facts of the case permeate the analytical process. Additionally,

Stephen Ziliak and Deirdre McCloskey bemoan the emphasis placed on statistical significance over relevance.[25] They argue that the focus should be on clinical, ecological, or forensic significance rather than statistical significance. Professional ethics require that the analyst acknowledge the limitations of empirical models and the influence of subjective matters and strive to strike a balance between a holistic approach and objective empiricism where possible.

The Formalism of Human Capital Theory

In labor economics, the asocial, apolitical, and ahistorical method of mainstream economics has fostered the rise of human capital theory. As an extension of price theory and utility maximization, human capital theory fits the description of a formalist theory. Most mainstream labor economists axiomatically accept that measures of human capital—primarily education and experience—represent productivity outcomes that determine the price of labor (wages or salary). The theory holds that rational individuals will delay their gratification to invest in human capital accumulation to increase future returns in the labor market. Nancy Folbre recognizes the pervasive influence of the theory in the context of discrimination studies:

> The bulk of empirical research on sex and race/ethnic discrimination adopts the assumption that education and experience are primary determinants of earnings, treating any residual difference in earnings as a measure of discrimination. This assumption does not necessitate agreement with the claim that earnings are primarily determined by productivity, but it certainly implies it.[26]

Given the positivist nature of human capital theory, it is somewhat paradoxical that it has gained traction as a component of forensic proof. In a case-driven arena such as the law, one would not expect much use of a theory detached from historical, social, and political influences. Yet, expert witnesses routinely appeal to human capital theory in quantifying and analyzing disparate wage claims and other employment discrimination disputes. In describing their earnings regressions, for instance, labor economists often defer to human capital theory as a rationale for including certain variables, or "productivity proxies." In some instances, human capital concepts are codified in employment regulations. The Equal Pay Act references three affirmative defenses for disparate pay related to individual productivity proxies: seniority, merit, and production. The law presumes that more experience (seniority), more credentials (merit), and more throughput (production) are observable and credible sources of disparate pay systems. The common use of human capital language suggests that practitioners many not appreciate the full meaning of the theory and use it euphemistically when describing mere skill and rank differences.

Although it has adopted some human capital terminology, labor law affords less reverence to the market forces of supply and demand than economics proper. The Equal Pay Act is incorporated into the Fair Labor Standards Act (FLSA) of 1938. The FSLA was implemented as a protective response to unacceptable market outcomes related to wages, hours, and child labor. In *Glenn v. General Motors Corporation*, the Eleventh Circuit ruled that "the argument that supply and demand dictates that women qua women may be paid less is exactly the kind of evil that the [Equal Pay] Act was designed to eliminate."[27] As Ian Ayres has argued, "Not all increments to profitability deserve equal judicial respect."[28] If market forces cannot be relied upon to accurately compensate a class of women, how can the metaphysical forces of supply and demand be a dependable assayer of individual productivity? Individual value is not individual if it is derived from aggregate market forces. Many legal practitioners may not view human capital theory as a positivist theory or recognize marginal productivity theory as its antecedent. They have adopted the terminology of human capital theory without a full appreciation of the neoclassical price determination paradigm on which it is founded.

When viewed from an alternative methodology, human capital theory is revealed as a cloak for labor market segmentation. Human capital theory amounts to a "re-packaging" of marginal productivity theory and a "new" theoretical mythology to rationalize extant labor market inequities. Productivity proxies provide employers with a convenient cover as they divide, queue, and conquer workers. Ignoring social, political, psychological, and historical influences, human capital theory instructs that delayed gratification, investment, and hard work will generate future returns.

Concerned with the ascendency of marginal productivity theory, institutionalists deny that wages and other payments relate closely to the individual attributes of an economic agent.[29] Clarence Ayres critiqued the atomistic view of marginal productivity theory and offered an alternative holistic view:

> In every society such [inalienable] "rights" derive from the mythology of agency, which is implicit in the system of beliefs to which the people of that society are emotionally conditioned, beginning in early childhood.

As a matter of fact, whatever any society accomplishes—however it gets its living and otherwise maintains itself—is a causal consequence of the functioning of that society as a whole. This is what anthropologists mean by insisting that all cultures can be understood only as functioning wholes... Economists should know better than anyone that no one creates anything except as a participant in the culture he shares with all the other members of the community, and that it is utterly impossible to determine how different the future of his society would have been if he had never been born.[30]

A holistic view of the labor market reveals that the price theory underlying human capital theory is tautological. It can only determine what the various participants of our economy "create" once it is "revealed" by what they "earn." In the context of employment discrimination, the factors contributing to the disparate treatment may simply be assumed away in the human capital model. Since what workers earn reflects a social value system, the atomistic approach of human capital theory offers little usefulness for the social scientist and the legal analyst.

Lester Thurow also delineated many limitations to marginal productivity theory, including economies of scale, monopoly power, and knowledge imperfections.[31] Moreover, the productivity of an economic input depends on its own productivity, its occupation's productivity, its industry's productivity, its region's productivity, and the productivity of the factor class to which it belongs. At the occupational level, it may be difficult for plumbers or doctors with superior talent to command a wage rate much higher than the going rates for common procedures. The same is true for a worker stuck in a low-wage industry. To earn more, workers often have to find a higher paying team in a different industry. Mancur Olsen underscores the regional productivity differences with his hypothetical immigrant worker:

> When an immigrant from, say, Bangladesh lands in the U.K., his earnings rise by a factor of fifty or more. Because the immigrant did not miraculously acquire either more human capital, or assume radically different cultural or religious values, during an 11-hour airplane flight, then the determining factors must lie in the institutional and policy differences between the two countries.[32]

The myriad factors impacting the "efficient" use of resources suggest that productivity is more closely linked to the position rather than the person.

Recognizing the importance of the job position rather than the person, comparative worth studies attempt to compare pay rates across industries for individuals with similar credentials. Such studies may offer a more holistic approach than regression analyses that attempt to "control for" a variety of human capital proxies. Analogous to social framework analysis, comparative worth analysis would need to incorporate detailed specifics of the case at hand to be admissible. Such case-specific research is expensive and time-consuming. Yet, Mitchell and his colleagues suggest that the research output is worth the effort and expense: "We understand that in some cases having an expert witness engage in speculation may be cheaper, quicker, and simpler then conducting original research, but those savings come at the cost of scientific reliability."[33]

Marginal productivity theory is also prominent in mainstream models of "efficient" income distribution.[34] In such models, individuals derive utility from consumption and disutility from labor. Their access to higher utility differs only in their relative productivity. As manifest in human capital theory and the Mirrlees model, marginal productivity theory has expanded its theoretical reach and serves as a foundation for individualist positivism on many fronts. Appeal to such individualism inflames distributional conflicts between groups that might otherwise display solidarity. Folbre writes that "in the 1980s and 1990s, the growing penetration of women and immigrants into managerial and professional occupations reduced prospects for the upward mobility of white males, creating a backlash against affirmative action and diversity efforts."[35] Growing acceptance of marginal productivity theory led to the expansion of means-tested social assistance in the United States and contributed to a lack of solidarity and growing economic inequities.

With their acknowledgment of abundance and technological progress, institutionalists realize that deprivation is not caused by natural scarcity but by artificial scarcity imposed through social conflict and power struggles. Since these power conflicts tend to find their full force in the labor market, credible wage determination models cannot ignore these influences. A positivist method that simply assumes that wage payments are a return to measurable productivity metrics alone ignores the complex dynamics of the labor market and the specifics of the case. A forensic model of wage determination would then require a holistic analysis of the manifold factors influencing earnings outcomes.

Conclusion

Since legal inquiry requires case-specific evidence and analysis, formalist methods that rely on general axioms and deductive reasoning are inappropriate. Positivist models rarely allow for the contextual detail and nuances required by forensic proof, forcing the model-builders to resort to "story-telling." Since the holistic approach starts with the story to build a pattern model, it is better suited to forensic analysis and testimony. Advocacy of holistic analysis is not intended to repudiate empirical or econometric analysis, but rather to encourage a balance between the rigor of formalist models and the realism of alternative methods. Incorporating the influence of social institutions (conflict, power, and path-dependency) into forensic analysis will reveal that many formalist models—such as human capital theory—are less reliable in revealing the truth than their proponents profess or their adherents understand.[36]

Notes

1. Wilbur and Harrison, "The Methodological Basis of Institutional Economics," 61.
2. *Int'l. Brotherhood of Teamsters v. United States*, 431 US 324 (1977).
3. Sahlins, *Stone Age Economics*, 1.
4. See particularly Samuelson, *Foundations for Economic Analysis*.
5. Friedman, *Essays in Positive Economics*, 4.
6. Wilbur and Harrison, "The Methodological Basis of Institutional Economics," 69.
7. Ward, *What Is Wrong with Economics?*
8. Available at http://federalevidence.com/rules-of-evidence#Rule702.
9. Wilbur and Harrison, "The Methodological Basis of Institutional Economics," 71.
10. See Kaplan, *The Conduct of Inquiry*, Chapter 9.
11. Herdnon, Ash, and Pollin, "Does High Public Debt Consistently Stifle Economic Growth?"
12. See Commons, "Institutional Economics."
13. Diesing, *Patterns of Discovery in the Social Sciences*.
14. Wilbur and Harrison, "The Methodological Basis of Institutional Economics," 84.
15. *Wal-Mart Stores, Inc. v. Dukes et al*, 131 S.Ct. 2541 (2011). Prior to this decision, it was increasingly common for social science experts to offer a more global analysis of the social forces that are likely to influence the outcomes at issue during employment discrimination cases. Testimony regarding general research results was intended to inform fact-finders about the conditions under which gender stereotypes and prejudices might influence impressions, decisions, behavior, and outcomes in organizational settings.
16. Ibid., 16.
17. Mitchell, Walker, and Monahan, "Beyond Context," 18.
18. *Int'l Brotherhood of Teamsters v. United States*, 340.

19. In a Title VII employment discrimination claim, for instance, the plaintiffs must first establish a prima facie case of disparate treatment by a preponderance of the evidence. Thereafter, the burden of production shifts to the defendants to articulate some legitimate, non-discriminatory reason for the employment practice or a flaw in the statistical analysis. If the defendants meet this burden, the plaintiffs must then show either that the defendants' statistical proof is inadequate or that the defendants' explanation for the practice is merely a pretext for discrimination.
20. See *Cicero v. Borg-Warner Automotive, Inc.*, 280 F.3d 579 (2002), 592–593.
21. Brockway, *The End of Economic Man*, 26.
22. See *EEOC v. Bloomberg L.P.*, 07 Civ. 8383 (2010).
23. Greiner, "Causal Inference in Civil Rights Litigation."
24. Ibid., 544.
25. Ziliak and McCloskey, *The Cult of Statistical Significance*.
26. Folbre, "The Political Economy of Human Capital," 282.
27. *Glenn v. General Motors Corporation*, 841 F.2d 1567 (1988), 1570.
28. Ayres, "Market Power and Inequality," 688.
29. In "The Political Economy of Human Capital," Folbre identifies the common ground that Institutionalists share with Marxists concerning the role of conflict as it relates to human capital theory when she writes that "the larger contribution of Marxian theory, in my view, lies not in attention to class conflict alone, but the more abstract notion of collective conflict over the distribution of the costs of creating and maintaining human capital, which represent a distinct form of surplus. Attention to this form of surplus helps explain the historic role of the nation-state as progenitor of socialized provision for health care and education, that pools risk, coordinates collaborative efforts, and captures the returns to human capital better than families or firms" (287).
30. Ayres, "Ideological Responsibility," 5–7.
31. Thurow, *Generating Inequality*.
32. Olsen, "Big Bills Left on the Sidewalk," 54.
33. Mitchell, Walker, and Monahan, "Beyond Context," 18.
34. See Mirrlees, "An Exploration in the Theory of Optimum Income Taxation."
35. Folbre, "The Political Economy of Human Capital," 290.
36. This discourse reflects the opinions of the author, and not the opinions or policies of the Department of Labor.

Bibliography

Ayres, Clarence. "Ideological Responsibility." *Journal of Economic Issues* 1 (1967): 3–11.

Ayres, Ian. "Market Power and Inequality: A Competitive Conduct Standard for Assessing when Disparate Impacts Are Unjustified." *California Law Review* 95 (2007): 669–719.

Brockway, George. *The End of Economic Man*. New York: W.W. Norton and Co., 1995.

Commons, John. "Institutional Economics." *American Economic Review* 21 (1931): 648–657.

Diesing, Paul. *Patterns of Discovery in the Social Sciences*. Chicago: Aldine-Altheron, 1971.

Folbre, Nancy. "The Political Economy of Human Capital." *Review of Radical Political Economy* 44 (2012): 281–292.

Friedman, Milton. *Essays in Positive Economics*. Chicago: University of Chicago Press, 1953.

Greiner, David. "Causal Inference in Civil Rights Litigation." *Harvard Law Review* 122 (2008): 533–598.

Herdnon, Thomas, Michael Ash, and Robert Pollin. "Does High Public Debt Consistently Stifle Economic Growth? A Critique of Reinhart and Rogoff." *Political Economy Research Institute*. Amherst: Working Paper Series, #322 (2013).

Kaplan, Abraham. *The Conduct of Inquiry: Methodology for Behavioral Science*. San Francisco: Chandler Publishing Co., 1964.

Mirrlees, James, A. "An Exploration in the Theory of Optimum Income Taxation." *Review of Economic Studies* 38 (1971): 175–208.

Mitchell, Gregory, Laurens Walker, and John Monahan. "Beyond Context: Social Facts as Case-Specific Evidence." *Emory Law Journal* 60 (2011): 1109–1155.

Olsen, Mancur. "Big Bills Left on the Sidewalk: Why Some Nations Are Rich and Others Poor." In *A Not-So-Dismal Science: A Broader View of Economies and Societies*, edited by Mancur Olson and Satu Kahkonen, 37–60. Oxford: Oxford University Press, 2000.

Sahlins, Marshall. *Stone Age Economics*. New York: Aldine de Gruyter, 1972.

Samuelson, Paul. *Foundations for Economic Analysis*. Cambridge, MA: Harvard University Press, 1947.

Thurow, Lester. *Generating Inequality*. London: Macmillan, 1976.

Ward, Benjamin. *What Is Wrong with Economics?* New York: Basic Books, 1972.

Wilbur, Charles, and Robert Harrison. "The Methodological Basis of Institutional Economics: Pattern Model, Storytelling, and Holism." *Journal of Economic Issues* 12 (1978): 61–89.

Ziliak, Stephen, and Deirdre McCloskey. *The Cult of Statistical Significance*. University of Michigan Press: Ann Arbor, 2008.

Chapter 5

Retributivist Justice and Dignity: Finding a Role for Economics in Criminal Justice

Mark D. White

Mainstream economics has long struggled with crime, an intrinsically moralized area of law that resists attempts to reduce all goals and motivations within it to considerations of efficiency. Legal philosopher Jules Coleman, in response to an attempt to explain the category of crime in terms of transaction structures, wrote that "such a theory has no place for the moral sentiments and virtues appropriate to matters of crime and punishment: guilt, shame, remorse, forgiveness, and mercy, to name a few. A purely economic theory of crime can only impoverish rather than enrich our understanding of the nature of crime."[1] Without mentioning economics outright, legal scholar Herbert Morris bemoaned an approach to the law that "subordinates principle to the realization of social goals, a mode of thinking that focuses, not upon exculpation of the innocent and conviction of the guilty, that is, upon justice, but upon keeping social disruption at an acceptable level."[2]

In the parlance of mainstream economics, "acceptable" would be interpreted as "efficient," recalling prominent jurist and law-and-economics scholar Richard Posner's statement that harsh punishments are inefficient, "but this is not say that there would be too much crime. There might rather be too little."[3] In fact, Posner once equated justice in general with efficiency:

> A second meaning of "justice," and the most common I would argue, is simply "efficiency." When we describe as "unjust" convicting a person without a trial, taking property without just compensation, or failing to require a negligent automobile driver to answer in damages to

the victim of his carelessness, we can be interpreted as meaning simply that the conduct or practice in question wastes resources.[4]

Whatever conception of justice is violated in the cases he mentioned— procedural, criminal, or corrective—few aside from economists would argue that the primary issue in any of them is the efficient use of resources. As we will see, economic efficiency, resource allocation, and analysis of trade-offs do have important roles to play in the law, especially in the area of crime, but not at the primary level that Posner saw it.[5]

This myopic focus on efficiency blinds practioners of the main-stream economic approach to the law to the normative richness of the law in terms of both actors and institutions. In terms of crime, spe-cifically, the consequentialist emphasis on efficiency to the exclusion of any principle-based or deontological concepts of duty, wrong, or desert renders law and economics inadequate in terms of both positive and normative analysis. Regarding the former, it cannot account for counterpreferential moral motivations that influence a person's choice to obey or disobey the law in particular circumstances, nor does it incorporate the many cognitive biases and dysfunction identified by behavioral economists that influence decisions that are more likely internally contentious than clinically rational. In terms of the latter, the efficiency goal does not correspond to the understanding of crime as a wrong that should be punished and prevented rather than a mere externality that should be accepted and optimized. We will see in this chapter that economics does have a role to play in the study of crimi-nal justice, but not the one it has presumed to play—and, nonetheless, a more legitimate role than it plays in the study of private law, in which it has assumed the position of pride for the past half-century.

Retributivism, Deterrence, and Normative Law and Economics

In legal philosophy, the two predominant goals of criminal punishment— and, by extension, of the criminal justice system itself—are deterrence and retributivism.[6] Under deterrence, punishments are designed to provide incentives to potential criminals not to break the law; often this goal is understood is the context of overall efficiency to generate "efficient punishments" that deter only those crimes that cost society more than do the penalties and associated enforcement. On the other hand, retributivism requires that punishment for crimes be exacted as a matter of right or justice, regardless of any impact on future behavior.

Deterrence and retributivism are often distinguished in terms of their outlook: the former is forward-looking, focused on increasing future well-being, while the latter is backward-looking, intent on correcting past wrongs. These two goals correspond to the broader ethical categories of utilitarianism and deontology insomuch as deterrence aims to reduce future harms by reducing current criminal activity while retributivism addresses the wrongs represented by past crimes. These goals are not mutually exclusive, of course—deterrent penalties also punish and retributive punishments also deter—but they are distinguished by their primary goal, either to promote "the good" (utility) or "the right" (justice).[7]

From this brief description it is easy to see why mainstream economics, with its utilitarian foundations, favors deterrence when studying criminal policy (especially given the direct precedents in the thought of Jeremy Bentham and Cesare Beccaria).[8] To many economists and legal scholars working in the economic tradition, retributivism is seen as a throwback to savage, unsophisticated, prelegal times. Richard Posner wrote that it is "widely viewed as immoral and irrational, or at least as primitive and nonrational" and concludes that "retributive theories of punishment appear to belong to particular historical circumstances rather than to have a timeless claim to be regarded as just."[9] Louis Kaplow and Steven Shavell declared that retributivism is nothing but "a philosophized version of tastes for retribution," largely because "the degree of alignment between their theory…and tastes for retribution seems too close to be due merely to chance."[10] Likewise, Cass Sunstein uses the term "outrage" to describe why juries base punitive damages on considerations of blame and condemnation (retributivist ideals) rather than on optimal deterrence.[11] All of these scholars argue forcefully that criminal sanctions need to be determined in order to provide efficient deterrence and that retributivist penalties will most likely be inefficient. This argument begs the question, however, assuming the primacy of efficiency and utility taken for granted in mainstream economics, the very position called into question here.

In contrast to mainstream economics and its utilitarian welfarism, social economics is uniquely concerned with human dignity and the role it plays in economics and society. In most conceptions, dignity accords a special status to the person that demands a certain respect and consideration; for instance, Immanuel Kant's version of dignity, deriving from a rational person's capacity to act autonomously, requires that the person is treated as an end in him- or herself and is not to be used merely as a means to the ends of others.[12] Since the pursuit of efficiency and welfare-maximization involves the sacrifice of the well-being of some to promote that of others, it offends this basic implication of human dignity. This also corresponds to criticisms of utilitarianism by philosophers such as Amartya Sen, Bernard Williams, and John Rawls that utilitarianism treats persons merely as "locations of their respective utilities" and of no special interest themselves.[13] As Ronald Dworkin famously wrote, in some cases, rights must "trump" welfare, protecting some aspects of the individual's choices and well-being from sacrifice to the interests of the collective (and the political forces in charge of it).[14] For these reasons, an "inefficient" social outcome that would be decried by mainstream economists (and similarly minded legal scholars) may nonetheless be just in terms of human dignity and preferable by that standard.

Despite the misgivings of economists and legal scholars who regard retributivism as barbaric, legal scholars and philosophers who study retributivism regard it as promoting human dignity in a way that deterrence does not.[15] Classical thinkers emphasized that retributivism holds persons responsible for their actions. Arguing against punishment based solely on deterrence, Hegel wrote that "to base a justification of punishment on threat is to liken it to the act of a man who raises his stick to a dog. It is to treat a man like a dog instead of with the freedom and respect due to him as a man."[16] Emphasizing his conception of dignity, Kant wrote that punishment "can never be inflicted merely as a means to promote some other good for the criminal himself or for civil society. It must always be inflicted upon him only *because he has committed a crime*. For a human being can never be treated merely as a means to the purposes of another."[17] To both Kant and Hegel, criminals "demand" their punishment as a matter of right based in their choice to disobey the law. This position is often caricatured as saying that criminals want to be punished, when it merely points out that by willing the act, the criminal also wills the consequences—and by enforcing those consequences through just punishment, the government respects the criminal as an person responsible for his or her own actions.[18]

Most generally, retributivism focuses punishment on the criminal for the crime he or she committed, whereas deterrence uses that person's punishment as a means to promoting the general welfare; in fact, as the traditional criticism of utilitarianism goes, an innocent person could potentially be subjected to "punishment" if it had beneficial effects on society as a whole (contra Kant's statement above). The extremity of this scenario aside, it makes the point that under deterrence, punishment is not about criminals themselves and fails to treat them as valuable persons deserving as respect (as well as punishment). Instead, they become a mere tool to the criminal justice system.

Following retributivism's focus on the criminal's act itself, punishments must be designed to "fit" each crime rather than to promote overall efficiency. This emphasis on proportionality in retributivism is often traced to the *lex talionis* and its prescription of "an eye for an eye, a tooth for a tooth." Kant endorsed this when he wrote:

> what kind and what amount of punishment is it that public justice makes its principle and measure? None other than the principle of equality…Accordingly, whatever undeserved evil you inflict upon another within the people, that you inflict upon yourself…But only the *law of retribution (ius talionis)*… can specify definitely the quality and the quantity of punishment.[19]

However, this strict identity of crime and punishment is rarely taken literally. In some cases, the thought of exact proportionality violates dignity itself (such as in case of torture or rape), literally impossible (serial murder), and nonsensical (unsuccessful attempted crimes). Even Kant acknowledged the shortcomings of the *lex talionis* and recommended that "what is done to [the wrongdoer] in accordance with penal law is what he has perpetrated on others, if not in terms of its letter at least in terms of its spirit."[20]

In modern times, the *lex talionis* is taken merely to be a quaint but antiquated symbol of retributivism's demand for proportionality. Modern retributivists are split depending on which direction of proportionality is emphasized. *Negative retributivism* is the more lenient, demanding only that the innocent not be punished and that the guilty not be punished too harshly. *Positive retributivism* agrees with these but asserts also that the guilty must be punished and not too leniently.[21] Some argue that negative retributivism is less a form of retributivism than a side-constraint on other philosophies of punishment such as deterrence, because it only restricts the practice of punishment rather than demanding it.[22] As such, it is often combined with deterrence in *hybrid theories* of punishment, such as that of H. L. A. Hart, who viewed deterrence as the "general justifying aim" of punishment and retributivism as governing the "distribution" of penalties, making sure the aim of deterrence did not violate basic ideals of justice such as not punishing the innocent or excessively punishing the guilty.[23]

While retributivist punishments are often assumed to be more severe than deterrent punishments—as evidenced by Richard Posner's concern that retributivist penalties would be inefficiently high—in many cases the mainstream economics of crime leads to higher punishments than are justified by the crime. Because of its emphasis of overall efficiency, mainstream economics recommends that when punishment has low marginal cost compared to enforcement, such as in the case of fines, penalties should be increased and enforcement lowered, which would (in theory) generate the same amount of deterrence at lower cost.[24] One common example is the high fines posted for littering, a penalty that is rarely imposed but is wildly disproportionate to the harm from the crime. While efficient deterrence may be achieved, a person who is prosecuted under this law is not merely punished according to his or her crime, but effectively for the crimes of many of those who were not caught. The economics of crime considers the probability of punishment as part of the operative penalty that deters potential criminal behavior, while retributivism looks only at the penalty exacted on the convicted—and in such cases, it is disproportionately high.

This is not to say, however, that the determination of just, proportionate punishments according to (positive) retributivism is clear-cut. There is no obvious scale or ordering of offenses that can be mapped onto a similar ranking of punishments.[25] Different degrees of murder, theft, or assault may be identified with more or less serious penalties according to each degree, but it is much more difficult to compare across crimes, such as a certain type of assault compared to a certain type of theft, to determine which is deserving of greater punishment. But the relative ease of determining deterrent punishment is illusory once the complexity of utilitarian logic is recognized; as we will discuss later, the amount of information about costs, probabilities, and behavioral reactions needed to calculate precisely efficient punishment is impossible to know with certainty. Judgment is required in either situation, whether qualitative or quantitative, deontological or consequentialist, retributivist or deterrent.

Retributivism, Models of Choice, and Positive Law and Economics

It is not only the sheer amount of information regarding costs and probabilities that makes the calculation of efficient penalties difficult, but the need for a good understanding of how people will respond to criminal laws, penalties, and the likelihood of being apprehended, prosecuted, and convicted, all of which are necessary to determine an efficient system of criminal punishment. It is in this sense that the positive analysis of criminal behavior is essential to the normative analysis of deterrence in the mainstream economics of crime, but the way economists model criminal behavior does not acknowledge factors that have a strong effect on these unique choice situations.

Paralleling the analysis of deterrent punishment based on welfare-maximization, economic choice is usually modeled as a process of utility maximization in which a person reaches the highest level of preference satisfaction within his or her resource constraints. Just as a quantitative focus on deterrence as welfare maximization renders the criminal justice system blind to qualitative considerations such as justice and desert, framing choice as a maximization problem makes it difficult to consider qualitative factors such as duties and principles. These factors may not be essential to consider in ordinary cases of consumer choice but are crucial to understand legal choices in a world in which many people take what H. L. A. Hart called an "internal view" of law, considering its prohibitions to be influential on their decision-making regardless of official sanctions or social penalties.[26]

The simplest example of this is the distinction between fines and prices. To the mainstream economics of crime, anything that lowers a person's wealth is treated as a disincentive with no regard to its normative status or implications. Accordingly, an expected ten-dollar fine for parking illegally will have the same effect on a person's choice as would a ten-dollar charge for parking legally. We see this very example in the Nobel address of Gary Becker, the founder of the economics of crime, when he described the situation that led to his thinking about the issue:

> I began to think about crime in the 1960s after driving to Columbia University for an oral examination of a student in economic theory. I was late and had to decide quickly whether to put the car in a parking lot or risk getting a ticket for parking illegally on the street. I calculated the likelihood of getting a ticket, the size of the penalty, and the cost of putting the car in a lot. I decided it paid to take the risk and park on the street. (I did not get a ticket.)[27]

Here, Becker considered the expected cost of a ticket as merely the cost of getting to the exam on time, not also as a violation of the law. Of course, many people think of misdemeanors such as traffic violations this way, as financial inconveniences rather than grievous societal harms. However, the economics of crime assumes that people treat fines as prices regardless of their size or the seriousness of the crime being punished (such as white-collar crimes for which fines are strongly recommended).

However, fines are more than mere prices; they are a particular representation of society's condemnation of a criminal act, no matter how minor.[28] People who consider the law internally will consider more than the monetary penalty associated with committing a crime but also the fact that it is a violation of the law. For such people, the fine will take on an additional dimension or weight and will have a larger effect on their decision-making than if it were instead a price for legitimate behavior. For a subset of these people, an illegal action will not even enter their opportunity set because in most circumstances they would not even consider it.[29] In both cases, a duty to obey the law changes the process by which they make their decisions away from a simplistic utility maximization calculus to one involving qualitative judgment.

Aside from issues of morality, the emotionally wrought nature of many choice situation involving law-breaking makes the insights of behavioral economics relevant. Persons with an internal view of the law will experience some measure of cognitive discomfort or dissonance when considering breaking the law, which is likely to trigger the irrational deliberations and actions described by psychologists and behavioral economists.[30] These findings have been incorporated into the mainstream economic analysis of law by scholars in the composite field of *behavioral law and economics*, exploring ways in which bounded rationality, willpower, and self-interest affect individuals' behavior (as well as how these results can inform normative policy decisions).[31] We can acknowledge the insight of these findings while nonetheless questioning their relevance to the analysis of decision-making among legal actors as well as policy, especially given their adherence to the standard preference-satisfaction framework on the mainstream economic model of choice and their refusal to consider the qualitative factors discussed earlier.[32]

These moral and behavioral aspects of choice are extremely difficult to model with any level of certainty and universality, which represents a theoretical problem for positive economics of crime but also a very practical one for normative analysis that presumes to inform criminal justice policy based on optimal deterrence. However, because retributivist punishments are designed to be just, proportionate to the specific crime committed, rather than efficient or welfare maximizing, such positive analysis plays no role in their determination. To the retributivist, it does not matter how well a given punishment deters future crime, although that is a positive side-effect; what matters is that the punishment was deserved and appropriate in form and degree. Therefore, legal decision-makers such as legislators, judges, and juries need no knowledge of how various penalties and probabilities will affect criminal behavior. They need only some idea of which penalties are proportionate to which crimes, which can then be modified for individual contingencies such as culpability or mercy.[33] Again, retributivist judgments pose their own problems, but they are problems of how to weigh the various principles that bear on just punishments, which depends on practical reason rather than specific knowledge of the motivations and behavioral patterns of potential criminals.

If both the positive and normative sides of mainstream economic analysis are irrelevant to retributive justice, does that leave any role for an "economics of crime" at all? Is there a way that economics can contribute to the study of crime consistent for those who, like social economists, prefer dignity and justice over instrumentality and efficiency? The answer is yes, but it lies in the most basic function of economics—speaking to resource allocation, opportunity costs, and trade-offs. The irony is that of all the legal areas treated by economics, including tort, property, and contract, economics has the most to contribute to the area of crime, the area about which the mainstream economic analysis of law has the least to say.

The Role for Traditional Economics in Retributivist Justice

What opens the door for economics to contribute to retributivist criminal justice is the recognition that retributivism, in its positive form, is an ideal system, mandating that *every* wrongdoer *must* be punished *according to* his or her crime. Of course, in order to be punished, this also implies that every wrongdoer must be convicted, and therefore that every suspect must be apprehended and prosecuted. Unsurprisingly, this is an "inefficient" use of resources compared to the deterrent ideal, because some of these crimes will not be worth the cost of apprehension, prosecution, and punishment. More relevant here is the fact that this perfect level of criminal justice cannot be achieved without absorbing all of society's resources (and even that would not be enough).[34] This should not be surprising, though, because there are few things on a societal level that can be achieved with *perfection* given limited resources. Furthermore, there are other goals and principles that society wants to further and maintain, and these also compete for resources that would be consumed by retributivist justice if the criminal justice system tried to do it "perfectly."

Given that retributivism cannot be implemented as much as its ideal form would demand, how are government leaders to decide where and how to make compromises within it? Again, the ideal nature of positive retributivism makes this difficult because no exceptions or allowances for other priorities are included in its conception. But given the impossibility of perfect implementation, compromises must be made, and the only questions are where and how.

One idea is to quantify retributive justice and then seek to maximize it within the constraints provided by scarcity and competing ends. Donald Wittman, one of the few economists to consider seriously the ramifications of retributivism within the economics of crime, made an early attempt at this by developing a model in which justice was a function of punishment, declining as punishment rose or fell from the just level for a given crime. Based on this, he analyzed the injustice from disproportionate punishment as well as from punishing the innocent or failing to punish the guilty.[35] More recently, legal scholar Michael Cahill proposed a less formal method of conceiving a *consequentialist retributivism* in which different policies are considered to produce "more" justice or "less" justice (without trying to quantify justice precisely), giving legislators, judges, and policymakers a rough idea of where trade-offs could be beneficial.[36] For instance, this could explain and justify instances of plea bargaining in which prosecutors cut a deal with a lesser criminal in exchange for information that helps convict a more serious one—or even to save on scarce prosecutorial resources that could be used to prosecute more serious crimes or simply more crimes.

Retributivists, however, are not often comfortable with conceptualizing justice as a quantifiable good rather than a qualitative principle or ideal.[37] In simple cases, it may seem easy to say that punishing a drug kingpin produces more justice than punishing a small-time drug dealer. But such comparisons become more difficult when the cases are not so similar, when cutting a deal with the lesser criminal seems distasteful even in the larger picture, or when the trade-off involves other principles altogether. Sometimes ideals of retributivist justice betray simple numbers, such as when it is said that "it is better than let ten guilty men go free than punish one innocent one," a ratio with uncertain origin and certainly no theoretical derivation.[38] Other times, retributivist justice conflicts with other principles of the criminal justice system that protect the rights of defendants, such as the exclusionary rule that forbids the introduction of evidence from an improper search or the Fifth Amendment right against self-incrimination.[39] Principles such as these may make it more difficult to secure convictions against the truly guilty in some cases, compromising the basic principle of retributivist justice—trade-offs that the court system has agreed are proper while they continue to debate the precise nature of them at the margins.

Not only must the criminal justice struggle with balancing retributivist principles against each other as well as other legal principles, but the government as a whole must decide how to balance the needs of the criminal justice system against the other goals and principles the government furthers. As we saw earlier, retributivist justice cannot be achieved with perfection in a world of scarcity, even it were the only role of government—and because it is not, even in a libertarian minimal state, compromises in retributivist justice must be made to enable other ends to be met, such as civil courts, national defense, education, infrastructure, and health care (depending on the political preferences of the electorate). But how can the principle of retributivist justice be balanced against, say, the right to a quality education? How do we compare prosecuting one more criminal suspect to funding a field trip for a high school class? If both promote an ideal or principle that resists quantification, how can a budgetary policymakers make such a decision (as, by necessity, they must)?

In his theory of judicial decision-making, Ronald Dworkin proposed a method of balancing principles at play in a "hard case" facing a judge.[40] In any case that is not clearly settled by established written law or past precedent, each judge deciding that case must consider the various principles invoked by the case, weigh each one according to its relevance and importance in the context of a broader legal-political philosophy, and render a decision, based on the most important principle, that maintains the integrity of the legal system. As with personal matters of difficult moral choice, there is no formula or algorithm to solve this problem—it is up to the individual's judgment. Furthermore, equally responsible and knowledgeable judges will disagree over the principles relevant to a case, how they are weighted against each other, and which one takes precedence. And, as has been pointed out recently, even a unanimous decision among a judicial panel may reflect different judgments favoring different principles that all indicated the same final decision.[41]

We can generalize this decision-making procedure to general questions of criminal justice within both the system itself and the broader governmental context in which it resides. Legislators, prosecutors, and other decision-makers within the criminal justice system need to

decide how they will balance the various demands of retributive justice (as in the example of plea-bargaining) as well as with the demands
of other types of justice (such as civil rights). All of these conflicts cast
one immeasurable instance of justice against another and cannot be
solved quantitatively with a formula or algorithm. This applies even
when the cause of the conflict is economic in nature, such as resource
constraints within a departmental budget or the higher-level allocation of budgets among departments; the currency may be the same
but the benefits of spending in different areas are incommensurable.

However, economics can and should play a role in such deliberations. Even in conflicts between intrinsically qualitative ideals and
principles such as justice, there is room and often need for quantitative analysis of costs, not as the primary level of decision-making, but
at a secondary, informative level. Even though problems regarding
justice and other ideals should not be forced into quantitative estimates at the primary level, quantitative aspects of the conflicts can be
useful to illuminate one dimension of them, one piece of information
to be combined with other considerations to help solve the problem.

For example, consider a police officer pursuing two thieves who
run down an alley. The alley ends at a "T," at which point the thieves
run in opposite directions. As implied by retributive justice, the police
officer has an equal obligation to apprehend each thief but obviously cannot catch both; she must use her judgment to decide which
one she will pursue. There is no principled way to make this choice
between two identically principled actions, but she still must choose,
so she must resort to some other aspect of the problem, including
consequential reasoning. For instance, she may know that one of the
thieves is also wanted for other crimes or has stronger ties to other
criminals than the other, or she may have seen that one was carrying
the stolen property that can be returned to the rightful owner. She
may simply choose the slowest runner whom she would be more likely
to apprehend! All of these are valid consequential reasons to split the
deadlock between principles (as long as there is no principle that can
solve the problem itself).

To be fair, these reasons are similar to those that would be generated by systems of consequential retributivism such as that of Cahill,
and this is no coincidence: both conceptions admit consequentialist factors but at different levels of decision-making. The approaches
result in different ways to frame the problem: Cahill's approach frames
justice in terms of a good that can be optimized while mine retains
its nature as an ideal. More symbolically, consequentialist retributivism incorporates trade-offs and compromises into the primary stage

of decision-making, which rejects the nature of justice as an ideal. In the approach inspired by Dworkin, on the other hand, principles and ideals are not compromised, but rather one is judged to be more important than another in a particular situation. Trade-offs are necessary, of course, but they are regrettable implications of conflicts of principles rather than an acknowledged feature of the basic decision-making process.

More broadly, although this difference between a consequentialist and principled approach to crime and punishment may be symbolic, that symbolism has important effects. For instance, scholars in the mainstream economics of crime often talk about an optimal or efficient level of crime, or that a society allows or "demands" a certain level of crime based on the inability to deter or prevent all crime. This inability is indisputable, of course, and is parallel to the impossibility of punishing all criminals under retributivism. But in the language of principles, the criminal justice system has the goal of punishing all criminals—a goal that is unattainable because of other principles and constraints, but a goal nonetheless. The consequentialist deterrent approach admits and accepts failure upfront, which may be realistic but is also defeatist when considered against the background of the principles that lie behind it. It is akin to the difference between telling someone you'll do something, even though there is a chance you will not be able to do as promised, and telling him or her that you'll try to do it. In the first case, the possibility of failure is understood but not explicitly acknowledged, while in the second case, it is explicitly stated as if failure is made acceptable before the attempt is even made.

Conclusion

Because of economists' traditional expertise in allocating scarce resources and emphasizing trade-offs, they can play an important role in helping authorities in the criminal justice system (as well as those higher up in government that fund it) to make judgments between irreconcilable principles and goals. Economics can help illuminate one aspect of the problem of implementing retributivist justice in a world of scarcity, granting a valuable perspective that, when combined with others, will help authorities make a decision that makes the best use of their available resources while furthering the goals and principles that are the primary focus of criminal justice. This is to be contrasted with the mainstream economics of crime that reduces *all* aspects of criminal justice to quantifiable benefits and costs and then optimizes among them. The approach outlined here maintains the principled framework of criminal justice while depending on economists for their traditional expertise in resource allocation toward predefined ends—in this case, retributivist justice that maintains the dignity of all involved.

Ironically, with its proper role so limned, economics becomes more valuable to the study of crime than to the areas of private law—tort, property, and crime—to which economics is widely held to be better suited. Because private law often deals explicitly with money and property, it seems to fit more comfortably within the consequentialist optimization framework of mainstream economics. This still assumes, however, that the goal of these areas of law is the maximization of welfare or wealth, which is a controversial assumption. Tort law, for instance, is seen by some to be the operationalization of corrective justice in the same way that criminal law implements retributive justice.[42] By the same token, contract law can be held to be about promise or consent, not generating efficient outcomes, and property law can be considered to be about respecting (not creating) property rights.[43] Seen in these principled frameworks, economics has very little contribution to make to these areas; decisions in private law cases come down primarily to rights and harm, and money is merely (and not exclusively) the currency of damages or remedies. Economics has more to offer to criminal law because the state plays an active role there, as opposed to the passive role it plays in private law in which private parties initiate and pursue their own cases based on their interests. Because the state enforces the law and assumes responsibility for apprehension, prosecution, adjudication, and punishment, all within the constraints of scarcity and principle, economics has the essential role identified earlier. In the matter of private law, however, it has no obvious contribution to make—which is a topic better left for another time.[44]

Notes

1. Coleman, "Crimes, Kickers, and Transaction Structures," 326.
2. Morris, "Decline of Guilt," 73.
3. Posner, "Retribution and Related Concepts of Punishment," 82.
4. Posner, "Economic Approach to Law," 777. The first meaning he cites, by the way, is distributive justice, which he interprets in terms of economic inequality.
5. Posner's views on this have moderated a bit, inspired by American pragmatists such as John Dewey and famous jurist Oliver Wendell Holmes; see Posner, *Problematics of Moral and Legal Theory*.
6. Braithwaite and Pettit, *Not Just Deserts*, emphasize that the entire criminal justice must be considered when debating philosophies of punishment; this line of thought will be seen throughout this chapter.

7. On the contrasts between deterrence and retributivism and their ethical bases, see Brooks, *Punishment*, Chapters 1–2; and Murphy and Coleman, *Philosophy of Law*, 117–124. For a collection of classic essays on the punishment theory, see Acton, *Philosophy of Punishment*.

8. Bentham, *Principles of Morals and Legislation*; and Beccaria, *On Crimes and Punishments*; on the nuanced views of the latter on punishment, see White, "On Beccaria, the Economics of Crime, and the Philosophy of Punishment."

9. Posner, "Retribution and Related Concepts," 92 and 83, respectively.

10. Kaplow and Shavell, *Fairness versus Welfare*, 366. For a critique of this point (and their book in general), see White, "Preaching to the Choir."

11. Sunstein, "On the Psychology of Punishment"

12. Based on the second formula of the categorical imperative; see Kant, *Grounding for the Metaphysics of Morals*, 429. For other versions of dignity used in social economics, see White, "Dignity."

13. Sen and Williams, "Introduction: Utilitarianism and Beyond," 4; for more on this point, see Rawls, "Social Unity and Primary Goods."

14. Dworkin, *Taking Rights Seriously*.

15. In addition to Kant and Hegel, see also Morris, "Persons and Punishment"; and Murphy, "Marxism and Retributivism."

16. Hegel, *Philosophy of Right*, 246 (addition to paragraph 99).

17. Kant, *Metaphysics of Morals*, 331 (emphasis in original). As Murphy points out, even the guilty are used as mere means if they are punished for deterrence alone: "those of a Kantian persuasion [must] object just as strenuously to the punishment of the guilty on utilitarian grounds as to the punishment of the innocent" ("Marxism and Retribution," 219).

18. Kant, *Metaphysics of Morals*, 334–335; Hegel, *Philosophy of Right*, 70. For more on Hegel's view on this point, see Johnson, "Hegel on Punishment," 153–155. Morris also gives a reasonable treatment of this position in "Persons and Punishment," contrasting punishment with a "therapy model" in which criminals are treated as flawed and needing help rather than responsible and deserving to "pay their debts."

19. Kant, *Metaphysics of Morals*, 332 (emphasis in original).

20. Ibid., 363.

21. This distinction is due to Mackie, *Persons and Values*, 207–208.

22. Cottingham, "Varieties of Retribution," 240–241.

23. Hart, *Punishment and Responsibility*; also see Brooks, *Punishment*, Chapter 5.

24. Becker, "Crime and Punishment."

25. See Davis, "How to Make the Punishment Fit the Crime" for such work, and Wertheimer, "Should Punishment Fit the Crime?" for a critique. For a lengthy critical discussion of proportionality, see Ryberg, *Ethics of Proportionate Punishment*.

26. Hart, *Concept of Law*; for an application to economics, see Cooter, "Intrinsic Value of Obeying a Law."
27. Becker, "Economic Way of Looking at Life," 389.
28. On this issue, see Cooter, "Prices and Sanctions"; Dowell et al., "Economic Man as a Moral Individual"; and White, *Kantian Ethics and Economics*, 64–65. On communicative theories of punishment that focus on punishment's role in expressing the community's condemnation to the criminal, see Duff, *Punishment, Communication, and Community*; in general, see Brooks, *Punishment*, Chapter 6.
29. See Baker, "Virtue and Behavior."
30. For accessible summaries, see Ariely, *Predictably Irrational*; and Kahneman, *Thinking, Fast and Slow*.
31. See Jolls, Sunstein, and Thaler, "Behavioral Approach to Law and Economics," for the initial foray into behavioral law and economics, and Sunstein (ed.), *Behavioral Law and Economics*, and Parisi and Smith (eds), *Law and Economics of Irrational Behavior*, for useful collections of early research in the area.
32. White, *Manipulation of Choice*, Chapter 2.
33. On culpability, see Alexander, Ferzan, and Morse, *Crime and Culpability*; on the role mercy plays within justice, see Holtman, "Justice, Mercy, and Efficiency."
34. White, "Retributivism in a World of Scarcity."
35. Wittman, "Punishment as Retribution."
36. Cahill, "Retributive Justice in the Real World" and "Punishment Pluralism."
37. White, "*Pro Tanto* Retributivism," 132–134.
38. Reiman and van den Haag, "On the Common Saying."
39. As Cahill writes, "The application of a retributive-justice scheme might give rise … to conflicts between retribution and other *principled* commitments. For example, a commitment to certain aspects of procedural justice or fairness may sometimes frustrate the system's ability to impose punishment on those who deserve it … Ultimately, resolution of such conflicts between principled commitments depends on some decision about which principle merits priority in the abstract" ("Retributive Justice in the Real World," 820n14).
40. Dworkin, "Hard Cases" (and, more generally, *Taking Rights Seriously*, in which it is included).
41. See, for instance, Sunstein, "Unanimity and Disagreement on the Supreme Court."
42. See, for example, Weinrib, *Idea of Private Law*; Coleman, *Practice of Principle*; and Wright, "Right, Justice, and Tort Law."
43. On contract law, see Fried, *Contract as Promise*; and Barnett, "A Consent Theory of Contract" (and, highlighting the difference between the two, Barnett, "Contract Is Not Promise; Contract Is Consent"). On property, see Nozick, *Anarchy, State, and Utopia*, Chapter 7; and Harris, *Property and Justice*.

44. I thank fellow presenters and attendants at various conference sessions at meetings of the Association of Social Economics/Allied Social Science Associations and the Law and Society Association. This chapter is dedicated to the memory of Dan Markel, a treasured colleague and an inspirational scholar.

Bibliography

Acton, H. B. *The Philosophy of Punishment: A Collection of Papers.* New York: St. Martin's, 1969.

Alexander, Larry, and Kimberly K. Ferzan (with Stephen Morse). *Crime and Culpability: A Theory of Criminal Law.* Cambridge: Cambridge University Press, 2009.

Ariely, Dan. *Predictably Irrational: The Hidden Forces That Shape Our Decisions.* New York: Harper Perennial, 2010.

Baker, Jennifer A. "Virtue and Behavior." *Review of Social Economy* 67 (2009): 3–24.

Barnett, Randy E. "A Consent Theory of Contract." *Columbia Law Review* 86 (1986): 269–321.

———. "Contract Is Not Promise; Contract Is Consent." *Suffolk University Law Review* 45 (2012): 647–665.

Beccaria, Cesare. *On Crimes and Punishments.* Translated by David Young. Indianapolis, IN: Hackett, 1986 [1764].

Becker, Gary S. "Crime and Punishment: An Economic Approach." *Journal of Political Economy* 76 (1968): 169–217.

———. "The Economic Way of Looking at Life." *Journal of Political Economy* 101 (1993): 385–409.

Bentham, Jeremy. *The Principles of Morals and Legislation.* Buffalo, NY: Prometheus Books, 1988 [1781].

Braithwaite, John, and Philip Pettit. *Not Just Deserts: A Republican Theory of Criminal Justice.* Oxford: Clarendon Press, 1990.

Brooks, Thom. *Punishment.* Abington, UK: Routledge, 2012.

Cahill, Michael T. "Punishment Pluralism." In *Retributivism: Essays on Theory and Policy,* edited by Mark D. White, 25–48. Oxford: Oxford University Press, 2011.

———. "Retributive Justice in the Real World." *Washington University Law Review* 85 (2007): 815–870.

Coleman, Jules L. "Crimes, Kickers and Transaction Structures." In *Criminal Justice: NOMOS XXVII,* edited by J. Roland Pennock and John W. Chapman, 313–328. New York: New York University Press, 1985.

———. *The Practice of Principle: In Defense of a Pragmatist Approach to Legal Theory.* Oxford: Oxford University Press, 2001.

Cooter, Robert D. "The Intrinsic Value of Obeying a Law: Economic Analysis of the Internal Viewpoint." *Fordham Law Review* 75 (2006): 1275–1285.

———. "Prices and Sanctions." *Columbia Law Review* 84 (1984): 1523–1560.

Cottingham, John. "Varieties of Retribution." *Philosophical Quarterly* 29 (1979): 238–246.

Davis, Michael. "How to Make the Punishment Fit the Crime." *Ethics* 93 (1983): 726–752.

Dowell, Richard S., Robert S. Goldfarb, and William B. Griffith. "Economic Man as a Moral Individual." *Economic Inquiry* 36 (1998): 645–653.

Duff, R. A. *Punishment, Communication, and Community*. Oxford: Oxford University Press, 2001.

Dworkin, Ronald. "Hard Cases." *Harvard Law Review* 88 (1975): 1057–1109.

———. *Taking Rights Seriously*. Cambridge, MA: Harvard University Press, 1977.

Fried, Charles. *Contract as Promise: A Theory of Contractual Obligation*. Cambridge, MA: Harvard University Press, 1981.

Harris, J. W. *Property and Justice*. Oxford: Oxford University Press, 1996.

Hart, H. L. A. *The Concept of Law*. 2nd ed. Oxford: Oxford University Press, 1994 [1961].

———. *Punishment and Responsibility: Essays in the Philosophy of Law*. Oxford: Oxford University Press, 1968.

Hegel, G. W. F. *The Philosophy of Right*. Translated by T. M. Knox. Oxford: Oxford University Press, 1952 [1821].

Holtman, Sarah. "Justice, Mercy, and Efficiency." In *Theoretical Foundations of Law and Economics*, edited by Mark D. White, 119–135. Cambridge: Cambridge University Press, 2009.

Johnson, Jane. "Hegel on Punishment." In *Retributivism: Essays on Theory and Policy*, edited by Mark D. White, 146–168. Oxford: Oxford University Press, 2011.

Jolls, Christine, Cass R. Sunstein, and Richard Thaler. "A Behavioral Approach to Law and Economics." *Stanford Law Review* 50 (1998): 1471–1550.

Kahneman, Daniel. *Thinking, Fast and Slow*. New York: Farrar, Strauss and Giroux, 2011.

Kant, Immanuel. *Grounding for the Metaphysics of Morals*. Trans. James W. Ellington. Indianapolis, IN: Hackett, 1993 [1785].

———. *The Metaphysics of Morals*. Trans. and ed. Mary J. Gregor. Cambridge: Cambridge University Press, 1996 [1797].

Kaplow, Louis, and Steven Shavell. *Fairness versus Welfare*. Cambridge, MA: Harvard University Press, 2002.

Mackie, J. L. *Persons and Values*. Oxford: Clarendon Press, 1985.

Morris, Herbert. "The Decline of Guilt." *Ethics* 99 (1988): 62–76.

———. "Persons and Punishment." *The Monist* 52 (1968): 475–501.

Murphy, Jeffrie G. "Marxism and Retribution." *Philosophy and Public Affairs* 2 (1973): 217–243.

Murphy, Jeffrie G., and Jules L. Coleman. *The Philosophy of Law: An Introduction to Jurisprudence*. Rev. ed. Boulder, CO: Westview Press, 1990.

Nozick, Robert. *Anarchy, State, and Utopia*. New York: Basic Books, 1974.

Parisi, Francesco, and Vernon L. Smith (eds). *The Law and Economics of Irrational Behavior*. Stanford, CA: Stanford University Press, 2005.

Posner, Richard A. *Economic Analysis of Law*. 6th ed. New York: Aspen Publishers, 2003.

————. "The Economic Approach to Law." *Texas Law Review* 53 (1975): 757–782.

————. *The Problematics of Moral and Legal Theory*. Cambridge, MA: Belknap, 2002.

————. "Retribution and Related Concepts of Punishment." *Journal of Legal Studies* 9 (1980): 71–92.

Rawls, John. "Social Unity and Primary Goods." In *Utilitarianism and Beyond*, edited by Amartya Sen and Bernard Williams, 159–185. Cambridge: Cambridge University Press, 1982.

Reiman, Jeffrey, and Ernest van den Haag. "On the Common Saying That It Is Better That Ten Guilty Persons than that One Innocent Suffer: *Pro* and *Con*." In *Crime, Culpability, and Remedy*, edited by Ellen F. Paul, Fred D. Miller, Jr., and Jeffrey Paul, 226–248. Oxford: Basil Blackwell, 1990.

Ryberg, Jesper. *The Ethics of Proportionate Punishment: A Critical Investigation*. Dordrecht, Kluwer, 2004.

Sen, Amartya, and Bernard Williams. "Introduction: Utilitarianism and Beyond." In *Utilitarianism and Beyond*, edited by Amartya Sen and Bernard Williams, 1–21. Cambridge: Cambridge University Press, 1982.

Sunstein, Cass R. (ed.) *Behavioral Law and Economics*. Cambridge: Cambridge University Press, 2000.

————. "On the Psychology of Punishment." In *The Law and Economics of Irrational Behavior*, edited by Francesco Parisi and Vernon L. Smith, 339–357. Palo Alto, CA: Stanford University Press, 2005.

————. "Unanimity and Disagreement on the Supreme Court." Working paper. Available at http://papers.ssrn.com/sol3/papers .cfm?abstract_id=2466057.

Weinrib, Ernest J. *The Idea of Private Law*. Cambridge, MA: Harvard University Press, 1995.

Wertheimer, Alan. "Should Punishment Fit the Crime?" *Social Theory and Practice* 3 (1975): 403–423.

White, Mark D. "Dignity." In *Handbook of Economics and Ethics*, edited by Jan Peil and Irene van Staveren, 84–90. Cheltenham, UK: Edward Elgar, 2009.

————. *Kantian Ethics and Economics: Autonomy, Dignity, and Character*. Stanford, CA: Stanford University Press, 2011.

————. *The Manipulation of Choice: Ethics and Libertarian Paternalism*. New York: Palgrave Macmillan, 2013.

————. "On Beccaria, the Economics of Crime, and the Philosophy of Punishment." *Philosophical Inquiries* 2 (2014): 121–137.

————. "Preaching to the Choir: A Response to *Fairness versus Welfare*." *Review of Political Economy* 16 (2004): 507–515.

White, Mark D. "*Pro Tanto* Retributivism: Judgment and the Balance of Principles in Criminal Justice." In *Retributivism: Essays on Theory and Policy*, edited by Mark D. White, 129–145. Oxford: Oxford University Press, 2011.

———. "Retributivism in a World of Scarcity." In *Theoretical Foundations of Law and Economics*, edited by Mark D. White, 253–271. Cambridge: Cambridge University Press, 2009.

Wittman, Donald. "Punishment as Retribution." *Theory and Decision* 4 (1974): 209–237.

Wright, Richard W. "Right, Justice, and Tort Law." In *Philosophical Foundations of Tort Law*, edited by David G. Owen, 159–182. Oxford: Oxford University Press, 1995.

Part II

Applications

Chapter 6

Female Genital Mutilation and the Law: A Qualitative Case Study

Regina Gemignani and Quentin Wodon

Female genital mutilation (FGM) or female genital cutting (FGC) is a cultural practice found across much of the African continent. (Both terms are used in the literature, but in this chapter we will use FGM.) Within the context of this book, it is important to highlight that the practice has potentially important economic consequences, not only in terms of the risks it creates for the girls' health and the associated potential medical and other costs, but also in terms of the broader gender roles it contributes to perpetuate, which tend to limit economic opportunities for women in a wide range of areas, including productive work.

According to a recent report by UNICEF, 30 million girls are at risk of suffering genital mutilation over the next decade.[1] The attention given to the issue of FGM is growing: for example, in July 2014, the United Kingdom and UNICEF jointly hosted the first ever Girl Summit to mobilize efforts to end female genital mutilation as well as child, early, and forced marriage. This chapter focuses on the social and cultural underpinnings of FGM, a practice that has deep roots in the social structures of many communities. Specifically, this chapter looks at the role played by culture and religion in shaping attitudes and practices around FGM, focusing on the relationship between FGM and Islamic law as well as national law.

First, consider Islamic law. The connection between Islam and FGM is by no means universal; FGM predates Islam and is found across many ethnic groups, regardless of religion. Some Muslim communities oppose the practice, including members of the Islamist group al-Ittihad in Somalia, the Hausa and Fulani in northern Nigeria, and some ethnic groups in the Sudan.[2] FGM is also not widely practiced across the Middle East, although it is found in Yemen and is reported to exist to a limited extent in Jordan, Oman, Gaza, and Kurdish communities in Iraq.[3] Generalizations regarding Islam and gender in Africa tend to be problematic.[4] And yet, in many countries Islam plays a role in the persistence of the practice, with ongoing support for cutting or mutilation—among both women and men—embedded in the interrelationships among religion, culture, gender, and the body. A better understanding of the relationship between religion and FGM requires investigation of these dynamic interrelationships.

Much of the debate regarding FGM in Muslim communities has centered on Islamic law. African religious scholars who support FGM suggest that it is mandated or at least recommended by religious doctrine. Some consider FGM as obligatory, while others consider it to be optional, recommended, honorable, or simply permitted. Still others argue that the practice is at variance with key Islamic tenets. In short, the literature on FGM in Muslim communities illustrates highly diverse interpretations of texts relating to the practice.[5]

While there is nothing related to FGM in the Qur'an,[6] reference can be made to the Sunnah (Way of the Prophet) and the narrative tradition of hadiths that relate Mohammed's sayings and doings. Unlike the Qur'an, which is regarded as divinely revealed, hadiths are historical accounts with various degrees of interpretive authority. Some communities refer to hidden sacred passages that communicate the importance of FGM.[7] Other communities that support FGM reference *ijtihad* (independent reasoning, one of the sources of Islamic law), which can be expressed by religious leaders through fatwas (religious rulings) instructing the faithful on behaviors considered morally obligatory. These fatwas are influential in the promotion (or, alternatively, the elimination) of the practice due to their plain language and accessibility, as well as their role in defining acceptable behavior for the population.

The hadith most commonly cited to support FGM describes a discussion between Mohammed and a former circumciser, in which Mohammed is reported to have stated, "Cut slightly and do not overdo it, because it is more pleasant for the woman and better for the husband."[8] Another hadith states, "Mohammed said: 'Circumcision is a *sunnah* (customary practice that confers blessings) for the men and *makruma* (honorable deed) for the women.'"[9] A third hadith in which Mohammed describes the behaviors defining *fitrah* (original, true nature) states that "circumcision is the sign of Islam." Islamic scholars have however criticized the ambiguous nature of these hadiths. They have pointed out that narrations defining fitrah contain only the Arabic term for male circumcision and mention another practice, that of moustache trimming, that is confined to men.[10] The other hadiths are viewed as possibly inauthentic, and in recent years, fatwas have been issued against FGM. For example, in 1996, the Grand Sheikh of Al Azhar University in Egypt pronounced a ban on FGM, and in 2006, at a large conference of leading Muslim scholars, the Grand Mufti of Egypt decried FGM as a punishable aggression and a crime against humanity.[11]

Unfortunately, the ability of fatwas to prevent FGM has been limited so far, including in Egypt where the practice remains widespread. This is because the question of whether FGM is mandated in canonical texts of Islamic law is not necessarily of central importance to populations. Many participants in our fieldwork for this chapter pointed out that their *marabouts* had already admitted that there are no clear references in the Qur'an or in the Sunnah that obligate believers to practice FGM. Nevertheless, they (and their religious leaders) continue to state that FGM is central to an Islamic way of life. Many referred to the fact that the practice is ancient and performed in accord with practicing Muslim members of the community. In other words, while scholarly discussions about the evidence (or lack thereof) in fundamental Islamic texts can be helpful, the connections between religion and FGM go beyond formal beliefs. A lack of ability to legitimize the practice with respect to religious texts does not negate what many in the communities still feel are religious aspects of the practice.

Today the practice remains highly prevalent in many countries, even if it has decreased.[12] In Burkina Faso, according to data from Demographic and Health Surveys as well as other data from the mid-2000s, about three in four women aged 15–49 are circumcised; the rates are lower for younger women. The nationwide survey by the National Committee for the Fight Against Excision conducted in 2006 suggests a rate for 15- to 19-year-olds of 54 percent, signaling a decrease in the practice.[13] But it remains common among some groups, especially in the north of the country; for the Mossi and Peulh, the main ethnic groups discussed in this chapter, about four in five women declare having been circumcised.

Furthermore, part of the apparent reduction in prevalence of the practice among younger groups may be overestimated due to the impact on survey response of another type of law: national law. A law was adopted in 1996 law banning the practice in Burkina Faso.[14] While the law has probably contributed to a reduction in the practice, there are also concerns that it may have led to the continuation of the practice underground and thereby to an overestimation of the decline in the practice over time.

This has happened in other countries. In a longitudinal study to compare responses about FGM in successive interviews in northern Ghana, a large share of women who reported being circumcised in 1995 denied this status in 2000 when 50 percent of women 20–24 years old who had earlier reported being circumcised said that they had not been.[15] This result was related to anti-FGM legislation enacted in Ghana in 1994. By 2000, when the second survey was conducted, a well-known local practitioner in the area had been jailed, and there was widespread awareness of the potential legal consequences of the practice. The effect of anti-FGM policies on survey responses was also revealed in focus groups sessions where girls described the importance of providing the "right answer" to interviewers. The denial of circumcision caused a decrease in measured prevalence from 88 percent to 77 percent.[16] For Burkina Faso, comparisons were made between respondents who know that the practice is illegal with those who do not know that it is illegal.[17] Only 10 percent of those who were aware of the law said that they would cut their daughters in the future, compared to 33 percent of those who were not aware of the law.

This chapter discusses the impact that both areas of law—Islamic law, including general religious values and interpretation, and national law—have on the practice, using Burkina Faso as a case study. The analysis is based on qualitative fieldwork data collected in 2008 in the northern Sahelian part of the country near the borders with Mali and Niger, a region where FGM continues to be widespread. Five sites where targeted in three provinces: Soum, Oudalan, and Yagha. The study also incorporates data from one additional site, Tanghin Dassouri, in the suburbs of Ouagadougou. The main ethnic groups in the communities visited for the study are the Peulh and Mossi. The data collection teams were composed of investigators familiar with the area and culture and fluent in the local language.

The research methods included semistructured interviews, in-depth interviews, and focus group discussions. For the semistructured interviews, the sample was stratified by age and gender and involved a random selection of interviewees. A total of 32 interviews (16 women and 16 men) were conducted in each of the sites, for a total of 192 respondents. Focus group discussions of 6–12 people were also organized with five focus groups in each of the six sites for younger men, older men, younger women, older women, and religious leaders. In the fieldwork the team asked respondents about community health concerns, women's reproductive health, the prevalence of FCC and details of the procedure, the perceived advantages and disadvantages of FGM, health beliefs related to the practice, and the social, cultural, and religious context currently contributing to its persistence. In focus groups questions were also asked about knowledge and views concerning the national law against FGM.

Religion, Culture, and FGM

In the communities sampled for this study, Islam is central to all aspects of life, and religious leaders and communities address a range of material as well as religious needs in their communities. Women are important agents in these processes; they do not merely respond to social forces but actively interpret and shape them. The intersections among religion, culture, and identity were clearly apparent in our discussions with community members. Several FGM-related themes are discussed in this section, including control over women's sexuality, feminine ideals of purity and modesty, and ethnoreligious identities.

Sexual Propriety

The view that women who are cut are more likely to be virgins at marriage and to remain faithful to their husbands is found in many Muslim communities that practice FGM, and is generally more common among men than women. It is a view that is closely linked to social, cultural, and religious structures, including, in some communities, patriarchal control over women's sexuality and reproduction. In most patrilineal groups in sub-Saharan Africa, kinship is traced through the male line for the purposes of inheritance, resource allocation, and the health and continuity of the lineage. Much effort is made to prevent children born out of wedlock. Because upholding personal and family honor through ideals and practices of sexual morality are central to Islam, communities may emphasize virginity and marital fidelity as reasons for practicing FGM. For example, it has been shown how Orthodox Islam contributes to infibulation practices in Somalia,[18] while in Somali communities in Kenya, FGM is practiced in order to enforce the cultural value of sexual purity in marriage.[19]

The linkage between FGM and sexual control is documented in the literature (e.g., in terms of the symbolic linkages between female circumcision and virginity in Sudan).[20] The literature suggests that women are however less likely than men to associate FGM with decreased sexual desire and activity.[21] This is also the case in our study, as 42 percent of Mossi male respondents—compared to only 4 percent of Mossi women—stated that FGM was practiced in order to control female "promiscuity" with men. Likewise, 13 percent of Peulh men—compared to less than 2 percent of Peulh women—listed sexual control as an advantage of FGM. While some Fulani men did state that FGM would help control women's sexual activities, especially during men's absences from home (many men engage in short-term work migration), this rationale was overshadowed by more explicitly religious and cultural factors that emphasized continuity with their past, the practice of one's faith, identity formation, and political struggle.

Modesty discourses are a fundamental aspect of morality in many parts of the Muslim world and may be expressed as respectful comportment, sexual propriety, concealing types of dress, and the emotions of shyness and embarrassment.[22] Those Peulh who discussed the role of FGM in sexual morality were likely to describe the importance of modesty and especially self-restraint. Men and women described those who had been cut as sensible and modest in their relationships with men.[23] As one female respondent from Petedga stated,

> Excision allows the control of women's sexuality. A good woman should not love sex. One must excise her to show her that a woman should be submissive and occupy herself with the education of her children. A woman that is not excised cannot control herself. She has no restraint and here in our place, the first thing that we teach to our children is restraint. Restraint is what gives you the respect of others.

Purity, Religion, and Community

In their discussions of FGM, many Peulh respondents focused less on sexuality or modesty and more on purity and the ability to pray and practice one's faith fully. For Muslims, ritual cleanliness is central to worship, and FGM is considered an essential act of purification. In the communities visited for this study, the clitoris is viewed as *haraam* (untouchable, forbidden, impure) and something that must be removed in order not only to practice one's faith but to be accepted into the Muslim community.

> If a woman is not excised, she does not have the right to pray. Her prayers will not be answered. The clitoris is dirty. If one does not cut it to make the girl pure, she will not be able to do her prayers...The clitoris is *haraam*, and everything that is *haraam* is impure...I am for excision because if a woman is impure she will not go to heaven, she cannot cook for her spouse because even if she were to do it, it is *haraam*. The fact that she is still carrying the clitoris makes her soiled. (Female respondent, Mansila)

Thanks to excision, you can say your prayers...[Excision] is above all due to the religion and our religion is our culture. You know, it is difficult not to conform to practices prescribed by our religion. Religion allows social integration within our community. (Female respondent, Petedga)

Finatawa (culture) is that which is done in agreement with all the community and for us, the Peulh, our culture is closely tied to our religion. If we abandon our *finatawa*, there is no more *yaage*, that is to say, "respect." If we stop excising our girls, how will we teach them to follow the principles of Islam since we must excise a girl before she learns anything of *faatiha* (initiation to adulthood). Here education follows Islamic rules and it is a whole, because everything works together. If one single rule is missed, it is a sin. (Female respondent, Petedga)

Among the Peulhs [excision] is important because it is an inescapable step for integration and to practice the teachings of the Qur'an. A non-excised women is impure and dirty. (Male respondent, Petedga)

The *marabouts* teach us that a non-excised woman is dirty and impure, her prayers are not valid and she is not a good Muslim. *Djoulnougol* [term for male and female circumcision, translated as "that which makes the person ready for prayer"] is obligatory and is parallel to *djoulnougol* for men. (Male respondent, Petedga)

You know that excision has the name *djoulnougol*. This means many things. A girl who isn't excised cuts herself off from religious faith. God does not count her among the faithful. (Male respondent, Bossey Barabe)

Among the Peulh, [excision] is a way to affirm the identity, the nobility of the Peulh culture. Among the Peulh, one should put purity, cleanliness first. (Male respondent, Petedga)

Thanks to excision, you can be counted among the believers and easily have a suitor. If not, it is like you have no faith, or even law—you are not part of any community. Excision is the first thing that you do for your daughter to prove that you are a believer and that your children will be the same. It is a precondition for the religious education of a girl. (Female respondent, Petedga)

Women who are circumcised are not only viewed as having a greater ability to pray, they are also seen as inherently more religious and more apt to follow religious values and precepts; both men and women emphasize these aspects of the practice. FGM is also linked to views of women as responsible and "serious" in regard to other areas of life such as their social roles in their family and community. Respondents suggested that a devout Muslim man could not eat food prepared by a noncircumcised women. One respondent in Sambagou said that "a non-excised woman is not a good Muslim or a good spouse. A good believer should not eat the food of a non-excised woman." This relates not only to purity itself but to its linkages with familial and social interdependence and belonging, as well as suitability for marriage.

Beliefs that draw on feminine sexuality and reproduction to contrast dirt and purity are deeply embedded in many indigenous religious traditions and can be found in African Christian religious communities as well (e.g., some of the African Instituted Churches). Menstruation is the classic example as it is often viewed as inherently powerful and dangerous, as illustrated by the example of an infibulated girl in Kenya who died from vaginal bleeding and could not have prayers offered for her by the Muslim community due to the presence of trapped blood.[24] Symbolic analysis of representations of the clitoris across sub-Saharan Africa is beyond the scope of this chapter, but it is important to point out that such understandings of purity and power have relevance to current discourses concerning FGM, which is viewed as a solution to the idea of compromised purity linked to physical maturation.[25]

Social identities are often constructed in opposition to an outside group. In our conversations, FGM as a symbol of Peulh identity was often contrasted with *kaado* (non-Peulh) and more often with *kefero* (pagan). Women of Bellah ethnicity were singled out for comparison. The Bellah, former slaves of the Tuareg, also live in the Sahel Region and most do not practice FGM; for the Peulh, they sometimes serve as the antithesis to the devout, circumcised believer. In discussing FGM, respondents returned again and again to the example of the Bellah.

Among the Peulh, when a girl or boy is not excised or circumcised, we say that he or she is no longer a Peulh, but a *kaado*, that is to say a non-Peulh. Therefore, among the Peulh, excision permits integration of the child into the culture. (Male respondent, Sambagou)

Among the Peulh, it is excision that differentiates from other communities. A good Peulh must be circumcised and a good Peulh woman must be excised. If it is not the case, they are treated as a *kaado* or *kefero*. (Male respondent, Sambagou)

A mother must excise her daughter. If not, she is viewed as *kefero*, a woman without cultural and ethnic identity. (Male respondent, Sambagou)

[Excision] permits us to be good Muslims and to distance ourselves from animism, called *keferakou*. (Male respondent, Sambagou)

There are no non-excised women in our place, but for comparison I can use Bellah women. I can say that a Bellah woman is not excised, she does not pray, she does not make any effort to be clean. Cleanliness is a religious requirement. Simply doing regular ablutions ensures the cleanliness of excised women. (Male respondent, Bossey Barabe)

We don't speak about that [nonexcised women] often here. It is certain that they would say that she is not a believer and that it would be better for her to join the Bellah women. (Female respondent, Petedga)

If you excise your child…the child is respected and has a place in the society, that is to say she is counted among Muslims and will easily be demanded in marriage. Here a non-excised girl could never be married. She is a Bellah. (Female respondent, Sambagou)

We always compare ourselves with the Bellah, because it is they who do not do what we do, and we believe that they are dirty, they are loose. There are always disputes among couples concerning infidelity. A man finds his woman with another man in the bedroom or in the bush. The men who travel come back to find their women pregnant because she is not serious. (Male respondent, Bossey Barabe)

Excision is an established custom among the Peulh and has always been practiced to spare the woman all the humiliation of being compared to Bellah women who are not excised. It is a form of exclusion among Peulh women. (Male respondent, Bossey Barabe)

When we speak of Bellah women, we say that she has an organ that is not of her age, because this organ only exists among children. We compare some of her behaviors to a child simply because she has refused to rid herself of that organ. (Male respondent, Bossey Barabe)

In all these conversations, FGM served to construct collective boundaries and difference, as excised Peulh women were positively compared—as clean, pure, serious, religious, or faithful—to unexcised Bellah women. Gendered concepts of the ideal woman play a central role in marking such boundaries and defining the specific attributes and identity of a community. For many Peulhs, FGM is not merely related to patriarchal control over wives' and daughters' reproduction. It is part of a wider system of cultural meaning that reflects and shapes social relationships. Again, concepts of purity, prayerfulness, responsibility, and respect are all bound up in the practice of FGM, as noted among others in Senegal.[26] In such communities, change can only be achieved very gradually, as the practice of FGM is intertwined with many benefits gained through the community and the practice of their faith.

National Law and Underground Practices

As mentioned in the introduction, accurate measures of FGM prevalence are difficult to obtain today due to the fear of reporting participation in a contentious or illegal practice. The qualitative field-work confirms a significant amount of secrecy surrounding the practice in northern Burkina Faso. The lack of openness in discussing FGM was especially pronounced in two of the six areas studied: a predominantly Mossi village in Soum Province and a Peulh village in Oudalan. Both were identified by local government officials as areas where the practice is known to be widespread. Yet, information about FGM was kept from the data collection team through avoidance of questions; ambiguous, misleading, or even false statements; and other methods of concealment not uncommon to such fieldwork.

In order to uncover information related to the prevalence of FGM, the semistructured interview contained several specially designed questions.[27] The first question did not implicate the individual directly and was about whether or not the practice was found in the village. Several additional questions were then asked about the respondent's position with regard to the practice and the intent to circumcise daughters in the future. Few individuals in Oundipoli (12.5 percent of men, no women) were willing to acknowledge the existence of the practice in the village, and respondents in both villages were reluctant to discuss their own personal views on the subject. During the interviews, women spoke in hushed tones about others villagers' engagement in FGM and denied their own support for FGM or their intent to circumcise daughters in the future. A small proportion of women (12.6 percent in Bossey Barabe and 6.3 percent in Oundipoli) said they were in favor of the practice. Many women (43.8 percent) in Bossey Barabe said that they did not know their position regarding FGM. Only 19 percent of women in Bossey Barabe, and none in Oundipoli, said that they would circumcise their daughters in the future.

Further discussions indicated that many women are not against the practice of FGM although the degree to which it is practiced was unclear. For example, several women described their position as a positive one. One woman stated:

> I was born into it, with my grandparents practicing it. For this reason, I can't abandon the practice...I'm afraid to practice excision in the future because it is prohibited. In a neighboring village, a circumciser was arrested. This is why there is fear...I was excised but I have never encountered any problems in my life. All my births were in the home without any problems.

A lack of arguments against FGM also pointed to underlying support for the practice. Although many women and men could list negative health consequences, these consequences were rarely mentioned by women in explaining their stated anti-FGM position. Instead, in explaining their position, they described "following" what they have been told. For example, one woman stated that she was against the practice but did not explain her view. In response to our question about long- and short-term health consequences of FGM, she replied: "They say that the excised woman is weak compared to the non-excised woman who is strong. That is what the village health officers have told us. But myself, I can't tell the difference. To me, all are the same. I think that the health officers are in a better position to give you this information."

Although it was very difficult to gain information from women in these two villages, interviews with men suggested that FGM is still widespread and that women play an important role in perpetuating FGM for reasons related to health, culture, religion, social acceptability, and marriage outcomes (as in other villages we visited). One male respondent stated: "Our area does not have circumcisers. They all come from other locations but with the repression it has become difficult to find them, if their conditions of safety are not met. Most often it is the women who have the responsibility to 'manage the dossier.' The men are not informed."

In both villages, the vast majority of respondents said that the decision to excise a daughter is made by women in the family—in most cases the mother or grandmother. Still, 13 percent of men in Oundipoli and 25 percent in Bossey Barabe said that the father also plays a role. Due to their greater comfort in the interview context and because they can more easily distance themselves from the practice of FGM and its legal repercussions (since it is considered "women's problem"), men were somewhat more open in interviews. Although they similarly denied their intent to circumcise daughters in the future (only 19 percent in Bossey Barabe and none in Oundipoli said they would do so), a larger percentage of men in each village openly discussed their support for FGM (50 percent in Bossey Barabe and 18.8 percent in Oundipoli). They did so only after being repeatedly reassured that they would not be imprisoned for their views and that the goal of the study was to better understand local perspectives on the practice, not to conduct a criminal investigation.

The respondents described in some detail how stated positions on the practice are influenced mainly by fear, noting the danger inherent in discussing a practice that has sent others in the community to prison. As one put it very simply, "Truth walks with your neck." Men's comments in Bossey Barabe concerning the fear and secrecy of the community when it comes to discussing FGM are found in the quotations that follow:

> It is a decision made by women but they are afraid because of sanctions that have been applied against the recidivists of [Sheik] Bossey Etage in 2006.

> Do you want to turn me in to the military police? I've already said a lot, but you haven't given me any guarantee. I don't want to say anything with respect to the future. The future does not personally engage me...We cannot keep quiet on this problem. People are afraid to talk about it even though we are all in favor of the continuation of the practice.

> I am "a little for" excision [rather than "totally for"—referring to response options] because we are in a situation of repression and I don't underestimate the power of the state. But in reality there are better things to do than be interested in cultural practices that do not kill anyone...My position hasn't changed but we are reduced to silence in the face of the state's force. Since you are humanitarians, I hope you're not going to turn us in to the law, because the state has all the means to gather information and to reach those who break the law.

> Today, it is too risky to speak of excision or to have a position other than being favorable toward its abandonment. There are ears everywhere. (*Il ya des oreilles partout.*)

> I am afraid to admit that I am totally for [excision] due to the risk of being arrested, since you [referring to the investigator] are against the practice. I don't understand why you are so interested in this practice although it doesn't hurt anyone. We are living according to our customs.

A male respondent in the other village of Oundipoli similarly stated:

> Excision is always about following initiation advice such as respect for elders and parents. Excision is never done without this advice. The advantage is respect for the elders...We don't say anything [about nonexcised women]. We are afraid to speak because of the law. But what I know is that one cannot control her because she doesn't respect people.

Among men and women who claimed that they are against FGM, a very large percentage cited the law as the sole reason for their position. Of 64 respondents in the two villages, 51 said that they were against FGM, and of these, 43 percent said that this was only due to the law. Among women alone, the percentage was 59 percent. One respondent explained that those who practice excision "are those who are not afraid of the law." Other comments about the role of the law in shaping current opinions and practices related to FGM are found in the following quotations:

> The people continue with excision because they don't know the reasons for which they've been told to stop. Those who have stopped are just afraid...To me, [excision] is a good thing, because I know its utility. Today we are told to stop so I don't have anything to say.

> I am convinced about the benefits I've talked about. It was not a long time ago. But the law came with new words and sanctions. I don't have a choice so I stopped.

> It is like I said, we have known excision and now they tell us not to practice it...Speaking honestly, when we see a child with a clitoris "up in the air," it is very evil. But, since there is repression, we are obliged to stop because we are afraid of being convicted.

> Personally, I cannot say anything. We are just following what we are told. Our parents said that it was necessary and now we've been told that it isn't good. So we are waiting to see what the future holds for us...We can no longer find circumcisers because everyone is afraid. So, I don't know if I'll do it or not, if I find a circumciser.

> I am against it because it is prohibited...Everything prohibited is fear-provoking. Otherwise, the people are born into it, and the white people have just forced us.

Similar findings have been reported in the Kolda Region of Senegal in 2001. A GTZ study shows that, despite ongoing programs against FGM, a large proportion of respondents stated that the law against FGM was the sole reason for renouncing the practice due to fear, but such fear can be overcome, in which case some may revert to the practice.[28]

The support for anti-FGM campaigns by the government, international organizations, and NGOs, as well as the active and visible way in which the law has been enforced in some places, has made it unlikely that men and women will openly discuss their participation in, or support for, FGM. Respondents were aware of the enforcement of the law and referred to instances of arrest, especially when these involved prominent local individuals and the imprisonment of women elders involved in the practice. In Bossey Barabe, many mentioned the local sheikh who arranged for the excision of his daughters and was arrested and heavily fined. Women described how in a neighboring village an older woman circumciser had been imprisoned—something that surprised them, perhaps because of her age and social status. Speaking about the incident, they emphasized that they did not want to be "taken to Gorom," the provincial capital where the prison is located. The military and police are known to work closely with the CNLPE (National Committee in the Fight against Excision) to eradicate the practice. Awareness campaigns conducted by mobile policy and army teams are a central part of state policy against FGM.[29] Rumors abound, heightening fears. In Oundipoli one woman stated, "It is difficult now to find the circumcisers, because they are afraid. We heard that if they catch a circumciser, they cut their two hands."

The relationship between women and health care providers also plays a role in promoting fear and a lack of openness on health-related issues. We found that women in many of the remote areas we visited feel uncomfortable with the health officers assigned to the village or nearby clinics. Women in one of our village surveys described this relationship:

> It's necessary to go frequently to the CSPS. If the nurses don't know you because you don't go often, they scold you. This is the reason women are afraid of visiting there.

> We haven't been to school and that is really a handicap for us. The women are ashamed to present themselves at the CSPS. Here, if you see that a woman has visited there, it is because her illness is now at a serious stage.

> It is a problem of distance and also the women are ashamed of speaking of those things. You know, our traditions contribute to our ignorance. You can never say what you feel. There is a lot of deceit and secrecy in our place, This makes it difficult to obtain information.

Women also lack a positive and open relationship with the health care system. In Oundipoli, as well, several respondents discussed the fear and avoidance that characterized their relationship with local health providers. They described the use of force, including the involvement of police, in children's vaccinations. One person stated, "People don't talk about [excision]. With the nurse who is there, everyone is afraid to say anything." Another described the local nurse as a "spy" who has instilled fear in all. In regard to FGM, some individuals said that health center personnel would refuse to treat girls who suffered complications from the practice. As a male respondent from Mansila explained, "It is the [medical personnel] who have told us in recent years that excision is not good for the health of the girl.

They have decided that they will not attend to a circumcised girl in the case of complications because the people have been warned of the dangers of excision."

Health personnel have taken note of local attitudes and strategies of avoidance. They described how many people are unwilling to communicate their health problems to professionals. As one health professional said, "When they have a headache, they say it is a footache." The position of health workers is a difficult one. On the one hand, they are expected to report FGM to the authorities and do what they can, with very few resources, to dissuade people from participating in the practice. On the other hand, their work is hindered by the lack of communication and trust with those that they serve.

In some cases, FGM has become a symbol of resistance in certain Muslim communities. Those who politicized FGM discussed their concerns regarding religious expression, community autonomy, and the right to self-determination. This was especially true for the northern province of Oudalan, where there has been significant legal enforcement of the sanctions against FGM. The state loomed large in conversations as an agent of force and restraint. Equally so were the "whites" (including Western-influenced Africans) who were seen to be imposing their values on the local population. Men were more likely than women to express their concerns regarding the need for cultural and religious expression. The following are quotes from men in Bossey Barabe:

> We need to help women to resolve the problem by discussing with authorities because tomorrow they can also tell us not to do it to boys. And after they can take away the right to pray, because the state has no religion.

> In my view, we no longer can have a position on something that is the object of repression. The law is stronger than everyone. That is what happened last year to the Sheik of Bossey [Barabe], Etage. He excised his daughters and the authorities found out.

> They told me that the reason for forbidding the practice of excision is because excised women have difficulties in childbirth. But that's how they scare someone who doesn't have the ability to understand medical problems—so that he is afraid and stops what he is doing. They have suggested a problem of childbirth in order to convince us, even though women in the past were excised and didn't have any problems.

> We don't speak about [nonexcised women] because we don't know about them. Our custom does not allow that a woman is not excised; it is the domination of "white people" [see definition given earlier] that

today makes us face this situation...I am for (excision) but if Islam were to overtly discourage the practice, we would abandon it because we are believers. But a state law may oblige communities to migrate to horizons that are favorable to their customs. Nothing obliges us to live forever in this location, tomorrow we can go somewhere else.

As a believer, we are held to our religious vow to die for our beliefs whenever an external force wants to take them away. But I wish that there was a dialogue to align the state law on the abandonment of excision with religious proscription in order to encourage a practice that does not create any victims...Any practicing Muslim is obliged to observe the religious proscriptions. I did my religious studies in Mali, so I can say that in this village very few people are more educated than me. I am a little influential here, but I keep quiet because there is repression. The great marabout of Bossey, Etage, has recently encountered problems with the justice system in Gorom because he let his girls be excised. It is unjust that people want to prevent us from following our religion.

Islam does not say that [excision] is good or bad. The Qur'an is mute on this...I already said that it is proper that a woman is excised in our place. It is ugly and dishonorable for a Peulh woman not to be excised. Today it is frustrating for us, to see the state reprimand us in the practice of our culture.

I said that [excision] is an element of our way of life. It is cultural like my scars and like the scars of my children...I don't know what you are going to do with my remarks, but I will not hide the truth from you, we practice excision because it is part of our way of life...Our neighbors the Bellah don't excise their girls because they are Bellah. We are Rimaibe. We also have our culture that was taught to us and that we have adopted. It is a belief with a spiritual dimension. I want to tell you that every element of our culture, of our customs, has its importance in the wellbeing of every member of our ethnic group and excision falls in the same category. You ask me to be against my own custom, what else remains for me? What will I be a part of? How will I educate my children? If I have the courage to respond to your questions, it is because I love my culture, and I am not embarrassed to present its form and content to anyone who wants to discover it...No one has shown me anything that proves the bad things they say about excision. I simply believe that they want to invert the order of things. We are in an era of entertainment and pleasure-seeking...there is a tendency towards the demoralization of human life. One must leave these women and men to amuse themselves and to engage in nothing else but pleasure.

But it was not only men who held such convictions. One woman described how her father, an imam, had been put in prison during the colonial era due to conflicts with the authorities. She proclaimed that she strongly supported FGM and said that "even if you threatened to cut off my head, I would still excise my daughters." She stated that she is following her father who was not afraid to openly express his beliefs. Work on FGM in Senegal has also shown that reaction against legal sanctions has led some imams and community members to take a strong stance in favor of FGM.[30] Even where leaders would like to take action against FGM, they may be constrained by popular opinion, especially by those who feel their religious and cultural identities are threatened. The same was observed in Kenya where Somali leaders are not willing to speak out against FGM for fear that they will be seen as "pro-Western" by the community members.

Because FGM is viewed as directly connected to the ability of women to pray and practice their religion, the national and global efforts to prevent FGM are controversial and seen as a direct challenge to an Islamic way of life. Similar findings were observed among women in Guinea-Bissau who felt that anti-FGM movements were an attempt by non-Muslims to take away their right to pray.[31] Especially in areas where groups are economically and politically disempowered (or perceive themselves to be so), FGM may be strongly promoted, and the draw toward FGM may be accentuated by its controversial nature since the very marginality of cultural representations can be powerful expressions of local identity and agency.

Conclusion

Religion is central to the social and cultural processes that shape women's opportunities and constraints, including in the economic and social areas. The practice has potentially high costs for girls and women, not only in terms of the medical complications that may ensue (and in some cases may be fatal), but also in terms of the contribution of FGM to the perpetuation of restrictive social and economic roles assigned to women in some societies.

Linkages between FGM and Islam, however, go well beyond interpretations of Islamic law. These linkages provide legitimacy to FGM despite widespread criticism of the practice, including among many Muslim men and women. While it is useful for FGM opponents to challenge the notion that FGM is a religious requirement, and especially to show the ways in which it runs counter to Islamic principles, one must also recognize that the practice is deeply embedded in the social, cultural, economic, and political life of communities. The local contexts surrounding FGM must be taken into account in order to promote human rights in such a way that communities can agree with and own these rights and to sustain progress toward FGM's abandonment.[32]

National laws against the practice can help, but they can also backfire. Due to the deeply seated cultural and religious underpinnings of FGM, successful prevention efforts tend to be participatory. Organizations at the forefront of prevention solicit community involvement, work with peer educators, facilitate discussion groups between community members, frame issues in culturally appropriate terms, and nurture long-term sustainability. Yet even with such approaches, progress in eliminating FGM has been mixed. In some areas, religious leaders have been quite open to change, often shifting from a positive to a negative view of the practice. Scholarly debates that reveal the contradictions between infibulation and Islamic doctrine can help. Prominent Muslim leaders in countries such as Kenya and Egypt have denounced FGM, pointing instead to Islamic teachings regarding physical health and wholeness, marital relations, and the care of children. These leaders have suggested that FGM conflicts with Islamic beliefs.

Elsewhere, however, there has been less enthusiasm for anti-FGM campaigns and religion continues to be a factor in the persistence of the practice. Male community and religious leaders may avoid the topic or decry outside intrusion into local affairs when the issue of FGM is raised. Whereas religious leaders in the past often legitimized FGM by citing teachings from the Qur'an or Sunnah that discuss male and female circumcision, they may now make more ambiguous statements about Islam's support for tradition. Some women also view and experience FGM as a key part of their cultural and religious identity. But statements of one's position for or against FGM collected through surveys may not adequately measure underlying support for the practice, since studies reveal that a position against cutting or mutilation may simply express fear of legal sanction.

This chapter has emphasized the need for better understanding of the validity of prevalence data and the factors influencing these data. Strict enforcement of the law against FGM has made it difficult to gather accurate prevalence data. The problem of secrecy is most acute for women who are directly implicated in the practice and have a history of exclusion from the public sphere. As a result, many are especially hesitant and fearful of FGM studies and are unable to discuss the practice openly. In Burkina Faso, due to the law, men as well as women are less likely to provide accurate information related to direct measures of prevalence such as women's and daughters' circumcision status. While the fear of arrest and prosecution probably help in reducing the practice, it makes it very difficult to gauge the actual level of decline. Discussions with local officials suggest that women continue to practice FGM when a circumciser is bold enough to come to the area or by themselves traveling to distant villages closer to national borders.

One common way to address the religious aspect of FGM has been to involve Islamic scholars who are against FGM in order to stimulate discussion on religious doctrine pertaining to the practice—emphasizing the dearth of passages supporting FGM as well as their ambiguity and lack of authenticity. This has had mixed results, with some local Muslim leaders showing much more interest and support than others. Recently, religious leaders in Mali and Mauretania who participated in such discussions were willing to admit that FGM is not an Islamic requirement. However, the meetings fell short of expectations in that they did not result in a religious decree against the practice.[33] Also, it has been common for leaders to advocate for a shift from infibulation to *sunnah* circumcision rather than for elimination of the practice altogether. Evaluations show that even in the case of the highly successful NGO TOSTAN, with its participatory and holistic framework, participants at the end of the program were *more* likely to say that FGM is supported by their religion than at the start (the percentage increased from 14 percent to 34 percent in the participant group and from 14 percent to 47 percent in the control group).[34]

For many African communities, FGM is interwoven with religious and cultural values and practices. The practice expresses notions of respectability, sexual propriety, religiosity, belonging, and continuity in ways that cannot be easily addressed through traditional methods of intervention which mainly inform communities about the medical complications of FGM. Ongoing challenges in preventing FGM in Africa suggest that the practice is best addressed with a long term approach that examines the religious, cultural, and social aspects of the practice in partnership with elders, religious leaders, and community members. Forums for religious and cultural leaders that take place alongside ongoing communication and training sessions for the entire community are helpful, particularly when leaders can play a role in identifying strategies and mobilizing the community. Because religion is inseparable from other aspects of daily life, both resistance to change and innovation toward new solutions are anchored in the religious sphere.

Work with religious and cultural leaders offers the opportunity to engage individuals in discussions not only about religious precepts but also about issues of morality, social change, cultural identity, and religious expression, all of which are implicated in debates about FGM. Intergenerational dialogue through which both elders and younger community members can express their concerns about the health and well-being of the community and explore solutions can also be very useful. This type of approach is currently being implemented with women elders among others in Senegal in order to provide an opportunity for intergenerational exchange. Elders are central to this work, not because of the need to overcome their resistance to change, but to chart out new directions as the community addresses multiple challenges—not only concerning health and human rights, but also economic struggle, declining ties of social solidarity, and the lack of moral, cultural, and religious education for children.[35]

Notes

1. UNICEF, *The Dynamics of Social Change.*
2. Renders, "Political-Social Movements"; Gruenbaum, *The Female Circumcision Controversy.*
3. Von der Osten-Sacken and Uwer, "Is Female Genital Mutilation an Islamic Problem?"
4. Mustafa, "Body: Female, Sub-Saharan Africa."
5. Asmani and Abdi, *Delinking Female Genital Mutilation/Cutting from Islam.*
6. Abu-Sahlieh, "To Mutilate in the Name of Jehovah or Allah."
7. See Johnson, "Becoming a Muslim, Becoming a Person," on the fact that some Muslims in rural Guinea-Bissau describe hidden, secret meanings beyond what is apparent or visible in readings of the Qur'an. Many of her informants explained that that the passages pertaining to FGM "are so sacred that they cannot be seen...with the naked eye." The notion of secrecy provides another way in which people may interpret and redirect discussions pertaining to religious doctrine. It also lends further legitimacy to the practice, since the message viewed as secret and concealed from public knowledge is considered to be even more profound and fundamental to religious belief.
8. Abu-Sahlieh, "To Mutilate in the Name of Jehovah or Allah."
9. See El Guindi, "Had This Been Your Face," on how the term *sunnah* helps to validate FGM for many Muslim communities in the Sudan since it suggests an Islamic basis, and this legitimacy is usually not questioned or challenged. FGM
10. Asmani and Abdi, *Delinking Female Genital Mutilation/Cutting from Islam.*
11. GTZ, "Female Genital Mutilation and Islam."
12. UNICEF, *The Dynamics of Social Change.*

13. CNLPE, *Plan D'Action National.*
14. See Population Council, "Using Operations Research," as well as UNFPA-UNICEF, "Burkina Faso Has a Strong Low against FGM/C."
15. Jackson et al., "Inconsistent Reporting of Female Genital Cutting Status."
16. Ako and Akweongo, "The Limited Effectiveness of Legislation."
17. Population Council, "Using Operations Research."
18. Abdalla, "My Grandmother Called It."
19. Jaldesa et al., *Female Genital Cutting among the Somali of Kenya.*
20. Gruenbaum, *The Female Circumcision Controversy.*
21. El Guindi, "Had This Been Your Face."
22. Abu-Lughod, "Modesty Discourses: Overview."
23. For Peulh men and women, *Pulaaku* or self-restraint is central to social life. In her ethnography of the Peulh, Helen Regis, who studied religion and gender in Cameroon, states that *"Pulaaku* requires that emotions such as anger, joy, grief and love—as well as feelings of thirst, hunger and pain—be displayed only among close friends and family. The public denial of physical need and vulnerability shapes how Fulbe men and women approach everyday life ... *Pulaako* encompasses meanings of reserve, restraint, self-mastery, and nobility."
24. Jaldesa et al., *Female Genital Cutting among the Somali of Kenya.*
25. Johnson, "Becoming a Muslim, Becoming a Person."
26. Aubel and Lombardo, *Cultural Values, Educating Girls and Female Genital Cutting.*
27. Questions regarding support for FGM were also asked during focus group discussions. Group participants in the two villages, however, were even more unlikely to discuss these questions and so we relied mainly on personal interviews.
28. GTZ, "Good Practice."
29. Diop et al., *Analysis of the Evolution of the Practice of Female Genital Mutilation/Cutting in Burkina Faso.*
30. Ibid.
31. Johnson, "Becoming a Muslim, Becoming a Person."
32. UNFPA, *Working from Within.*
33. GTZ, "Good Practice."
34. Diop, et al., *The TOSTAN Program.*
35. The authors are with the World Bank. Comments from Mark White are gratefully acknowledged. The opinions expressed in the chapter are those of the authors and need not represent those of the World Bank, its executive directors, or the countries they represent.

Bibliography

Abdalla, Raqiya D. "My Grandmother Called It 'The Three Feminine Sorrows': The Struggle of Women Against Female Circumcision in

Somalia." In *Female Circumcision: Multicultural Perspectives*, edited by Rogaia M. Abusharaf, 187–204. Philadelphia: University of Pennsylvania Press, 2007.

Abu-Lughod, Lila. "Modesty Discourses: Overview." In *Encyclopedia of Women and Islamic Cultures, Volume 2: Family, Law and Politics*, edited by Suad Joseph, 494–498. Leiden: Brill, 2005.

Abu-Sahlieh, Sami A. A. "To Mutilate in the Name of Jehovah or Allah: Legitimization of Male and Female Circumcision." *Medicine and Law* 13 (1994): 575–622.

Ako, Matilda A., and Patricia Akweongo. "The Limited Effectiveness of Legislation against Female Genital Mutilation and the Role of Community Beliefs in Upper East Region, Ghana." *Reproductive Health Matters* 17 (2009): 47–54.

Asmani, Ibrahim L., and Maryam S. Abdi. *Delinking Female Genital Mutilation/Cutting from Islam*. New York: Population Council, 2008. Available at https://www.unfpa.org/webdav/site/global/shared /documents/publications/2011/De-linking%20FGM%20from%20 Islam%20final%20report.pdf.

Aubel, Judi, and Bridget Lombardo. *Cultural Values, Educating Girls and Female Genital Cutting: A Qualitative Community Study*. Rome: The Grandmother Project, 2006.

CNLPE (National Committee in the Fight Against Excision). *Plan D'Action National de Promotion de L'Abandon des MGF dans la Perspective de la Tolérance Zéro*. Ministry of Social Action, Burkina Faso, 2007.

Diop, Nafissatou J., et al. *Analysis of the Evolution of the Practice of Female Genital Mutilation/Cutting in Burkina Faso*. New York: Population Council, 2008. Available at http://www.popcouncil.org/uploads/pdfs /frontiers/FR_FinalReports/BurkinaFaso_FGMAnalysis.pdf.

Diop, Nafissatou J., et al. *The TOSTAN Program: Evaluation of a Community Based Education Program in Senegal*. New York: Population Council, 2004. Available at http://www.popcouncil.org/uploads/pdfs/frontiers /FR_FinalReports/Senegal_Tostan%20FGC.pdf.

El Guindi, Fadwa. "Had This Been Your Face, Would You Leave It as Is?" In *Female Circumcision: Multicultural Perspectives*, edited by R. M. Abusharaf, 27–46. Philadelphia: University of Pennsylvania Press, 2007.

Gruenbaum, Ellen. *The Female Circumcision Controversy: An Anthropological Perspective*. Philadelphia, University of Pennsylvania Press, 2001.

GTZ. "Female Genital Mutilation and Islam." GTZ Supra-Regional Project: Ending Female Genital Mutilation. Eschborn: GTZ, 2009. Available at http://www.intact-network.net/intact/cp/files/1296995492 _FGM%20&%20Islam-%20GTZ.pdf.

GTZ. "Good Practice: Information, Education and Communication Strategies to End FGM within the Context of Reproductive Health in Senegal." GTZ Supra-Regional Project: Ending Female Genital Mutilation. Eschborn: GTZ, 2008.

Jackson, Elizabeth F., et al. "Inconsistent Reporting of Female Genital Cutting Status in Northern Ghana: Explanatory Factors and Analytical Consequences." *Studies in Family Planning* 34 (2003): 200–210.

Jaldesa, Guyo W., Ian Askew, Carolyne Njue, and Monica Wanjiru. *Female Genital Cutting among the Somali of Kenya and Management of Its Complications.* New York: Population Council, 2005.

Johnson, Michelle C. "Becoming a Muslim, Becoming a Person: Female 'Circumcision,' Religious Identity, and Personhood in Guinea-Bissau." In *Female "Circumcision" in Africa*, edited by Bettina Shell-Duncan and Ylva Hernlund, 215–234. Boulder, CO: Lynne Rienner, 2000.

Mustafa, Hudita N. "Body: Female: Sub-Saharan Africa." In *Encyclopedia of Women and Islamic Cultures, Volume III, Family, Body, Sexuality and Health*, edited by Suad Joseph, 40–43. Leiden: Brill, 2006.

Population Council (Frontiers in Reproductive Health). "Using Operations Research to Strengthen Programmes for Encouraging Abandonment of Female Genital Cutting." Report of the Consultative Meeting on Methodological Issues for FGM Research, April 9–11, 2002, Nairobi, Kenya. Available at http://www.popcouncil.org/uploads/pdfs/frontiers/nairobi_fgcmtg.pdf.

Renders, Marleen. "Political-Social Movements: Islamist Movements and Discourses: Sub-Saharan Africa." In *Encyclopedia of Women and Islamic Cultures, Volume 2: Family, Law and Politics*, edited by S. Joseph, 611–614. Leiden: Brill, 2005.

UNFPA. *Working from Within: Culturally Sensitive Approaches in UNFPA Programming.* New York: UNFPA, 2004. Available at http://www.unfpa.org/webdav/site/global/shared/documents/publications/2004/Culture_2004.pdf.

UNFPA-UNICEF Joint Programme on FGM/C. "Burkina Faso Has a Strong Law against FGM/C, but Winning Hearts and Minds Remains Crucial." New York: UNFPA and UNICEF, 2010. Available at https://www.unfpa.org/gender/docs/fgmc_kit/burkinafaso.pdf.

UNICEF (Innocenti Research Center). *The Dynamics of Social Change: Towards the Abandonment of Female Genital Mutilation/Cutting in Five African Countries.* Florence: UNICEF, 2010. Available at http://www.unicef-irc.org/publications/pdf/fgm_insight_eng.pdf.

UNICEF. *Female Genital Mutilation/Cutting: A Statistical Overview and Exploration of the Dynamics of Change.* New York: UNICEF, 2013. Available at http://www.unicef.org/esaro/FGCM_Lo_res.pdf.

Von der Osten-Sacken, Thomas, and Thomas Uwer. "Is Female Genital Mutilation an Islamic Problem?" *Middle East Quarterly* 14 (Winter 2007): 29–36.

Chapter 7

An Unexamined Oxymoron: Trust but Verify

David George

Early in my introductory economics classes, I go through the various roles of government in the economy. I start with "property rights" and present it as the least questioned government function, agreed to by liberals and conservatives alike. My purpose is in part strategic: a desire to counter the conventional view conveyed by the texts that government only comes into the economy *after* the establishment of robust markets and not before. Rhetorically, governments is described as "intervening" and "interfering" and is portrayed as a late arrival into the economy.[1] Missing from this version of history is consideration of the evidence that enforceable property rights must exist before it is even possible for markets to succeed. What belongs to one must be a matter of fact, not opinion, and accepted as legitimate by others. Perhaps theft should be relegated to the status of an oxymoron when property rights are absent.

Looking more broadly not just at the law but also at the executive branch of government, I provided evidence more recently that the strengthening grip of libertarian rhetoric has coincided with a decline in government's status and legitimacy.[2] As I discovered, the use of the pronoun "our" serves as a rough measure of the speaker's regard for the subject. It was much more common for favorable adjectives, such as "beautiful," "thoughtful," and "conscientious," to be preceded by "our" than it was for unfavorable adjectives, such as "ugly," "thoughtless," and "dishonest." Consider this: since 1960, the chance that "government" was preceded by "our" in *The New York Times* fell by half. Over the same period, the chance that "corporations" was preceded by "our" rose fourfold. And prior to 1980, favorable description of "voters" and "citizens" occurred 50 percent more often than favorable descriptions of "consumers." Since 1980, the picture has reversed, with "voters" and "citizens" only one-third as likely to be described favorably as "consumers." This and other rhetorical changes offered strong support that, even in a newspaper generally regarded as liberal, respect for the private sector has grown while the public sector has fallen into disfavor.

Social economists and heterodox economists in general like to stress that markets cannot work well without strong institutions—government most of all—providing strong support. The mainstream, in contrast, sees less need for government and tellingly fails, at least in its most read textbooks, to even distinguish democracies from dictatorships. Adding to this, the failure of the mainstream to distinguish between representative and nonrepresentative government, my strong support for a better portrayal of government becomes understandable. Moving away from my usual support for government, I will be arguing in the sections that follow that a closer look at the uses of the legal system and property rights in recent years suggests this part of government is perhaps less in the business of keeping the dark side of *homo economicus* in check than in serving as an enabler for this dark side.

The Law and Economics Movements

Two schools of thought that connect economics and the law, one primarily positive in its orientation, the other primarily normative, have flourished over the past several decades. The public choice school, most associated with Gordon Tullock and Nobel laureate James Buchanan, is the primarily positive one.[3] It has built upon the simple idea that economic principles should be used to better understand how the actors within the government—the executive branch and legislative branch more so than the judicial branch—can be better understood if they are treated as simple maximizers rather than as people sworn to act in the public interest. While I am unaware of any studies that have sought to reveal the contributions that this school of thought has had on the spreading cynicism directed at government, it may be more than coincidence that politicians are regarded less favorably than ever before.

The primarily normative school of thought is the law and economics movement usually associated with the University of Chicago. The central theme of this movement has been the application of efficiency criteria in evaluating the law. By their account, if the benefits of the existence and enforcement of a law can be shown to be less than the costs of legislating the law into existence and enforcing it, then the law cannot be justified on efficiency grounds. By their reasoning, moving in the direction of efficiency represents a Pareto improvement where some gain and no one loses, or, following the less ambitious compensation criterion, where the gains of the winners are greater than the losses of the losers, with the winners, in principle, being able to compensate the losers and still be better off.

Each of these ambitious movements contains a particular assumption that makes questionable much of each movement's conclusions. The positive public choice school treats utility maximization as a testable proposition rather than as a tautology. Since the time of Adam Smith, the limits of narrowly self-interested *homo economicus* have been largely ignored by many outside the field.[4] Smith rejected Bernard Mandeville's vision of people despite its being superficially similar to his own. Mandeville, a mercantilist, took narrow self-interest to be the norm, and concluded that strong government was necessary to counter the destruction that such selfishness would likely cause. In contrast, Smith implied that the adoption of free markets presupposed a minimal amount of "moral development." A century later the great synthesizer Alfred Marshall sought to acknowledge other-regarding behavior by treating narrow self-interest as reasonably descriptive of market behavior but not of other areas of life.

As the increasingly mathematical approach to economics took off in the twentieth century still another strategy took hold. Maximizing utility was essentially treated as a tautology, consistent with absolutely any behavior, from the most selfish to the least. Findings of the public choice school largely rest on the assumption that the narrower, selfish sort of utility maximization prevails in all areas of life. It leaves out the possibility that political actions might be motivated by behaviors inconsistent with simple self-interest and thus treats proclamations that one is "acting in the public interest" as little more than posturing.

Turning now to the law and economics movement, a shaky assumption is that Pareto improvements are necessarily desirable even when looked at fairly narrowly. The problem bears some resemblance to the distinction between an individual's "intrinsic" and "overall" preferences. Intrinsic preferences focus on immediate costs and benefits, while overall preferences bring into account the costs and benefits contingent on the action but far in the future. Thus, a recovering alcoholic might announce that he prefers a drink but will not act upon it. Another way of making the same point would be to say that while he has an intrinsic preference for the drink, the overall preference that takes into account the longer term is to not have the drink. This preference, as I have argued previously, is the more relevant one, the one that moves the agent to take action.[5] Prescriptions that follow from the law and economics paradigm might reflect a failure to think "overall." Bypassing a trial because of its cost might be wise in terms of immediate costs and benefits, but unwise when the long-term implications of such an action are considered.

This brief history and critique of current movements have been intended to provide a context within which an understanding of the law based on social economics can situate its critique. I have fairly reflexively defended government against the libertarian animosity toward nearly all collective action.[6] And in the spirit of full disclosure, I will admit that my strong defense of government might be an example of "the enemy of my enemy is my friend." Market zealots don't like government, therefore I must, went my reasoning. In the next section, I'll offer some experiences that have caused me to think more about this position.

Distrust, Accountability, and Resentment

Some recent personal experiences have caused me to reconsider my largely uncritical acceptance of the law as a counterweight to the market. The capture theory of government has a grain of truth: those making governmental decisions might be those representing the interests of the powerful.[7] The experiences that follow are intended to show how the spread of "legalistic" thinking can signal (and itself create) a weakening of broader institutions.

The apartment complex in which I rent has a pool, and there is a small fee for joining. Only when it became unbearably hot last summer did I decide to join the pool. The complex is primarily a co-op and renters are offered little information regarding which privileges they have and which they don't. When I went to the main office to pay my membership fee, I was told that membership was possible only with approval from the apartment's owner. It seems that fear of a lawsuit prompted such defensive policy. I didn't get to swim on this 98-degree day, and something just didn't seem right about the whole experience.

A second unpleasant experience occurred at my university. After 35 years at La Salle, I only recently became aware that tenure was not a legally binding agreement. In addition, La Salle has updated student evaluations of their professors by going to an online evaluation process. As a member of the Faculty Senate, I proposed that professors seeking tenure or promotion be able to challenge evaluations that they strongly dispute. I had little support from my fellow senators. The importance of anonymity for students caused some opposition as did the implicit "students can't be trusted" message. After discussion, the Senate concluded the promotion and tenure committee could be trusted to spot the rare vindictive evaluations and discount them accordingly.

This experience had me occupying a different role than the one I played in the apartment experience. In that case, I was the one asking for permission from the condo owners' association. Their legalistic response reflected, I felt, a distrust of me that I might file a lawsuit against them. While I expected trust, they insisted on a legally binding agreement. In the Senate case, the university had held the legal right to dismiss me or to base considerations of promotion and tenure on anonymous evaluations. The apartment and university experiences had in common a tension between an individual and an institution, but the roles were reversed in the two cases. The university had the legal right to do things that I might regard as grossly unfair, but until fairly recently I had trusted that they would never wrongly exercise this right. In contrast to this, it was I who had the legal right to sue the apartment had I suffered an injury while swimming. Rather than trust that I would not sue, management took a legal approach that would guard against the possibility of a lawsuit. Note that in the La Salle case, I was the one who lost faith in the institution to act according to the spirit rather than the letter of the law. I simply no longer trusted my university to not abuse its legal right to dismiss me and felt the need to become more legalistic in any future interactions with the institution. It is true that in both cases an individual was confronting an institution, but in the university case it was the institution that was no longer trusted by the individual, while in the apartment case it was the individual who was no longer trusted by the institution.

It took a while for me to recognize the case for extralegal solutions to market inefficiencies, solutions such as trust and, when appropriate, shame. As something of a rhetorical device in the framing of my work on metapreferences, I drew upon the lack of property rights in one's preferences to show that markets were inefficient in shaping tastes.[8] When one has something of value, it can't be taken away, at least not legally. But when one has an internal state—such as a preference for healthy food—one has no property claims upon this state. For marketers to cause a person to prefer unhealthy food is harmful since it involves changing a preference that a person likes having with a preference that she does not like.

Demonstrating market failure of this sort does not necessitate that we always turn to the law to solve the problem. The legal nightmare that would be created if people were given the right to sue when their tastes are harmed is more than enough to reject a legal solution. In the language of economics, the transactions costs would be so great as to make inaction better than an otherwise more efficient outcome.

In continued attempts to demonstrate that there is a problem in the way that markets shape our taste, I took into account informal solutions that might lessen preference pollution. The task I faced was to provide reasons for rejecting the unqualified claim that the occurrence of unwanted tastes was simply the "human condition" rather than something to attribute to the culture encouraged by the market. My goal was to show that informal institutions that censured the creation of unwanted desires had historically been the way in which the problem was avoided. Social censure for, say, serving alcohol to an alcoholic or selling cigarettes to a minor were sufficient to keep the forces of "preference pollution" in check. What appeared to be happening with the spread of markets was a fading awareness of the very idea of preferences about one's preferences. Thus, pornography and gambling have been legitimized as "victimless crimes" when in fact it is often the user who is the victim when the desires for these activities are unwanted and caused by their availability. Laws can do something, but so can social censure for selling things that people would prefer not to prefer.

As another example of how social pressure can sometimes stand in place of the law as a prevention against harmful actions, consider the fact that prior to the transportation revolution, markets were extremely limited in size, particularly in retail trade. With a single bank, dry goods store, grocery store, and so on, the conditions for monopoly abuse were certainly there. Yet the evidence suggests that monopoly profits were not earned.[9] An interesting area of research might be to find if the failure to charge such prices followed from simple social pressure. Making excessive profits might simply have provided an income that seemed "unfair" to one's customers.

The trouble with instituting property rights where they were previously absent can perhaps be seen best with the spreading phenomenon of "intellectual property rights." The idea that the absence of monetary rewards would lessen the creation of new ideas should be challenged, especially by academics. How many of us do the research that we do because of the monetary income it might provide? It is not that we are less materialistic and self-centered than profit maximizers.

Rather, the currency of our realm is different, manifested in citations, praise, and respect. And the advantage of not establishing property rights in ideas is simple efficiency as defined by the most mainstream economists. With the marginal cost of allowing one more person to "consume" an idea being zero, any benefit this person might derive is worth allowing. Otherwise, the marginal benefit of letting those valuing the idea by less than the price being asked would not be allowed to consume the "idea," despite valuing the knowledge more than its zero marginal cost.

Employing Lawyers More while Respecting Lawyers Less

Returning to the experience at the apartment complex, was the management's fear of lawsuit justified? If so, what has changed over time that has increased the fear of lawsuits? That they are more in the public eye and in the news is borne out by trends in *The New York Times*. "Lawsuit" appeared fewer than 1,000 times per decade from 1900 through 1959, from around 600 times in the 1930s to 987 times in the 1950s. The 1960s showed a sudden doubling as the word appeared 1,835 times, and in the 1970s the trend continued, as "lawsuit" appeared 7,702 times, a fourfold increase. Over the last decade this number had risen to 24,650, a tripling of the occurrences since the 1970s. Not surprisingly, the actual number of lawsuits has also risen significantly, doubling between 1990 and 2006.

Along with this increase in lawsuits has come an increasing mention of "frivolous lawsuit." Prior to 1969 this expression did not appear in *The New York Times*, and by 1980 it had appeared only three times. In the three decades since, "frivolous lawsuit" has appeared 75 times (1980s), 265 times (1990s), and 325 times (2000s). To check if other words were used before "frivolous" became so widespread, I did a search for "questionable lawsuits" and "unjustified lawsuits" but found use of these to be miniscule, in single digits every decade since 1900. The huge increase in "lawsuits" in the *Times* over the century certainly contributed to the rising use of the word "frivolous" over the same period, but this explains only a small part of the increase in use of this word. In the 1970s, "frivolous" appeared before "lawsuit" approximately once every 500 times, increasing in frequency to once every 400 in the 1980s, and then to once every 127 times since.

Are the rise in lawsuits lessening the opinion of lawyers in general? The increased interaction with lawyers would not be expected to change the ratio of positive to negative experiences with lawyers since for every lawsuit there's a "winner" and a "loser," suggesting that favorable and unfavorable experiences should approximately balance. A look at the ratio of favorable adjectives preceding "lawyer" ("honest," "outstanding," "respected," "distinguished," and "excellent") to unfavorable adjectives ("dishonest," "mediocre," "corrupt," "undistinguished," and "incompetent") shows the ratio of favorable to unfavorable rising from 9 between 1900 and 1925, to 23 between 1925 and 1950, to 34 between 1950 and 1975. Yet, since 1975, the ratio has plummeted to 6.

Initially, this appeared to be strong evidence that lawyers were suddenly held in low, rather than high, esteem. Politicians (senators and governors) showed a very similar 110-year trend as the ratio of favorable to unfavorable went from 9 to 24 to 16 before falling all the way to 5 since 1975. Somewhat surprisingly, doctors showed a similar trend. (Teachers, however, were the one exception with the ratio of favorable to unfavorable actually rising significantly post-1974.)

Further exploration revealed another effect: namely, that the pattern observed for lawyers, politicians, and doctors were part of an overall trend in use of the adjectives. The relative use of positive adjectives increased from 1900 through 1975, but dropped significantly since. The cause of this general trend—a growing pessimism? evolving styles of reporting?—is not something that will be pursued here. Table 7.1 provides an alternative way of summarizing these findings that abstracts from the overall historical trend from favorable to unfavorable adjective use. The numbers reflect how the ratio of favorable to unfavorable descriptions compares over time and across professions when compared with overall trends in the change in favorable and unfavorable adjective in general. So, for example, the first number indicates that for lawyers the ratio of favorable to unfavorable was equal to 0.55 of the overall ratio. For three of the professions, the trends are similar. Note that doctors are the only one of the professions shown that had a favorable-to-unfavorable ratio that exceeded the overall one. For all three of these professions, a fairly precipitous drop in the number has occurred since 1975.

Table 7.1 Relative use of positive to negative adjectives for professionals

	Lawyers and attorneys	Teachers and professors	Senators and governors	Doctors and attorneys
1900–1924	0.55	0.78	0.57	1.52
1925–1949	0.73	0.57	0.77	1.74
1950–1974	0.67	0.65	0.31	1.10
1975–2009	0.32	2.50	0.28	0.62

Regarding the rising reliance on lawsuits, what does this data reveal, if anything? The main thing to note is that over the same period when reliance on the civil law to resolve conflict and to deter bad behavior has been rising, the legal profession (as well as politicians) have been regarded less favorably. It is thus not a growing popularity of lawyers that is at work but more likely an increasing reliance upon the courts to settle disputes. This might seem counterintuitive, but a different way of looking at this suggests the declining respect for lawyers may be fully consistent with the growing dependence on their services. With trust declining, there is perhaps a long-term trend away from "compact" and toward "contract."[10] Legal approaches and legal protection have increased over the same period when less formal social forms of social control were decreasing. To this I turn in the next section, where the relative status of the legal relative to the moral is considered.

The Rise of Hierarchies and Decline of Collegial Trust

As a society matures, it is not surprising that legally enforceable contracts replace the social contract and, related to this, that thinking legally replaces (or crowds out) thinking morally. A search of *The New York Times* shows "illegal" appearing 5 times as often as "immoral" from 1900 to 1910, 10 times as often in the 1930s, 18 times as often in the 1980s, and 25 times as often in the 2000s.

One likely cause of this trend is the rising use of "unethical" as a somewhat less self-righteous condemnation. While business ethics has become a requirement for business students, one would be hard pressed to find much talk of "business morality." "Immoral" went from appearing 15 times as often as "unethical" in the *Times* between 1900 and 1920 to just twice as often over the next 20 years, and to less than twice as often ever since. From 1980 to 2000 "immoral" appeared only 13 percent more often than "unethical," and since 2000, "unethical" took the lead for the first time as "immoral" appeared 20 percent less often than "unethical." Going to a wider source, ProQuest, we see the two terms running neck and neck since 1980 at about 42,000 appearances each.

The reasons for the gains of "unethical" relative to "immoral" are of course complex. It is worth considering though how much closer the term "ethics" connects with the law. Much unethical behavior can be characterized as having to do with not acting in the spirit, if not the letter of the law. "Immoral" behavior, in contrast, casts a wider net. Some of what might be called "immoral" has no identifiable victims. So, for example, taking no actions to live in a more environmentally sustainable way seems much more like a "moral" matter than an "ethical" one. Most of those who will be harmed by this inaction are not yet born, but acting unethically usually has to do with more immediate effects on specific people.

Even after taking these considerations into account, the move toward thinking legally instead of morally is supported after combining "immoral" and "unethical" into a single category. From 1900 to 1930 "illegal" appeared 4.3 times as often as "immoral" and "unethical." In the 30 years that followed the number rose to 6.6 and in the next 30 years to 8.5. Since 1990, "illegal" has appeared 11.5 times as often. Not only is the law replacing less formal social constraints, but these formal constraints are leaning in a more legalistic direction, from the "immoral" to the "unethical," from acts with hard to identify victims to acts with clear victims.

Changes in the relative usage of words can be informative but a richer picture is possible if attitudes toward the words can be uncovered. One way to approach this is by observing the frequency of "-istic," a suffix that is almost always used pejoratively. For example, those who spread the scientific approach beyond its usual boundaries are sometimes labeled "scientistic." At least one text book refers to the "economistic" ambitions of some to use economic concepts to describe behavior outside of the traditional economy. In short, to be called "whatever-istic" almost always conveys a judgment that one is approaching "whatever" in a faulty way.

Trends in the use of "legalistic" vis-à-vis "moralistic" are shown in table 7.2. The first line shows data from *America's Historical Newspapers* from the period 1900–1923 and the second is post-1980 drawn from ProQuest. The first two columns show the number of times "legal" and "legalistic" appeared and the third shows the ratio of the two; the last columns do the same for "moral," "moralistic," and the ratio of the two. For example, we see that "legalistic" appeared once every 2,012

Table 7.2   Relative appearance of "-istic" terms

	Appearances of "legal"	Appearances of "legalistic"	Ratio of "legal" to "legalistic"	Appearances of "moral"	Appearances of "moralistic"	Ratio of "moral" to "moralistic"
AHN (1900–1923)	396,511	197	2,012	222,810	65	3,427
ProQuest (since 1980)	2,619,254	3,941	684	386,911	4,028	96

times that "legal" appeared from 1900 to 1923, while "moralistic" appeared even less, just once every 3,427 times that "moral" appeared.

Using the modern ProQuest data, we see that both "legalistic" and "moralistic" became much more frequent, with the latter increasing much more than the former. While the relative frequency of "legalistic" was increasing roughly threefold (to once every 684 times that "legal" appeared), the relative frequency of "moralistic" was rising roughly thirtyfold (to once every 96 times that "moral" appeared). The evidence is quite strong: although both "legal" and "moral" have become steadily more subject to negative portrayals by attaching "-istic" to them, the negative view of "moral" has risen far more rapidly than the negative view of "legal."

What social forces can best explain the shift away from informal compact based on trust and toward legal contracts in lieu of trust? Earlier I attributed the trends to the simple economic maturation of society. Regardless of whether one is considering the now defunct Soviet-style communism, the "extreme capitalism" that has become so dominant, or anything in between, the reality of population growth, technological change, and urbanization all point in the direction of interacting with strangers more often than with acquaintances and thus suggest increasing reliance on contract rather than social pressure as the way to guide behaviors.

Another force at work connects in some ways with John Kenneth Galbraith's writings from the early 1950s through the 1970s that saw large hierarchical organizations and the planning that went with them replacing smaller businesses. Yet, since 1980, the popular narrative has said the opposite—that "entrepreneurialism" continues to spread. Never has "entrepreneur" been used so frequently. Yet, conventional wisdom to the contrary notwithstanding, there has been a steady decline in small, "entrepreneurial" businesses.[11]

The belief that there has been a certain flattening of social roles in recent years is a strong one. There has indeed been a movement away from ranking people on the basis of on race, gender, ethnicity, or sexual preference. Even though the well-known prejudices haven't gone away, the political incorrectness of suggesting group superiority is very evident. While the current conventional wisdom has it that the information society has broken down elites and, basically, allowed for a certain leveling, there are reasons for strongly doubting this.[12] There has been a clear "leveling" in the household going on for many years now. Patriarchy is rare, especially in the more educated and affluent parts of society. What is striking, however, is that at the same time the very idea of "superiors" and "inferiors" in the household has fallen out of favor, there has been no similar retreat from hierarchy in the workplace. And with these hierarchies come the need for binding rules for one ranking above another to tell the underling what to do. Thought of differently, as with law, not following specific directions can be cause for dismissal. While the law requires abstaining from certain behaviors, less formal social compacts steer one in certain directions through more amorphously defined social pressure rather than enforceable laws. Taking the property of another can lead to fines or jail. Eating more than one's fair share of food at a party can earn one the disgust of others but not defined punishments.

Recently, I took issue with someone asking who my "boss" was. I explained that the department chair or the dean of the school could make demands but could not involve themselves in most of what I do. Independence, after all, has been a defining feature of the professions, or so I thought. In addition, we took turns, at least in our department, at being chair. Even were one to accept that a chair was somehow "superior" to other department members, rotating roles meant taking turns being on top. Just as any inequality of income or wealth that is attributable to one's age and stage of career is not unfair since all expect to occupy higher paying positions as one ages, so too the collegial model might have had a degree of hierarchy, but not of the type where one might be locked into a relative position indefinitely.

My interest in what seemed to be an increase in the use of the term "boss" led me to do another word search, and the results were more striking than I had expected. Since 1900, the likelihood that "his" or "her" would be followed by "boss" has risen markedly. Also interesting is the similarity of the trend across genders. The data in table 7.3 show how often the relevant pronouns were followed by "boss" over time. The first column of data divides the number of times that "his" appeared by the number of times "his boss" appeared, and the second does the same for "her" and "her boss." The increasing use of "boss" crosses gender lines. Prior to 1940, "his" was more often followed by

Table 7.3 Frequency of "boss" following "his" and "her"

	"His"/"His Boss"	"Her"/"Her Boss"
1900–1919	2,940	17,903
1920–1939	2,271	3,592
1940–1959	1,154	1,278
1960–1979	619	491
1980–1999	271	251
2000–2009	163	161

"boss" than was "her," largely because men were far more likely to be employees. Since 1940, the frequency of "boss" has risen steadily for both genders, sevenfold for men and eightfold for women. At the same time that the idea of a boss in the household fell so out of favor, its apparent role in the workplace became ever more common; being told what to do lessened in one sphere while increasing in the other. The informal (though gender specific) roles in the household were becoming less common at the same time that the legalistic, clearly hierarchical world of work was becoming more common. The workplace has been portrayed as "fairer" since the individual's opportunity to occupy a top place in the hierarchy is (or is slowly becoming) more merit based than gender based.

Concluding Comments

The public choice and law-and-economics movements have played major roles in the several decades long trend away from informal mechanisms based on trust and toward formal legal ways to accomplish similar results. "Trust but verify" has become a simple truism and there has been a failure to consider that any other way of linking these two words is even possible. Perhaps the expression should be changed to "trust *or* verify," with each making the other unnecessary. Connected with the movement away from trust is the conventional wisdom that all must be "accountable" for what they do. It may be awkward to announce that one is accountable to no one, yet a social ideal must surely be a movement away from the reliance on "accounting" for one's actions and toward letting trust often serve as an efficient substitute.

Personal experiences suggest to me that moving from a relationship of trust to one relying on the law comes at a cost, namely, the resentment such a shift can cause to parties on either side of the relationship. Yet even in the absence of these resentment costs, there is another problem with moving away from trust: inefficiency. In making my initial case for market failure I operated within the categories of thought associated with mainstream economics. Following a law and economics perspective leads to the troublesome conclusion that insufficient formal property rights is where the problem lies. But any reasonable solution to the problem of market failure in the shaping of our tastes would have to rely on trust. Enforcing property rights in preferences would be a bureaucratic nightmare difficult to even contemplate.

Much of what governments provide in their economic role is by its nature communal or intended to correct for the market's shortcomings. But government's first economic role, enforcing property rights through the force of the law, has had a role in the weakening of trust. Adam Smith recognized that in the absence of developed "moral sentiments," free markets were a luxury that many societies could not afford. The Hobbesian war of all against all could only be tempered by a strong government deciding what belonged to whom and enforcing the rights of property. In an over-extended reliance on the law as a means to lessen market failures, we may be weakening the habits of trust that are critical for the survival of markets.

Notes

1. See George, "The Rhetoric of the Economics Texts."
2. George, *The Rhetoric of the Right*, Chapter 2.
3. Their pioneering work was *The Calculus of Consent*.
4. For a readable work of fiction that demonstrates Smith's broader view of people, see Wight, *Saving Adam Smith*.
5. George, *Preference Pollution*.
6. The most extreme libertarian dream is perhaps the Bitcoin popularity. For a devastating critique of reliance on Bitcoin, see Posner, "Bitcoin's Bandwagon Has Never Been More Crowded."
7. This phenomenon is likely in part due to the cynicism that public choice theory has caused by treating those in government as narrowly self-interested. See Marwell and Ames, "Economists Free Ride, Does Anyone Else?" for some evidence that narrow self-interest appears to describe economists more than any other group.
8. George, *Preference Pollution*, Chapter 3.
9. I have been unable to find the source for this claim that monopoly profits were absent. I definitely recall reading this and ask for the reader's trust.
10. See George Will's *Statecraft as Soulcraft*, though his views have changed in a more libertarian direction since then.
11. See, for example, Weissman, "Think We're the Most Entrepreneurial Country in the World? Not So Fast." The reasons for the decline in small businesses are many. David Kinkade ("Banishing Act"), writing for US Chamber of Commerce, attributes the trend not to the power of corporations but to such things as overtaxation and overregulation.
12. See, in particular, Frank, *One Market under God*.

Bibliography

Buchanan, James M., and Gordon Tullock. *The Calculus of Consent: Logical Foundations of Constitutional Democracy*. Ann Arbor, MI: University of Michigan Press, 1962.

Frank, Thomas. *One Market under God: Extreme Capitalism, Market Populism, and the End of Economic Democracy*. New York: Random House, 2000.

George, David. *Preference Pollution: How Markets Create the Desires We Dislike*. Ann Arbor, MI: University of Michigan Press, 2001.

———. "The Rhetoric of the Economics Texts." *Journal of Economic Issues* 24 (1990): 861–888.

———. *The Rhetoric of the Right: Language Change and the Spread of the Market*. Abingdon, UK: Routledge, 2013.

Kinkade, David. "Banishing Act: The Decline of American Entrepreneurship." US Chamber of Commerce, June 2, 2014. https://www.uschamber.com/blog/vanishing-act-decline-american-entrepreneurship.

Marwell, Gerald, and Ruth E. Ames. "Economists Free Ride, Does Anyone Else? Experiments on the Provision of Public Goods, IV." *Journal of Public Economics* 15 (1981): 295–310.

Posner, Eric. "Bitcoin's Bandwagon Has Never Been More Crowded." *The New Republic*, December 3, 2013. Available at http://www.newrepublic.com/article/115801/bernankes-bitcoin-comments-signal-growing-acceptance.

Weissman, Jordan. "Think We're the Most Entrepreneurial Country in the World? Not So Fast." *The Atlantic*, October 2, 2012. Available at http://www.theatlantic.com/business/archive/2012/10/think-were-the-most-entrepreneurial-country-in-the-world-not-so-fast/263102/

Wight, Jonathan B. *Saving Adam Smith: A Tale of Wealth, Transformation, and Virtue*. London: Financial Times/Prentice Hall, 2001.

Will, George R. *Statecraft as Soulcraft: What Government Does*. New York: Touchstone, 1984.

Chapter 8

On the Question of Court Activism and Economic Interests in Nineteenth-Century Married Women's Property Law

Daniel MacDonald

In the early years of the American republic, most married women did not enjoy any rights over their property or earnings. According to the common law, a married woman was a *femme covert* or "covered woman," meaning that when she married she was placed under the "protective wing" of her husband and had no independent legal status. Furthermore, any contract that a married woman entered into was considered void precisely because she was under "coverture," carrying no independent agency status; if she wanted to enter into an apprenticeship or convey property, she needed the permission of her husband.

While the common law—and thus the common law conception of *femme covert*—remained a part of American legal treatises and case law throughout the nineteenth century, legislatures began overturning it via statute beginning in the 1830s. Initially, the cause for concern was abuse of the marriage estate by the husband: if the wife had acquired property via dower or through the death of a family member, the husband would try to use that property to satisfy his personal debts. Giving married women ownership rights over their part of the estate would protect them against this kind of behavior.

A second wave of legislation was intended to give married women additional rights to control and conveyance of their separate property.[1] These laws were more focused on assigning a positive set of rights for married women to freely allocate their property as they wished. Referred to as the "married woman's property acts" or MWPAs for short, most of these laws awarded married women rights over any real or personal property they might acquire via gift, devise, or inheritance.

A third wave gave married women ownership and control rights over their labor market earnings. In most states, these laws were passed along with, or shortly after, the passage of an MWPA. Many scholars have argued that the third wave was a significant expansion of a married woman's rights. For example, the freedom granted over labor market earnings may have ultimately increased her involvement in paid work outside of the household. This process, in turn, would increase her bargaining power in the household.

The second and third waves have received a significant amount of attention from researchers interested in the effects of these laws on economic and social outcomes. The reason for the attention is simple: these laws represented an expansion of married women's self-ownership and the supposed overturning of the common law default of *femme covert*. It is only natural then to hypothesize that the laws could have increased household wealth and investment in girls' human capital. Others have tested whether the laws increased labor supply as well, though the evidence supporting this hypothesis is not as strong.[2]

Nevertheless, estimating the laws' impact along any particular dimension is complicated by the fact that many state courts still operated under the common law default principle of *femme covert*. While we know that the common law could and often did bend to prevailing social and economic developments in the nineteenth-century political economy, to conclude without any inspection of the judicial side of the issue that the laws had direct social and economic effects is unwarranted. At the very least, we can investigate whether courts may have used an efficiency criterion or some other mode of justification in support of the married women's legislation, as we know they did in the areas of property and contract law earlier in the century.[3] But we might also find that courts held on to the common law conception in certain circumstances, resisting the expansion of a married woman's rights.[4]

This chapter contributes to the research on the economic impacts of the laws in two ways. Overall, I explore the extent to which court activism limited the potential of the laws to lead to real social and economic change. First, using court records from 48 states I review and suggest revisions to an authoritative data set from Richard Geddes and Sharon Tennyson on the "dates of passage" of the MWPAs and Earnings Acts.[5] Since many statutes were rewritten and revised in subsequent sessions of the legislature, leaving it unclear which statutes held the most force, Geddes and Tennyson developed and applied a transparent set of criteria for determining the dates of passage of both MWPAs and Earnings Acts between 1848 and 1920. Their criteria is based on statutes that—for both the MWPAs and Earnings Acts—granted married women explicit ownership and control rights over their separate property or earnings. After obtaining their data set, I reconsidered these "dates of passage" from the judicial perspective, based on the argument that including the judicial perspective on all 48 states prior to 1920 is crucial for any test of the economic impact of the laws.

In many cases, I simply confirm the validity of the years recorded in the Geddes and Tennyson data set for each state's MWPA and Earnings Act. In other cases, I suggest minor revisions to the dates based on how judges, in their recorded opinions, assessed the development of their state's legislative history. The minor revisions are mainly based on the judges' assessment of loopholes and qualifications in the existing statutes, which violate the ownership and control criteria. In one case, for instance, I found that an MWPA was repealed six years later, though there is no record of this in Geddes and Tennyson's data set. Many of my revisions are drawn from the fact that these judges had a more practical and direct knowledge of the statutes. Regardless of any particular political bias each judge may have harbored, then, there were technical irregularities that were missed by Geddes and Tennyson, justifying a slightly revised data set on dates of passage.

The second way in which this chapter contributes to the research on the laws' economic impacts is through a content analysis of state Supreme Court records. In other words, I am not simply interested in how the judges assessed the legislative record, but also in whether judges systematically found ways to argue against the statutes or otherwise limit their scope, as has been suggested in the legal historiography of married woman's property law. For example, a judge may accept that the relevant Earnings Act was passed in 1872 but still uphold a husband's claim to the wife's earnings, on the grounds that the wife's work was done in connection to her duties and obligations to her family and were thus part of the family's wealth, which was understood to be in control of the husband. Reviewing court records from 48 states, I find several such qualifications on a wife's property rights being employed by state courts. These results call into question the arguments by economic historians that the laws had significant social and economic effects.[6]

This chapter builds on about 20 years of scholarship in economic history on the effects of the MWPAs and Earnings Acts. Authors of the early studies constructed their own "dates of passage" data sets relying mainly on contemporary legal treatises on the MWPAs and Earnings Acts written in the early 1880s. Most of the laws had been passed by the time that the legal treatises were written but a few were not, so it is presumed that the authors performed their own research via direct reference to statute books as well as secondary legal histories for filling in the remainder of their data set. The dates of passage data set received an update in recent research by adopting explicit criteria of an effective law: namely, one that granted both ownership and control rights over the wife's separate property.[7]

Some economic historians developed a working model with which to understand the intuition behind their argument that the laws led to an increase in economic activity.[8] They argued that a property rights framework provides the clearest way of understanding the timing of the laws: as returns to education for young women increase, the incentives for them to enter the labor market increase. The government responds to those incentives by passing the appropriate legislation, with the result of an increase in investment in human capital for young women. Empirical results using historical data on schooling, in conjunction with the dates of passage data set, provide evidence for their property rights hypothesis.

The legal historical research on the MWPAs and Earnings Acts started earlier than the economic history research and gives more attention to nuance in how the courts shaped the key marital relations issues brought out by the law, instead of trying to generalize about their impact. More recent surveys dive more deeply into deeper issues such as qualifications to a wife's right to her earnings, the empowerment of effects, and some of the specific social movements that helped lead to the laws being passed.[9] While it is outside the scope of the present chapter to summarize this body of research, it suffices to say that a key concern of both the older and more recent research was on understanding the ways in which the judicial system exerted its own forces on the path of the laws.

Thus, there are two main contributions of this chapter to existing research. First, I consider the extent to which state courts affected the effective dates of passage of the MWPAs and Earnings Acts. More broadly, I use the court records data to assess the validity of the property rights framework—that is, I test whether the process of court activism limited the social and economic potential of the MWPAs and Earnings Acts.

Constructing the Data from Court Records: Analysis and Main Results

Data were collected from an online database containing digitized records of state Supreme Court cases for 48 states between 1848 and

1920.[10] The records themselves are drawn from digests that were usually written a year or two after a court had completed its circuit. The digests normally contain, for every case heard, a summary of the counsel's arguments and the main questions of law that the case resolved. In addition, an account of the court's opinion (as well as any dissents) is usually given.

The records are fully searchable, so data were initially collected by searching for relevant strings in specific years around which an MWPA or Earnings Act was passed, according to Geddes and Tennyson's "dates of passage" data set. For example, to pull records relevant to MWPAs, combinations of the words "married" or "wife" and "property" were searched in a state's court records around the year that the MWPA was passed. I also draw on the secondary legal history literature for citations to popular cases and later cases that cited them. However, since many states' histories of this issue have not been studied in a comprehensive manner, references to secondary literature served as a limited complement to the database search.

The result of these efforts is a data set of over 150 court cases containing information on the nature of a dispute, how the case was ruled, the basis for the court's opinion, nature of any dissent, and historical facts useful to constructing a legislative history of the legislation of a particular state. On this last point, references were compared to the discussion of the legislative history in Geddes and Tennyson's work. Analysis first focused on comparing Geddes and Tennyson's "dates of passage" data set to my own assessment of the legislative history based on the court records.

The results of that analysis are presented in the appendix. It is important to note that, at this point, the suggested revisions are purely technical. I am not analyzing judges' political positions taken for or against the MWPAs and Earnings Acts; I am only considering how an incorporation of the judicial perspective changes the economic historians' assessment of the legislative history. For example, an Arizona court found that the MWPA in that state initially awarded married women ownership and control rights over her property, but not over the rents, issues, and profits derived from the use of that property; the original act was revised in 1885 to address this technicality.[11] In California, the initial MWPA was found to leave out the possibility that a married woman might exchange property for the payment of money; this too led to a revised statute two years later.[12] Finally, for some states, such as Florida, there simply appears to be an error in reviewing the legislative documents that may have caused Geddes and Tennyson to overlook the crucial statutes.

In short, we learn a great deal more about the legislative history of the MWPAs and Earnings Acts from a consideration of the judicial perspective. I have clarified and updated Geddes and Tennyson's analysis using their same criteria of "ownership" and "control," but with a richer analysis of the legal sources. The broader goal of this chapter, however, is to shed light on the laws' social and economic significance, and to that end, in the following section I perform a more detailed content analysis of the judicial record.

Generalizable Trends in the Judicial Perspective on the MWPAs and Earnings Acts

I summarize two particularly visible trends in the judicial record and I elaborate on each issue. Analysis of the trends suggests that courts *did* play an activist role in limiting social reform. The first trend I address is the issue of labor performed in connection to a married woman's obligations to her family, and the second is how the courts handled cases involving a married woman entering into contracts involving debt obligations.

On Labor Performed in Connection with the Family Wealth

Courts often ruled that if a wife had performed services in connection to her duties to the household, she was not entitled to ownership and control rights over any acquired property or earnings. To explore this issue, it is useful first to understand the two ways in which the legal system attempted to handle the idea of family wealth—that is, property that belonged to the household as a whole. Courts either addressed family wealth explicitly through the concept of "community property," or implicitly through reference to the family estate. Community property states such as California and Arizona borrowed their legal system from the civil law tradition rather than the common law one. In these states, the earnings of either the husband or the wife would fall within the community property, over which the husband had exclusive rights. A similar concept of a common pool of family assets, in the exclusive ownership and control of the husband, was present in common law states. Judges used the concepts of community property and family assets to restrict the impact of the MWPAs and Earnings Acts.

Previous economic histories of the laws suggested that community property states would, on average, pass MWPAs and Earnings Acts later than noncommunity property states. However, no reason was given for why they would do so. In an earlier paper that Richard Geddes wrote with Dean Lueck, it is suggested that married women in community property states may start out with more rights than in noncommunity states (making the incentives to grant additional rights to the wife lower than in common law states), supposedly because the property in community property states was already seen as held *equally* by both husband and wife.[13] Historically, however, husbands were the only ones with ownership and control rights over the community property.[14]

It follows from the historical definition and operation of community property outlined in the previous paragraph that significant reform could be achieved in community property states if and only if the wife enjoyed ownership and control rights over both her own property *as well as* the community property. First a state must grant the wife rights over property that she personally acquired and which was seen as her own. Then the state must grant her rights over the community property, which was any property that she may have acquired but which was seen as going into the community "pool" of property. There is, in a sense, an additional barrier formed by the fact that some property that the wife may have in theory "earned" is actually under the exclusive ownership and control of the husband, due to its classification as community property.

This theoretical observation in turn implies that community property law would actually be *more* restrictive of women's rights before and after the passage of an MWPA or Earnings Act, not less, as some economic historians suggest. While this observation does not change the prediction that community property states would pass an MWPA or Earnings Act after noncommunity property states, the interpretation of the rule clearly matters for an accurate assessment of the history and nature of married woman's property reform in the nineteenth century.

How did these ideas operate historically? In community property states, if a married woman had obtained rents or profits from her separate property,[15] or if she had performed a service such as a nurse for one who had deceased (and in whose home the services were rendered),[16] then that property was assumed to be community property. In both cases, it was ruled that the property or earnings were acquired during the marriage (i.e., not brought with her prior to the marriage), and should therefore fall within the scope of community property. It was then ruled that the husband had full control and ownership rights over the community property, erasing any rights the wife may have initially had over her property or earnings. Since courts were not willing to "break up" the economic basis of the family, community property law generally acted as an additional barrier to women's property ownership.

In the California Supreme Court case *Smith v. Furnish* in 1886 (after the date that Geddes and Tennyson list for the relevant Earnings Act), the husband and wife had lived in the house of an owner and the wife had performed services as a nurse.[17] When the owner passed away, the wife sued his estate for the services performed. The court argued that the suit was improperly made under the assumption that the wife had rights to her earnings. In fact, the husband should have sued under the community property rule. Justice Ross's ruling in the case is informative:

> It is provided by...[Section 162] of the Civil Code that "all property of the wife owned by her before marriage, and that acquired afterwards by gift, bequest, devise, or descent, with the rents, issues, and profits thereof, is her separate property"...By section 164 it is declared that *"all other property acquired after marriage*, by either husband or wife, or both, is *community property.*"[18]

This last section is what Justice Ross used in forming his opinion: as long as the wife is living with her husband, it is assumed that her earnings are devoted to either the community property or family estate, which in either case is in the exclusive control of the husband. In 1900, the California Supreme Court arrived at a similar decision:

> Prior to her injury by the wrongful acts of defendant carrier, plaintiff's wife did all her housework, but by such injury she was rendered wholly unable to do such work. Civ. Code, § 155, provides that *husband and wife contract to each other's mutual support.* Held that, *since the earnings from the wife's services are a part of the community property,* the husband, as the head of the community, could maintain an action for the loss of such services.[19]

In noncommunity property (common law) states, when similar disputes arose, a similar principle was applied of preserving the husband's control over the family's assets.[20] The justification in these cases was that the husband had an obligation to provide for his family and a right to the services of his wife, and these entitled him to full control and ownership rights over any enterprise related to reproducing the household. For example, if it could be established that the wife's earnings from services or rents and profits from her property were related to her familial duties, then the husband often retained rights over them. The category of "duties" often involved anything performed in the household, such as caring for and feeding boarders.[21]

However, precisely because the common law contained no institutionalized conception of ownership rights over the pool of family assets, there *were* cases and states in which the wife enjoyed unqualified rights over her separate property.[22] Nevertheless, the dominant view was to restrict the MWPAs and Earnings Acts by qualifying married women's rights in cases in which some connection to family assets or wealth was made. In a representative case from Delaware in 1886 defending the husband's ownership rights over the wife's earnings, the court argued that "whatever, therefore, a wife does, in the performance of the duties devolving upon her as such (as all of you no doubt know what they are in the case of a farmer's wife in good health), cannot be looked upon otherwise than as her wifely service."[23] Delaware passed its Earnings Act in 1873, while over a decade later the court's opinion was still shaped by the traditional concept of the husband's exclusive ownership over the family assets.[24]

The unifying theme in both community property and common law states is that the separate property rights of married women were qualified by traditional norms of the husband's duty to provide for his family, and the wife's obligation of service to her husband. The feature was simply more institutionalized in community property states and therefore more difficult to overturn, providing a historically accurate explanation for why community property states were slower to award full ownership rights to wives. In a few cases, an explicit "family assets" principle counter to the MWPA or Earnings Act can be found, while in most other cases judges simply suggested that the MWPA or Earnings Act could not overturn the entire doctrine of coverture. In Missouri, for example, we see an explicit recognition of the "family assets" principle: "where the work and business are carried on by husband and wife in co-operation, the labor of the husband being united with that of the wife, the business and its proceeds will be regarded as belonging to the husband."[25]

On the Validity of Contracts Involving Debt Obligations

Courts often prevented a wife from entering into contracts involving debt, such as the issuance of a promissory note, under the assumption that she is incapable of acting as an independent economic agent. In other cases, courts ruled that a wife could enter into such contracts, but only if she used her separate property as equity. In most cases, it was assumed that women did not hold the capacity to enter into such contracts.[26] By excluding women from contracts involving a debt obligation, courts proved that they were willing to sacrifice the potential expansionary social and economic effects of the statutes for the maintenance of traditional gender norms.

An example of a restrictive court ruling on debt contracts was the Arizona Supreme Court's position in *Stiles v. Lord* in 1886. A married woman had endorsed a promissory note to another individual in exchange for money. The individual then failed to recover from the initial issuer of the note, and sued the married woman. The court held that, within the scope of the 1871 MWPA, married women did not have the right to enter into a general contract regarding the endorsement of a promissory note because the note was not a valid form of property within the meaning of that statute. The justice ruled that "we are not prepared to extend [the meaning of the 1871 statute] beyond such a simple contract as is necessary to the sale of personal property."[27]

In *Pippen v. Wessen*, the North Carolina Supreme Court argued that married women do not fall under the category of "obligors *pleni juris*," meaning they do not enjoy the contracting rights of a full citizen.[28] A suit to recover on a bond that was sold by a married woman was not upheld, due to her legal inability to enter into contracts regarding debt obligations. In an early Pennsylvania case, *Mahon v. Gormley*, Justice Lewis argued that a married woman could not enter into debt contracts generally because the statutes were primarily designed "for [a married woman's] protection, not for their injury, and must receive such a construction as shall promote that object."[29] Lewis went on to note that "in her dependent condition, with duties which preclude and habits which unfit her for out-door business of life, to give her these extensive powers [to enter into debt contracts] would be an injury instead of a benefit to her, and would be altogether at variance with the benevolent purposes of the legislature."[30]

Lewis's reasoning is instructive for understanding the general perspective on women's capacities to enter into contracts in the nineteenth and early twentieth centuries. Lewis based his argument on the assumption that it would be dangerous to let her enter into a contract regarding a debt obligation. Debt contracts, while an integral part of a growing economy, contain elements of risk and uncertainty of future performance and payment. In order to minimize these factors, the law must prevent persons who are not of a "sound mind" from entering into such contracts. Thus, women should not be allowed to issue bonds or endorse promissory notes because then they are taking on a risk in the obligation to pay.[31] Speaking of the article in the constitution that served as the MWPA and Earnings Act in South Carolina, Justice McIver asserted that "the main object of the provision was not so much to give positive rights to the wife, but to negate some of those of the man."[32] This perspective summarizes the traditional view of the wife's capacities as well as the impact of that view on her rights.

Some states endorsed a less-strict construction of a married woman's right to enter contracts in which debt obligations *could* be sustained, but only as long as her separate property was used as equity. In Nebraska, it was ruled that the wife was allowed to give a promissory note to another person as a debt which would be recoverable on her separate property; courts in Arkansas ruled similarly.[33] The uniting feature in all these cases was that a married woman was free to enter into such contracts as long as they were made with respect to her separate property. In other words, she needed to supply the equity at the time of signing to prove that she could pay off the debt, bringing the contract closer to a simple exchange contract than a debt contract.

In New York, a series of cases revolving around *Yale v. Dederer* included a discussion of the logic behind the idea that married women had a right to enter into contracts of debt as long as they are made with respect to her personal property. As Justice Comstock wrote,

> I think it is plain, however, that the [MWPA] does not remove her incapacity, which prevents her from contracting debts. She may convey and devise her real and personal estate, but her promissory note or other personal engagement is void, as it always was by the rules of the common law. *This legal incapacity is far higher protection to married women than the wisest scheme of legislation can be, and we should hardly expect to find it removed in a statute for "the more effective protection of her rights."*[34]

The allowance of a married woman to enter into debt contracts respecting her personal property, Comstock goes on to note, is within the logic of the "rights to disposal of property," which the MWPA does grant.

In summary, it is apparent from the discussion in this chapter why courts were willing to accept that a married woman could own, control, and even convey her property, but not enter into contracts in which she would be liable for debt: assumptions regarding (the extent of) her capacity to make contracts, and specifically, to continue to be protected under the law given the incapacities. This tradition in the common law had not been overturned by either the MWPA or the Earnings Acts.

Conclusion

Quantitative estimation of the effects of the Married Women's Property Acts and Earnings Acts is complicated by the fact that courts sought to enforce traditional conceptions of *femme covert*. I provide a judicial history of the MWPAs and Earnings Acts in all states that had passed a law before 1920. I find that while most courts did not overturn the laws via judicial review as some have suggested, judges did limit the laws' potential for reform by maintaining the husband's traditional ownership rights over the family estate and maintaining the idea of a wife's incompetence as an independent economic agent.

Legal change is always a difficult phenomenon to assess because successful enforcement usually must overcome one or more institutional channels before the laws can be carried out. In this case, the interests of both courts and society placed significant limitations on legal reform. While the social and economic benefits of distributing property rights may be recognized by scholars today, there were other social and political reasons, highlighted earlier, for maintaining the common law default of *femme covert*. This historical account thus highlights the contingency of an economy embedded in social norms, which is a cornerstone of social economics.[35]

Appendix

Dates of passage (based on the work of Geddes and Tennyson with suggested revisions based on the new case analysis research)

State	MWPA	Revision	Earnings	Revision
Alabama	—		1887	
Arizona	1871	1885[36]	1973	
Arkansas	1873		1873	
California	1872	1874[37]	1872	–?[38]
Colorado	1861		1861	
Connecticut	1877	1878–1882, then 1887[39]	1877	1878–1882, then 1887[40]
Delaware	1873	1875[41]	1873	1875
Florida	1943	1885[42]	1892	1906[43]
Georgia	1873	1866[44]	1861	1866[45]
Idaho	1903		1915	
Illinois	1861[46]		1869	
Indiana	1879		1879	
Iowa	1873		1873	
Kansas	1858		1858[47]	
Kentucky	1894		1873[48]	
Louisiana	1916		1928	
Maine	1855		1857	
Maryland	1860		1842[49]	
Massachusetts	1855		1846	1855[50]
Michigan	1855		1911	
Minnesota	1869		1869	
Mississippi	1880		1873	
Missouri	1875		1875	
Montana	1887		1887	
Nebraska	1871		1871	
Nevada	1873		1873	
New Hampshire	1860		1867	
New Jersey	1852		1874	
New Mexico	1884		—	
New York	1848		1860	
North Carolina	1868	1911[51]	1913	
North Dakota	1877		—	
Ohio	1861		1861	
Oklahoma	1883		—	
Oregon	1878		1872	

continued

Continued

State	MWPA	Revision	Earnings	Revision
Pennsylvania	1848		1872[52]	1887[53]
Rhode Island	1872		1872	
South Carolina	1868		1887	
South Dakota	1877		—	
Tennessee	1919		1919	
Texas	1913		1913	
Utah	1872		1897	1888[54]
Vermont	1881	1884[55]	1888	
Virginia	1877		1888	
Washington	1881		–?[56]	
West Virginia	1868		1893	1891[57]
Wisconsin	1850		1872	
Wyoming	1869		1869	

Notes

1. Chused, "Married Women's Property Law," refers to the fact that many of these laws were passed around a similar period, thus the term "wave."
2. See Roberts, "Women's Rights and Women's Labor"; Khan, "Married Women's Property Laws" and "Property Rights and Patent Litigation"; and Geddes, Lueck, and Tennyson, "Human Capital Accumulation."
3. The most widely cited source in the legal history literature regarding the ability of the common law to adapt to economic interests is Horwitz, *The Transformation of American Law.*
4. There is a tradition in legal history that emphasizes the feudal nature of nineteenth-century law; see, for example, Orren, *Belated Feudalism.*
5. See Geddes and Tennyson, "Passage of the Married Women's Property Acts." This contribution is not particularly at odds with how legal historians have studied the social and economic impacts of legal change. Legislatures played an increasingly active role in American politics after the American Revolution, but so did courts, according to Horwitz, *Transformation.* Thus, it is only natural to consider how courts viewed the MWPAs before considering the laws' broader impact on society.
6. Khan, "Married Women's Property Laws" and "Property Rights and Patent Litigation"; also Geddes and Lueck, "Gains from Self-Ownership."
7. The most recent paper, which draws on the data used in this chapter as well, is Geddes and Tennyson, "Passage of the Married Women's Property Acts."
8. Geddes and Lueck, "Gains from Self-Ownership."
9. Basch, "Legal Fiction" and *In the Eyes of the Law*; Chused, "Married Women's Property Law"; Lazarou, *Concealed under Petticoats*; Salmon,

Women and the Law of Property; Shammas, "Re-Assessing"; Siegel, "Home as Work" and "Modernization"; also Warbasse, *Changing*.

10. In 1848, New York passed the first effective MWPA (by Geddes and Tennyson's criteria). All 48 states had passed either an MWPA or Earnings Act by 1920.

11. *Woffenden v. Charauleau*, 2 Ariz. 44 (1885).

12. *Wood v. Orford*, 52 Cal. 412 (1877).

13. Geddes and Lueck, "Gains from Self-Ownership."

14. Siegel, "Home as Work" and "Modernization."

15. *Woffenden v. Charaleau*, 2 Ariz. 91 (1886).

16. *Smith v. Furnish*, 70 Cal. 424 (1886) is a representative case; see also *Clinton Station General Merchandise and Manufacturing Company v. Hummell and wife*, 25 N.J. Eq. 45 (1874) for an earlier example of restricting the wife's separate ownership rights in New Jersey.

17. *Smith v. Furnish*, 70 Cal. 424 (1886).

18. Ibid. (emphasis added).

19. *Martin v. Southern Pac. Co.*, 130 Cal. 285 (1900) (emphasis added).

20. *Hemingwray v. Todd*, 5 Kan. 660 (1865); also *Riley v. Mitchell*, 36 Minn. 3 (1886): "An agreement between husband and wife that the latter shall receive the compensation to be earned by her in nursing a boarder in the family, who pays the husband for his board, vests in her any claim accruing on account of such nursing, and, there being no question of set-off or counterclaim, it is immaterial that the boarder does not know of such agreement."

21. . *Valentine v. Tatum*, 7 Houst. 402 (1886), a Delaware case which addresses the issue. In *Sampson v. Alexander*, 66 Maine 182 (1876) the court ruled that "we think it reasonable to allow her interest upon the sums advanced by her, for the reason that a considerable amount of rent seems to have been indirectly received from the property, besides its enjoyment for mere family use." In other words, the court had to frame the issue within the default rule that a wife's labor is done in service of the family's wealth and the ownership right is therefore the right of the husband. For a more extreme position in which the husband recovers for his wife's debts and injuries, see *City of Wyandotte v. Agan*, 37 Kan. 528 (1887). Similarly, see *Norfolk & W.R. Co. v. Prindle*, 82 Va. 122 (1886): only the husband can recover for injury to the wife.

22. From a Pennsylvania court ruling in favor of the wife: "the earnings of a wife, by taking in boarders, belong to the wife and not to the husband" (*Rafferty v. Rafferty*, 5 Pa. D. 453, 1896). See also *Barry v. Teel*, 12 R. I. 267 (1879) as another favorable ruling for married women.

23. *Valentine v. Tantum*, 7 Houst. 402 (1886).

24. Another important piece of evidence in support of the argument in this section is the fact that while Arizona's (a community property state) initial MWPA gave a married woman ownership and control rights over her separate property, according to the courts it did

not give her ownership and control rights over the *rents and prof-its derived from that separate property*, presumably because the gains were made in some way in connection to the household. This "gap" in the legislation, which was not found in other community property states, was eventually rectified in 1885.

25. *Plummer v. Trost*, 81 Mo. 425 (1884). MWPAs or Earnings Acts in common law states often contained phrases such as "other than work done in service to her family" as a qualification on her separate prop-erty rights. So as long as the laws did *not* contain such wording, it was harder for courts to maintain the husband's ownership rights (for an in-depth study of this rule in several state Supreme Courts, see Siegel, "Home as Work" and "The Modernization of Marital Status Law."

26. Some state courts did support contracts involving a debt obligation, though they are rare cases.

27. *Stiles v. Lord*, 2 Ariz. 154 (1886).

28. *Pippen v. Wessen*, 74 N.C. 437 (1876).

29. *Mahon v. Gormley*, 24 Pa. 80 (1854).

30. Ibid. The entire opinion is illustrative, but here is one more quote to give one a sense of the court's position under the *strict* interpretation: "The Act of 1848 gives her a right to acquire property by 'deed of conveyance or otherwise,' and therefore by implication confers upon her the right to charge it with the payment of the purchase-money, for that is a part of the act of acquisition; but it has been held that she cannot charge her other estate with the debt."

31. Examples of the more "strict" view where it was ruled that married women could not enter into any kind of debt obligation are *Boyett v. Potter* (mortgage contract, 80 Ala. 476, 1887), *Bank of Commerce, Ltd. v. Baldwin et al.* (general debt contract, 12 Idaho 202, 1906), *Ames v. Foster* ("a married woman can contract only in respect to property conveyed to her sole and separate use, free from the control and interference of her husband. She can not contract in anticipation of any such purchase to her sole use," 42 N. H. 381, 1861).

32. *Bridgers v. Howell*, 27 S.C. 425 (1887).

33. *Buckner & Co. v. Davis*, 29 Ark. 444 (1874); *Webb v. Hoselton*, 4 Neb. 308 (1876).

34. *Yale v. Dederer*, 21 Barb. 286 (1855), as quoted in *Cartan v. David*, 18 Nev. 310 (1884) (emphasis added).

35. The author thanks the Association of Social Economics for financial support through the William Waters Grant.

36. A series of cases in Arizona shows that while the 1871 law did give own-ership and control rights of the property to the wife, the ownership and control rights over the *rents and profits derived from that ownership* were assigned community property status: "by [1871] act it is provided that the wife shall have the sole and exclusive control of her separate prop-erty, with power to sell, etc.; nothing is said about the rents and profits, while the other portion of the statute stands in full force, making the

rents and profits common property." This "rough edge" in the law was smoothed by an 1885 statute. The specific wording of the 1885 statute is that "the rents, issues, and profits of the husband's separate property shall be his separate property, and the rents, issues, and profits of the wife's separate property shall be her separate property."

37. I revise to 1874 because in that year there was a revision of the original statute cited by Geddes and Tennyson which allowed the wife's property to be sold for money. Selling for property was not permitted beforehand, meaning that a married woman did not have complete ownership and control over her property at that time. See *Marlow v. Barlew*, 3 P.C.L.J. 68 (1879): "A married woman's power under Civ.Code, § 158, to 'enter into any transaction respecting property,' includes giving a note and a mortgage of her separate estate to secure it...She was deprived of the capacity to make a contract *for the payment of money* by sec. 167 of the Code as first adopted; but the section was repealed in 1874" (emphasis added). Also see *Wood v. Orford*, 52 Cal. 412 (1877): "As it stood at first, a married woman could not bind herself by any contract for the "payment of money," *even if that contract was respecting her separate property.* As amended, it leaves a married woman to make such contracts as sec. 158 provides that she may make."

38. It is not clear when control and ownership rights over earnings was granted: *Tobin v. Galvin*, 49 Cal. 34 (1874) references an 1869–70 Act in rejecting a married woman's case: "Act March 9, 1870, St.1869–1870, p. 226, which provides that while the wife lives separate and apart from her husband she shall have the sole use of her property, and may sue and be sued, etc., does not apply to a case where the wife is temporarily absent from her husband with his consent, but to cases where there has been an abandonment on the part of the husband or wife, or a separation which is intended to be final." While the dispute in this case is not directly relevant to earnings ownership and control, one can see by implication the perspective of the law toward earnings in a traditional marriage. Furthermore, as late as 1886, her control ownership of earnings was questioned, since the earnings were allocated to the community property, which was under the husband's control (see *Smith v. Furnish*, 70 Cal. 424, 1886). The wife's earnings were, since section 168 of the Code referenced by Geddes and Tennyson, protected from the debts of the husband, but that is the extent of her ownership rights (see *Finnigan v. Hibernia Sav. & Loan Soc.*, 11 P.C.L.J. 362, 1883, for additional support of this claim). It is, at the very earliest, after 1886 that a fuller earnings act could be passed.

39. For a brief period, 1878–1882, wives had ownership and control rights over their separate property, including earnings, but an 1882 statute repealed the 1878 one: in *Shea v. Maloney*, 52 Conn. 327 (1884), "The act of 1878 (Session Laws 1878, ch. 61), since repealed

[in 1882 according to Justice Granger], provided that 'all property' thereafter acquired by any married woman should be held by her to her sole and separate use. Held that money due for the personal services of a married woman in washing and house cleaning, was property acquired by her within the meaning of the statute." In short, the wife won this case because it fell within the time that the 1878 statute was in force. No other relevant cases after this one, either upholding the acts or not, can be found. But the repeal of the 1878 is certain. From the *Public Statutes Laws of Connecticut*, 1882: "Chapter sixty-one of the public acts of 1878, which reads as follows: 'All property hereafter acquired by any married woman shall be held by her to her sole and separate use,' is hereby repealed" (approved, March 9, 1882). A new statute was passed five years later, in 1887 (Peck, *The Property Rights of Husband and Wife under the Law of Connecticut*).

40. See previous note.

41. *Moore v. Darby*, 6 Del. Ch. 193 (1889) shows that there were two acts in question, 1873 and 1875, and the latter is broader by including women who were already married and who acquire property and earnings *after* the date of passage of the statute. Given that New York courts initially struck down their statute on the basis of the claim of abrogation of an already-existing contract, extending married women's rights to property already acquired is an important extension that warrants the suggested revision. Note that Geddes and Tennyson also find this minor distinction in the language, saying the two statutes are "almost identical." But as I have just argued, there is a big difference both in theory and legal application.

42. According to a court case from 1911, the 1885 constitution gave ownership and control rights to a married woman over her property.

43. The clause in the 1885 constitution was followed up with a statute in 1906 that gave the wife control over her earnings *(Lerch v. Barnes*, 61 Fla. 672, 1911).

44. The reason for a suggested revision to 1866 is based on several cases that referenced the statute in that year (as well as the state's constitution in 1868) as the point at which a married woman obtained all rights of ownership and control over her property. See, for example, *Dunnahoo v. Holland*, 51 Ga. 147 (1874) for property and *Eichberg v. Bandman*, 74 Ga. 834 (1885) for earnings. From *Eichberg*: "Where a married woman, living with her husband, owned a separate estate, which consisted in part of a house and lot where they resided, and she carried on the business of keeping a boarding-house, since the act of 1866, her earnings in that enterprise belonged to her, and she was entitled to sue and recover in her own name from one who boarded with her and failed to pay the amount due therefor."

45. See previous note.

46. Not a suggested revision, only a particularly strong support for the Geddes and Tennyson date as well as the laws in general. A court case

from 1870, *Musgrave v. Musgrave*, 54 Ill. 186 (1870), affirms without question the validity of both property and earnings acts: "Prior to the act of 1861, a married woman could not own separate property in her own name and right. But that act invests her with her property, free from the control of her husband, and gives her the same power over it as if she were sole and unmarried. Again, in 1869 (Pub. Laws, 255), it was enacted that any married woman shall be entitled to receive, use and possess her own earnings, and sue for the same in her own name, free from the interference of her husband or his creditors, etc. These acts have manifestly radically changed the common law. Under them, she may hold, use and enjoy separate property, and her earnings free from the interference of her husband."

47. While I have no direct evidence to dispute the 1858 date, I first note that there are no recorded cases at the state level that occurred prior to 1865 (there was a case that enforced a part of the 1858 statute that only protected the wife from the husband transferring property to her to avoid paying creditors). Second, I note that several later cases explicitly refer to an 1862 statute as "authorizing married women to perform labor and services on their sole and separate account, and making their earnings their sole and separate property." See *Larimer v. Kelly*, 10 Kan. 298 (1872). Since I can neither confirm nor deny that any statute prior to 1862 did not carry the same force, I accept the 1858 date for the Earnings Act.

48. Several early cases clearly rule that the wife had no right to her earnings unless the husband agreed to give her the right ("if a married woman desires to secure the fruits of her own labor or accumulations, she must in conjunction with her husband pursue the mode pointed out by the statute authorizing her to trade as feme sole," *Strowd v. Stanley and Son* 1876), or in a related set of cases (*Brown v. Casbier*, 1882) unless the husband and wife went through the court of Chancery. These cases do not reference an act from 1873. Nevertheless, I cannot find anything that explicitly overturned the 1873 law, and indeed eventually the courts were recognizing the wife's ownership of earnings based on the 1873 statute (*Bullock v. Commonwealth*, 16 Ky.L.Rptr. 806, 1884). I cannot determine why the earlier cases did not reference the 1873 statute.

49. Not a revision, but I briefly note that an 1859 case confirms the strength of the 1842 law giving rights over earnings: a married woman had undertaken a business from which she was earning some money. Her husband was sued and the sheriff tried to take her property. Ruling for the wife, the court referenced the 1842 law (*Bridges v. McKenna*, 14 Md. 258, 1859).

50. In Massachusetts, many of the cases after 1855 referenced the 1855 statute as the more salient one when it came to earnings. In *McKalvin v. Bresslin* (8 Gray 177, 1857) justice stated that "before the St. of 1855, c. 304, the earnings of the personal labor of a wife, even when

living apart from her husband, were his property, and might be recovered by him from one to whom she had assigned them without value." See also *Gerry v. Gerry,* 11 Gray 381 (1858). The difference seems to be that the 1846 case was a "protection" statute, that is, was primarily intended to further protect the wife's property or earnings from a husband's debtors (see, for example, *Maxwell v. McGee,* 66 Mass. 143, 1853). This is confirmed in the secondary literature on the laws, though some remark that there were still qualifications in the 1855 Act for work done in service to her family (Siegel, "Home as Work").

51. The 1868 act required that women gain consent from her husband before she had ownership and control rights (*Pippen v. Wessen,* 74 N.C. 437, 1876). The next relevant case dates confirms the 1911 date: "Under Const. art. 10, § 6, Revisal §§ 952, 2107, 2112, 2113, and Laws 1911, c. 109, repealing section 2094 and substituted therefor, a married woman may make a valid contract for the conveyance of her land without the assent of her husband, and in case of breach, is liable for damages" (*Warren v. Dail,* 170 N.C. 406, 1915).

52. A dilemma arises in Pennsylvania, as well as in Montana (see *Barger v. Halford,* 10 Mont. 57, 1890), regarding whether to categorize a law that required a woman to register with the court before she could have ownership of her earnings, as a full Earnings act. Since qualifying rights with the husband's consent is not the same thing as awarding full control and ownership rights, the issue is complicated. Because there were several other laws, including one in 1887, which the court claimed to have "confer[red] on married women the same power over their property and earnings, and the same rights and remedies incident thereto, that men have" (*Small v. Small,* 129 Pa. 366, 1889). In the case *In re Bowler's Estate* (20 Phila. 44, 1890) Justice Hanna also makes reference to the "proceedings" that a married woman had to follow in order to be granted rights to her separate earnings. Since an explicit date of a more expanded statute can be found for Pennsylvania, I adopt it as a suggested revision. But either case may be used, subject to this caveat.

53. See previous note: either date may be used, subject to the caveat.

54. From *Compiled Laws 1888,* Vol. II, Part 5 on Domestic Relations, Section 2528: "All property owned by either spouse before marriage, and that acquired afterwards by purchase, gift, bequest, devise or descent, with the rents, issues, and profits thereof, is the separate property of that spouse by whom the same is so owned or acquired; and separate property owned or acquired as specified above, may be held, managed, controlled, transferred and in any manner disposed of by the spouse so owning or acquiring it, without any limitation or restriction by reason of marriage." As quoted in *Culmer v. Wilson,* 13 Utah 129 (1896).

55. Geddes and Tennyson's explanation for 1881 is somewhat confusing (pp. 184–185). They immediately state 1881, but never give a

reference. They go on to cite an 1884 statute that was "stronger" but didn't include earnings. I agree that the 1884 act does not award earnings rights, but I also think that the MWPA date should be set to 1884, based on the following assessment of the history of the laws from Justice Start in *Fletcher v. Wakefield* (75 Vt. 257, 1903): "by No. 21 of the Acts of 1867, p. 29, a married woman was authorized to hold to her sole and separate use all personal property and rights of personal action acquired by her during coverture, by inheritance or distribution. This right to hold separate personal estate was, by No. 140 of the Acts of 1884, p. 119, enlarged so that she could hold all personal property and rights of action acquired before or during coverture, except those acquired by her personal Industry or by gift from her personal industry or by gift from her husband, and by No. 84 of the Acts of 1888, p. 98, the exception of property acquired by her personal Industry was removed."

56. In *Yake v. Pugh*, 13 Wash. 78 (1895), the court ruled that "the earnings of the wife, as well as those of the husband, where they are living together, belong *prima facie* to the community." The reason why the wife's property was not subject to the husband's debts in this case is because the husband had consented to her ownership of her earnings.

57. I list 1891 due to the following justice's opinion: "A wife's earnings, at common law prior to chapter 109, § 14, Acts 1891, belonged to the husband" (*Roberts v. Coleman* 37 W.Va. 143, 1892). Another case, also from 1892, confirms a married woman's rights to her separate earnings (*Trapnell v. Conklyn*, 37 W.Va. 242).

Bibliography

Basch, Norma. *In the Eyes of the Law: Women, Marriage, and Property in Nineteenth-Century New York.* Ithaca, NY: Cornell University Press, 1982.
———. "The Legal Fiction of Marital Unity in Nineteenth Century America." *Feminist Studies* 5 (1979): 346–366.

Bishop, Joel P. *Commentaries on the Law of Married Women under the Statutes of the Several States, and at Common Law and Equity.* Boston: Little, Brown and Co., 1875.

Chused, Richard H. "Married Women's Property Law: 1800–1850." *Georgetown Law Journal* 71 (1982–1983): 1359–1425.

Doepke, Matthias, and Michele Tertilt. "Women's Liberation: What's in It for Men?" *Quarterly Journal of Economics* 124 (2009): 1541–1591.

Geddes, Rick, and Dean Lueck. "The Gains from Self-Ownership and the Expansion of Women's Rights." *American Economic Review* 92 (2002): 1079–1092.

Geddes, Rick, Dean Lueck, and Sharon Tennyson. "Human Capital Accumulation and the Expansion of Women's Property Rights." *Journal of Law & Economics* 55 (2012): 839–867.

Geddes, Rick, and Sharon Tennyson. "Passage of the Married Women's Property Acts and Earnings Acts in the United States: 1850–1920." *Research in Economic History* 29 (2013): 145–189.

Horwitz, Morton. *The Transformation of American Law*. Cambridge, MA: Harvard University Press, 1979.

Kelly, John F. *A Treatise on the Law of Contracts of Married Women*. Jersey City, NJ: F.W. Linn & Company, 1882.

Khan, B. Zorina. "Married Women's Property Laws and Female Commercial Activity: Evidence from the United States Patent Records, 1790–1865." *Journal of Economic History* 56 (1996): 356–388.

———. "Property Rights and Patent Litigation in Early Nineteenth-Century America." *Journal of Economic History* 55 (1995): 58–97.

Lazarou, Kathleen Elizabeth. *Concealed under Petticoats: Married Women's Property and the Law of Texas, 1840–1913*. New York: Garland, 1986.

Orren, Karen. *Belated Feudalism: Labor, the Law, and Liberal Development in the United States*. Cambridge: Cambridge University Press, 1992.

Peck, Epaphroditus. *The Property Rights of Husband and Wife under the Law of Connecticut*. Hartford: Dissell Publishing Co., 1904.

Roberts, Evan. "Women's Rights and Women's Labor: Married Women's Property Law Reform and Labor Force Participation." Unpublished manuscript (obtained from author), 2014.

Salmon, Marylynn. *Women and the Law of Property in Early America*. Chapel Hill: University of North Carolina Press, 1986.

Shammas, Carole. "Re-assessing the Married Women's Property Acts." *Journal of Women's History* 6 (1994): 9–30.

Siegel, Reva B. "Home as Work: The First Woman's Rights Claim Concerning Wives' Household Labor, 1850–1880." *Yale Law Journal* 103 (1994): 1073–1217.

———. "The Modernization of Marital Status Law: Adjudicating Wives' Rights to Earning, 1860–1930." *Georgetown Law Journal* 82 (1995): 2127–2211.

Warbasse, Elizabeth Bowles. *The Changing Legal Rights of Women, 1800–1861*. New York: Garland Publishing, 1987.

Chapter 9

Divergent Outcomes of Land Rights Claims of Indigenous Peoples in the United States

Wayne Edwards

Land is one of the most important, valuable, and versatile assets in human endeavor. The ability of a party to own land enhances its opportunity for economic growth and wealth acquisition in many ways including through resource extraction, agricultural production, and as use for collateral to finance economic projects. Land also provides a physical place for people to exist momentarily or over time, the latter affording the opportunity for the development of cultural identity and the accumulation of a people's history. The value of land, therefore, can be evaluated in many ways and its market value represents only a portion of its meaning to the people who inhabit it.

The right to own land is a property right, which is usually considered a bundle of rights as described here by Robert Cooter and Thomas Ulen: "These rights describe what people may and may not do with the resources they own: the extent to which they may possess, use, develop, improve, transform, consume, deplete, destroy, sell, donate, bequeath, transfer, mortgage, lease, loan, or exclude others from the property."[1] Private ownership of land is not the same as sovereign control over land. For example, private ownership may or may not convey rights to exploit subsurface resources. More generally, sovereign control in its broadest form allows for the creation of laws, including taxation, that govern the use of the land, while private ownership requires the owner to comply with existing laws. It is important to observe that ownership and sovereignty imply different bundles of rights.

In this chapter, the concept of land and ownership is taken at an aggregated level and the analysis focuses on land rights and ownership of land by political entities rather than individuals. In particular, this essay surveys the legislative and treaty outcomes of the US government's acquisition and dispensation of land in North America and Hawai'i with respect to the people who lived on the land prior to the arrival of Europeans. Because land is such a fundamental asset, differences in land rights settlements among these groups have contributed to differences in observed economic outcomes. At an aggregated level, group differences can be seen in poverty rates and other statistical measures, although there is considerable variation within each group. As hinted earlier, a significant corollary issue is sovereignty and therefore the opportunity for self-determination. These concepts relate to land rights in the sense that, if the US government is dealing with sovereign entities, the rights transferred through land ownership are different than those transferred to individuals (or nonsovereign institutions) through land ownership. In addition, in many cases the rights transferred through land ownership (or at least occupancy) have been inhibited by the "trust relationship" the US government has declared with recognized indigenous people. Cooter and Ulen's description of rights to property (including land) is useful because these acts of acquiring and/or transferring land often included restrictions on its use and title.

Three Populations Described: Legal Status and the Level of Aggregation

When referring to native peoples with whom the US government has had land agreements (or disagreements), I use standard terms and definitions used in the literature and by federal authorities. The term "American Indian" refers to native peoples in the contiguous United States, while the general term "native" will refer to any indigenous group or individual considered, including American Indians, Alaska Natives (Native Alaskans), and Native Hawaiians. The Census Bureau considers "a person having origins in any of the original peoples of North and South America (including Central America)...who maintains tribal affiliation or community attachment" to belong to the American Indian and Native Alaskan (AINA) category.[2] While the AINA category is treated as an homogenous group by the Census Bureau, it must be noted that in fact the AINA category encompasses hundreds of tribes, vast geographical space, and many language groups.[3] In terms of land claims, there are stark differences between the settlements with people in Alaska and those in the Lower 48, so they are treated as separate groups here. For indigenous people with ancestral roots in the Hawaiian Islands, the major census category is Native Hawaiian and Other Pacific Islander (NHPI). Because of the geographic isolation of the Hawaiian Islands from the rest of the United States, there is less confusion about membership in this group. Although separate bands and subgroups of people certainly do exist among Native Hawaiians, their treatment with respect to land rights and the US federal government has been, for the most part, homogenous.

The issue of sovereignty is in some ways a question of the *degree* of sovereignty that groups possess. A higher level of sovereignty might allow a group to construct rules for its society that better suit its specific needs than the rules that bind the broader society. At the same time, if sovereign status results in limited interaction with the rest of the national economy, then group members might be worse off in a number of ways. In terms of political status—which is a necessary but not sufficient condition for sovereignty—Native Hawaiians have never been recognized by the Bureau of Indian Affairs (BIA) as having valid tribal status, while American Indians and Native Alaskans have been so recognized (separately). For the most part, the reservation system, which identifies specific tracts of land and sets them aside for certain groups of people, has been used in the contiguous 48 states to establish areas of "Indian Country" for American Indians. In Alaska, reservations are rare and generally not widely used in legal agreements to resolve disputes and claims of Native Alaskans against federal and state entities. Rather, in the Alaska Native case, a separation between economic interests and political interests was made, leading to a different sovereign political impact.[4] Sovereign rights in land claims, then, apply to a greater extent to American Indians, secondarily to Native Alaskans, and to Native Hawaiians in a much smaller sense, although all three groups have similar origin histories of ancestral occupancy.

Issues of historic governance vary between the groups. While Native Hawaiians had a system that seemed "national" in the sense that the islands had a monarch and a functioning government by the middle of the nineteenth century, Native Alaskans and American Indians were primarily organized in tribes and bands and therefore observed local authority prior to being dominated and absorbed by the United States.[5] The contemporaneous relationship between existing native governing bodies and the United States hinges on the degree of sovereignty negotiated between them. The current legal basis for tribal governance extends back at least to the 1970s when the federal government adopted the policy of what President Nixon called "self-determination of Indian people" while maintaining the trust relationship the government held over Indian land.[6] The main law addressing self-governance is the Indian Self-Determination and Education Act of 1975, which authorizes tribal entities to administer funds provided through the federal budgetary process. Many other pieces of legislation address sovereign authority. For example, tribes organized under the Indian Reorganization Act of 1934 can conduct their affairs as they see fit in Indian Country provided federal laws are not broken. Tribes are not entirely separate governments from the United States because they are allowed to pursue self-determination only within stated boundaries and remain subject to federal law.[7]

Land ownership in general, as well as the type of land ownership (that is, which bundles of rights are included), matters for numerous economic, social, and political reasons, as mentioned earlier. The comparative study of the differences in the types of ownership amongst groups that follow suggests that real consequences result from the disparate treatment of groups with similar claims.

Important Treaties, Legislation, and Group Outcomes

The US government inherited its relationship with American Indians from England and therefore initially approached land rights issues in continental expansion through treaty negotiations, treating American Indian groups as sovereign nations.[8] In Hawai'i, the United States backed a coup based on economic interests of Americans in the islands and subsequently acquired the islands through a treaty that annexed them to the United States.[9] In Alaska, the land was acquired simply by purchasing it from Russia with little thought given to the people who were living there at the time.[10] Today, all people in these groups are US citizens and most, but not all, have legally recognized tribal affiliations. The path out of the past into the present has been very different for each of these groups. The following is a brief discussion of some of the major events and legislation that affected each group and led to the current status of its members.

The Contiguous 48 States

At the moment of the Declaration of Independence, the British law specifying the western boundary between the 13 colonies and the recognized land belonging to indigenous people was the Line of Royal Proclamation of 1763. By 1776, the effective boundary was being pushed west by the colonies. Under the Articles of Confederation, tribes were treated as sovereign nations, even though the western concept of sovereignty did not well describe the social and political institutions of American Indian tribes and bands.[11] The Treaty of Paris (1783) made no mention of American Indians at all, and within ten years the federal government had taken away the authority of states to negotiate any land agreements with Indian nations.[12] During this time American Indians were thought of and generally treated as entirely separate nationalities and sharp lines were drawn and enforced. Indeed, early treaty agreements between the United States and the Creeks and the Cherokees required American citizens to have a passport to enter Indian lands.[13] When land title was in dispute, courts typically ruled in favor of the United States. For example, in the 1923 case of *Johnson and Graham's Lessee v. William McIntosh*, the plaintiff claimed ownership of a tract of land based upon a purchase from American Indians while the defendant's claim to ownership of the same land rested on a grant from the US government.[14] The court decided the grant held sway on the basis of the federal government having the right to grant land regardless of tenancy and specifically that absolute title of the "crown" extinguishes any title Indians might hold.[15] Therefore, in 1823, even though tribes had been considered separate nations in treaties, the court system placed tribes in a subordinate position to the US government, implying that the sovereignty of Indian nations did not carry the same weight as the sovereignty of the United States.

In 1825, President James Monroe suggested a voluntary removal policy to address the calls of southern and eastern states to extinguish Indian land title: "The great object to be accomplished is the removal of these tribes to the territory designated on conditions which shall be satisfactory to themselves and honorable to the United States."[16] It was under the Andrew Jackson administration that the removal and relocation of American Indians accelerated precipitously. The Indian Removal Act of 1830 established as public policy the relocation of eastern and southern tribes to lands west of the Mississippi, specifically authorizing the exchange of land in the West for land occupied by Indian tribes in territory or state.[17] One example is the "Great Removal" of southeastern native peoples wherein about 100,000 individuals were moved. Plains peoples experienced similar pressure to relocate and, over time, the conflicts became increasingly violent.[18] The reservation land that was established conveyed limited political autonomy. For example, the Supreme Court refused to hear a complaint from Cherokee Indians when the state of Georgia extended political authority of Cherokee lands in 1831 because the Cherokee

Nation was not a foreign nation. The court described Indian tribes as "domestic dependent nations."[19]

The removal of Indians westward followed the basic concept of Indian Territory being west of a line established in the Intercourse Law of 1796 that was simply pushed farther and farther west over time. By the 1840s this idea was no longer functional due the rapid expansion of white settlements. Between 1845 and 1848 enormous spans of land came under direct federal control with the additions of California, Oregon, Texas, and the Mexican Cession. The solution was to create reservations that initially were meant as a stop-gap approach to conflicts between white settlers and Indian peoples. The point of view the federal government held was that Indians maintained title to the land they occupied and that the title could be extinguished only through treaty. The treaties themselves tended to be unilaterally proposed and enforced rather than negotiated, resulting in shrinking land holdings of Indians.[20]

A parallel intent of treaty and legislation was to "civilize" and assimilate Indians into US society. Questions of sovereignty and self-determination became increasingly problematic. The political organization of tribes was localized and, for a time, the federal government tried to establish a territorial organization for Indians that would allow territorial government, American citizenship, and land in severalty. This was a challenging hurdle for many reasons, not the least of which was the fact that so many different treaties and arrangements existed between the federal government and separate individual tribes.[21] To further the assimilation policy under these circumstances, the US government adopted a policy of allotment. The General Allotment Act of 1887 (the Dawes Act) splintered tribal control of existing reservations. Under that act, certain tracts of land within reservations were given to individual American Indians and held in trust by the US government, while other tracts of land were sold to non-Indians. The Dawes Act resulted in substantial land loss for American Indians at the aggregated level. It also weakened the institutional position of tribes because some reservation land was owned by individuals, but other land was owned by individuals or the tribe and was now held in trust by the BIA. The policy lasted into the 1930s.[22] Land held in trust is not as economically productive as land owned by private individuals or institutions because there are numerous legal and bureaucratic obstacles involved in utilizing this land. For example, investors may be hesitant to loan money for the development of land held in trust because in the event of a default it might be difficult to repossess.[23]

The Indian Reorganization Act was passed in 1934. The act was an attempt "to rehabilitate the Indian's economic life and give him a chance to develop the initiative destroyed by a century of oppression and paternalism."[24] This act ended the allotment process and encouraged a new focus on self-determination and economic development. After a period of attempts to terminate tribal authority and governance in the 1950s and 1960s, self-determination again came into focus late in the Johnson administration and then in the Nixon administration.[25]

Presently, any land in the Lower 48 held by American Indians is known as Indian Country and represents the remnants of an ever shrinking ancestral space. These places hold a measure of sovereignty and the leadership can conduct the affairs of the people as they see fit, to a limited degree and as long as activities remain within federal law.[26] The laws of states that surround reservations do not necessarily apply, although the differences between laws on reservations and state laws are typically small except in some cases involving issues of commerce and taxation. Large administrative problems do exist because of jurisdictional overlap between the tribal authority, the state, and the federal government, frequently resulting in a lack of services on reservations and persistent social and human poverty.[27] The land is not equally productive in every place, and the size of reservations varies enormously. Management of the land suffers from jurisdictional confusion, historical arrangements, and differences in management style and ability from one tribe and reservation to another. Contracts for mineral extraction and other land uses are sometimes negotiated by federal agencies to a less than optimal conclusion for tribes. Some tribes choose business models such as casinos that others shun. The net results for revenue generated by the land are determined by a multitude of factors affecting each tribe unequally.[28]

Alaska

In 1867, Alaska was purchased from Russia by the United States in what was popularly known at the time as "Seward's Folly" in reference to Secretary of State William Seward, under the presumption that there was no value or use in buying millions of acres of land in the far north. The people who had been living in Alaska for thousands of years were not consulted and might have been completely unaware that the land they lived on had been transferred from one foreign nation to another. The United States appeared not to have much interest governing in Alaska seriously until mineral wealth was discovered, first notably in 1897 when news that gold was found in the Yukon and that relatively easy access to the Klondike strikes was available through southeastern Alaska, which neighbors British Columbia, first got out. Alaska Natives had little involvement in the gold rush or the further development that came in the early part of the twentieth century leading eventually to statehood in 1959.[29]

Similar to American Indians in the Lower 48, the legislative history concerning land rights of indigenous peoples in Alaska is long and convoluted. Laws and agreements overlap and conflict with each other, sometimes disappearing only to later reappear.[30] Some of the major laws with important consequences for land rights are summarized here.[31]

The Native Allotment Act (1906) was one of the earliest laws addressing land rights of Natives. Under this act, Alaska Natives were authorized to acquire individual allotments of up to 160-acre parcels of unreserved and unappropriated land in what was essentially a type of homestead legislation. Approximately 10,000 applications were filed by Alaska Natives for 16,000 parcels of land under the law. The Alaska Statehood Act (1958) had a much larger impact in that it added a newly created economic unit, the State of Alaska, into the land rights issue by giving it legal standing and claim to land formerly in federal hands. This act allowed the new state to select for ownership approximately 104 million acres of unclaimed and unreserved federal land. The single act that had by far the largest impact on Native Alaskans was the Alaska Native Claims Settlement Act (ANCSA) of 1971. The law was designed to settle the claims of the aboriginal peoples of Alaska by transferring approximately 44 million acres of public land and nearly $1 billion to them. The land and cash were distributed through 12 newly created regional Native corporations and approximately 200 village corporations.[32] This approach established a remedy in the form of private compensation rather than creating a political entity such as a tribal government and a reservation to address past wrongs. All Alaska Natives (people who could prove they were at least one-quarter native) born on or before December 18, 1971, were allowed to enroll in one of the corporations, receiving ownership through corporate shares. ANCSA prohibited the sale of any shares in a corporation for a period of at least 20 years.[33] Conceptually, the distribution of land returns to natives ancestral heritage and subsistence ability. The cash transfers were included because it was thought that not enough land was made available through the act to achieve these goals.[34]

The acquisition of the land assets allowed for potential economic gains through land use but no sovereignty. The distribution of land to the regional corporations, however, was not uniform. The corporation receiving the smallest allotment was Sealaska at 0.3 million acres; the largest distribution was 12.5 million acres to the Doyon Corporation. The potential market value of the land varied widely as well. Some corporations received land with valuable surface or subsurface products, like the Arctic Slope Corporation receiving land with real and potential oil and gas deposits, Chugach Natives Corporation receiving land rich in timber, and NANA Corporation receiving land with zinc-lead deposits. Other regional corporations, like Aleut, Bering Straits, and Koniag, took title to land with no known marketable products other than the land itself.[35] This disparity is important because the regional corporations received "fee simple" title to the land, meaning they controlled rights to both the surface and subsurface of the land.[36] Remote land in Alaska with no harvestable trees and no subsurface assets has a market value that is, for all intents and purposes, zero. The disparity is addressed and somewhat overcome by the requirement that 70 percent of all net earnings from subsurface and timber resources made by each Native corporation must be distributed equally among all other corporations.[37] The cash settlement was divided among the corporations and individual natives: the regional corporations received 45 percent of the distribution, as did the village corporations, and the remaining 10 percent went to individuals as an immediate transfer.[38] Land has value beyond its market price, but in the absence of any associated sovereignty the nonmarket value resides entirely in the murky sphere of personal utility arising from preference satisfaction.

Like any major legislation, ANCSA faced repeated legal challenges and was periodically revised over the years to address unforeseen problems that emerged.[39] ANCSA was substantially revised through legislation during the Reagan administration. The so-called 1991 amendments allowed important changes such as including shareholder control to issue stock to natives who missed out on the original enrollment (those individuals who were born after the initial deadline established by the law), a continuation of restrictions on the sale of stock after the expiration of the initial 20-year prohibition period, the protection for undeveloped land became automatic and did not require other specific legislation, authority of shareholders to change benefits to elders, and several other minor corporate structure changes.[40] Because of the extraordinary scale of money involved in the settlement, it is not surprising that litigation continues on many aspects of both the initial ANCSA legislation and the many subsequent amendments to it. Even with this apparent turmoil and uncertainty, ANCSA provided legal property rights to natives that did not exist prior to the law.[41]

Land use activities were addressed separately in the Alaska National Interest Lands Conservation Act (ANILCA) of 1980. The law gave people living in rural places in Alaska, the overwhelming majority of whom were Alaska Natives, priority in hunting and fishing on public lands.[42] While ANILCA was written mainly to address land conservation issues, it was also designed to preserve native culture by protecting the opportunity to engage in a subsistence lifestyle of land use.[43] In rural Alaska, subsistence activities account for a large share of final food consumption goods. According to the Alaska Department of Fish and Game, 86 percent of rural households used game from subsistence hunting and 95 percent of rural households used fish from subsistence fishing in 1999.[44] These traditional activities are also practical, given the rugged nature of the rural environment in Alaska. Urban residents in the state also participate in hunting and fishing activities, but on a much smaller scale and not for a primary subsistence purpose. In addition, the impact of subsistence activity rests disproportionately on the native population because natives make up the majority of the rural population and a much smaller proportion of the urban population.[45] Therefore, any change in legal access to subsistence goods affects proportionately more natives than any other racial group in Alaska.

Part of the intent in the original conception of ANCSA was to preserve the lifestyle of natives. It has nevertheless been seen by some as a failure, especially with respect to subsistence guarantees.[46] ANILCA, then, can be easily seen in part as a response to the perceived need to protect rural residents' rights to subsistence access left unaddressed by ANCSA. Because the highest priority goes to Alaska Natives more than any other group, an entitlement is created specifically for natives as it eliminates competition for game and fish from commercial and sport activities and excludes non-natives (people without customary and direct dependence) from the highest priority subsistence rank.[47] These definitions provided by ANILCA of exactly which group has what specific rights in the use of the land in question refines the land rights attributes Alaska Natives own.

While ANCSA is notable in the context of this chapter for providing specific property rights and cash transfers to a vulnerable population in Alaska, ANILCA is remembered for defining fundamental land *use* rights.[48] In each case, the laws can be interpreted as providing a particular bundle of rights to a specific group of people. The arrangements are very different in Alaska than they are in the Lower 48 states, and tribal governance, as such, occurs primarily at the village level while the bulk of economic distributions to members comes from the regional corporations, each of which spans many villages.[49] Some village corporations do generate large revenues, but they are in a small minority.[50]

Land owned by Alaska Native Corporations does not constitute Indian Country.[51] In Alaska, then, the ownership of the land operates much more like private ownership than the political public ownership nature of reservations in the Lower 48. For the reasons noted earlier, average earnings per member of Alaska Native Corporations is higher than earnings per member of tribal entities outside Alaska. It is clear that average economic production value from the land is higher in Alaska while at the same time the functional sovereignty is considerably lower. Whether this outcome constitutes a relative success or not depends on what goal is being examined: economic performance or self-determination. Alternately, the question of success can be said to rest on how relative value is assigned to the separate components of sovereignty and revenue generation. Ancestral and cultural activities can certainly be preserved through private ownership of land that is subsequently used for such activities. Self-determination, however, is severely limited in the case of private ownership as compared to sovereign control because the laws of the surrounding government supersede local laws.

Hawai'i

The Hawaiian Islands were annexed by treaty to the United States in 1898. This process of acquisition makes the history of Native Hawaiians unique from that of AINA peoples. Before its annexation, Hawai'i was a nation with an independent functioning government, although the government and the society were experiencing considerable turmoil.[52] Even with the strife, this stands in stark contrast to the historical situation in both Alaska and the Continental United States whose native peoples were organized in separate autonomous communities rather than in a broader macro-political institution. Queen Lili'uokalani was the last ruling monarch of the sovereign nation of the Kingdom of Hawai'i when it was overthrown in 1893 by insurgents, many of whom were American businessmen in the sugar industry. The resultant "Republic of Hawai'i" was established solely for the purpose of transferring the island chain to the United States as a territorial claim. This strategy was adopted to avoid the politically difficult alternative of directly annexing the islands. Hawai'i became a state in 1959 after a referendum vote favored statehood. Most areas in the islands approved statehood by a comfortable margin. There was one precinct that voted to reject statehood status: Ni'ihau, the only island populated entirely by Native Hawaiians.[53]

Native Hawaiians became US citizens when the islands were annexed in 1898. This political status stands in contrast to the other groups examined in this essay, not all of whom were granted citizenship until the Indian Citizenship Act of 1924. The BIA does not recognize any Native Hawaiian group as a tribe or band for federal purposes, although people of Native Hawaiian ancestry are eligible for some federal programs. Trust lands in Hawai'i amount to 200,000 acres that were ceded as part of the annexation of 1898. Initially, the lands were administered by the federal government, but authority over ceded land was transferred to the state as part of the statehood process in 1959. The land is now managed by the Department of Hawaiian Home Lands, a state department.[54]

There have been many attempts to gain both federal recognition of Native Hawaiians as a political entity and reclaim ancestral land in Hawai'i, none of which has been successful. The most well-known attempt is the Akaka Bill, named for Daniel Akaka, the senator from Hawai'i who introduced it. At the state level, there has been more progress. The Hawai'i state constitution was amended in 1978 to provide that previously ceded lands would be held in a public trust for Native Hawaiians and the general public. The amendments also established the Office of Hawaiian Affairs (OHA) that was charged with managing and administering the pro rata portion of the public trust set aside to benefit Native Hawaiians. In 1979, the definition of "public land trust" was made clear. Laws enacted that year in Hawai'i defined the land trust as all proceeds and income from the sale, lease, or other disposition of ceded lands. At the same time, the OHA was authorized to collect, administer, and expend 20 percent of all funds derived from the "public land trust" for the betterment of the conditions of Native Hawaiians. Still, there have been no land rights transferred to any tribal entity in Hawai'i and no sovereign recognition.[55]

Native Hawaiians as a group tend to fare better than AINA groups in most measured categories of well-being including health, longevity, and income.[56] There are many factors that contribute to the observed differences in well-being outcomes, and it can be argued that the social integration that resulted from the denial of land claims and any sovereign status has, in the long run, benefitted Native Hawaiians. In terms of economic outcomes, the data are difficult to refute. Consider, for example, poverty rates: table 9.1 shows poverty rates for several different Census groups of people from 2006 to 2010. While

Table 9.1 Poverty rates among Native Americans (all families), 2006–2010 (in %)

Year	American Indian and Alaska Native alone	American Indian and Alaska Native alone or in combination with one or more other races	Native Hawaiian and Other Pacific Islander alone	Native Hawaiian and Other Pacific Islander alone or in combination with one or more other races	Total population	White alone	Black or African American alone
2006	21.2	19.2	16.1	14.5	10.2	7.5	22.8
2007	21.6	18.6	14.4	13.1	9.8	7.2	21.8
2008	20.9	18.1	13.4	11.9	9.6	7.2	21.2
2009	21.2	18.4	12.9	11.5	9.9	7.5	21.6
2010	22.0	19.4	13.7	12.4	10.5	8.0	22.0

Sources: American Community Survey, S0201, three-year estimates for 2007–2010; American Community Survey, S0201, one-year estimates for 2006. Three-year estimates are not available for 2006, so one-year estimates (generated from a smaller sample) are used for that year. Edwards, "Native American Poverty during the Great Recession."

the poverty rates for Native Hawaiians (alone or in combination with another race) are higher than the rate for whites or the average in the population, they are far less than AINA rates and the poverty rates for black or African American groups. This is true before, during, and after the 2008–2009 recession. Additionally, while the poverty rates for the other minority groups reported in table 9.1 are about the same in 2006 as in 2010, the rates for Native Hawaiians have fallen.

Why, then, is there still a movement to reclaim ancestral space when integration seems to have had an aggregate positive effect on Native Hawaiians? The answer is complex and difficult to pin down. Certainly the individuals who seek land rights for Native Hawaiians have a preference for some level of sovereignty for the group. A cynical view might be that the push for land is simple asset acquisition; a standard economic assumption is people prefer more rather than less of most commodities and so it might be natural to desire more land. But the transfer of land to a tribal group for sovereign control, rather than into individual private hands, would not necessarily bring economic benefits in excess of those presently available through lease arrangements for the use of set-aside land. Also, while table 9.1 does show that Native Hawaiians are statistically better off than the other groups examined in this essay, they are still among the least well-off groups in the state of Hawai'i and, in the absence of specific land rights, they face formidable economic development challenges.[57]

No group comprised of individuals speaks with a singular voice. What any particular Native Hawaiian might want could easily be very different from what another particular Native Hawaiian wants. The aggregated concerns of individuals in a group can only be assessed on a majority (or perhaps a plurality) basis, and even then there is always the danger of misunderstanding the desires of some or simply not hearing them. An assessment of the merits of a land rights claim might then revert to historical facts and legal precedents. If so, it is difficult to understand why the outcomes of land rights initiatives by Native Hawaiians have been so much less successful than those of American Indians and Native Alaskans.

Outside the System: A Private Partnership Approach to Ancestral Land Acquisition

In the land that is now Vermont, the first permanent European settlement was built at Fort Dummer by Massachusetts Bay colonists in 1724.[58] Large numbers of Europeans did not enter Vermont until about a decade before US independence, and most were from

Massachusetts. French settlements were established north in Quebec and on the western shore of Lake Champlain. Most of the natives in the area were Western Abenaki. By the time of European settlement in Vermont, the Abenaki had already been significantly influenced by Western culture through trade and conflict resulting in large changes in their movements and economic activities. The largest factor that pushed Abenaki peoples out of Vermont was the repeated violent encounters with other tribes, the French, and, finally, the British in the War of Conquest that ended in the early 1760s.[59]

More war followed, notably the Revolutionary War. Natives in Vermont were systematically pushed out of their land like their fellows had been in southern New England one hundred years before. As early as 1789, some Abenakis did request compensation for lost land, but were unsuccessful. As time passed, the Abenaki people who remained near ancestral places assimilated into the European culture that surrounded them as a survival strategy.[60] Ultimately, this approach worked against them in terms of future land claims and the quest for sovereignty and self-determination. The main reasons given for the denial of federal recognition of Abenaki people in Vermont were the assimilation into the US society outside of tribal separatism and the "weight of history," meaning that they had not maintained a separate existence for so long that they had given up any sovereign right to it contemporaneously.[61] While the "weight of history" argument has been criticized by some legal scholars, it remains a citable precedent.[62] The ultimate result is there are no federally recognized Abenaki people or lands in Vermont now. One group, the Nulhegan Band of the Coosuk Abenaki Nation, has received Vermont state recognition, but no land has been officially returned or set aside for any Abenaki group.[63]

Faced with dim prospects for land rights claims, the Nulhegan Band partnered with the nonprofit land conservation organization the Vermont Land Trust and the Sierra Club to raise money for the purpose of buying land in ancestral areas of Vermont. In 2012, the project was successful in acquiring a small parcel of forestland in Orleans County in the northern part of the state, title to which is privately held by Abenaki Helping Abenaki, Inc., a nonprofit organization. In addition, the Vermont Land Trust holds a conservation easement on the forestland in perpetuity to ensure it is not developed for other purposes. The land represents the first tribal communal land held by Abenakis in 200 years, and they intend to use it for small-scale traditional agriculture in existing clearings, for hunting opportunities, for firewood harvesting, and for other nondestructive usages.[64]

The Abenaki arrangement carries no political authority or sovereign implications. It does however address some of the goals of reestablishing cultural identity and represents an innovative approach to what appeared to be an untenable situation. The strategy of the private purchase of land by an unrecognized American Indian organization and the granting of a conservation easement to a land trust is an innovative attempt to address land rights issues. Many land trusts exist throughout the United States, but they generally do not specifically attempt to set aside land for native peoples. If the Nulhegan Band initiative proves successful, it might serve as a productive template for other peoples throughout the United States who find themselves in similar circumstances.

Conclusion

Through its long history of land rights disputes with indigenous peoples, the United States government has reached a wide variety of settlements. Existing agreements today take many forms: manifesting in paternal trust arrangements, appearing to be payoffs for previous and contemporaneous takings, or resulting in the outright denial of cultural legitimacy. Although the three groups of people examined— American Indians, Native Alaskans, and Native Hawaiians—all have in common the fundamental loss of ancestral lands to the US government, the attention and compensation each has received are widely disparate. American Indians have received some reservation land carrying the partial sovereignty of Indian Country, which allows for limited self-determination. The distribution of land to tribes and bands is not the same and the uses and economic returns to the land vary widely generating measurably different outcomes for American Indian groups. Land compensation to Native Alaskans was issued primarily through Native Corporations rather than tribal governments. As with land reserved for American Indians, the amount and economic potential of the land distributions to Native Corporations in Alaska varied widely. Tribal control exists in relatively small ways at the village level; the corporate structure of the land settlement conveys no sovereignty. Land owned by Alaska Native Corporations is not Indian Country. No land has been specifically set aside or awarded to any Native Hawaiian group. Some ceded land does exist in Hawai'i as trust land, but its specified uses are not exclusive to natives. The lack of land settlements in the case of Native Hawaiians is due in large part to the absence of tribal recognition by the BIA.

Ownership of land, and the nature and extent of the bundle of rights held in any transferred title, has real economic consequences for group members. A higher level of sovereignty allows a group to construct rules for its society that best suit its specific social and cultural needs rather than simply adopting the rules that bind the broader external society. At the same time, if sovereign status results in limited interaction with the rest of the national economy, then group members might be worse off in a number of ways. The balance is difficult to analyze and achieve because individual group members will naturally place different values on separate characteristics. That is, some group members might value maintaining a separate cultural identity over integration and economic development while others might hold the opposite view. How then is the group to decide what to do? Viewing outcomes and existing entitlements through an historic lens might offer some clarity as to how the arrangements came to be, but a knowledge of the evolutionary process does not change the reality of the cultural and wealth effects of the property right to ancestral land or its absence. An understanding of the consequences of the differences might inform future policy and court decisions, and if it does, the study of the issues surrounding land rights of indigenous peoples in the United States has the potential to benefit group members.

Further research that establishes the extent to which these differences have affected economic and social outcomes of group members would be an important step in understanding the consequences of historic land settlement decisions. Some data do exist that have the potential to reveal relationships between groups characteristics and group outcomes. These public data sets can be augmented with additional survey data collection that asks the people in question specifically what their experiences have been and what their desires and preferences are today. Additional information uncovered in this way has the potential to inform public policy decisions to the betterment of native peoples.

Notes

1. Cooter and Ulen, *Law and Economics*, 77.
2. Norris, Vines, and Hoeffel, "The American Indian and Alaska Native Population: 2012."
3. *Federal Register* Vol. 75 No. 190; Edwards and Natarajan, "ANCSA and ANILCA."
4. Edwards and Natarajan, "ANCSA and ANILCA."
5. Daws, *Shoal of Time*, 107; Pevar, *The Rights of Indians and Tribes*, 1; Getches, Wilkinson, and Williams, *Cases and Materials on Federal Indian Law*, 893.

6. Prucha, *The Great Father*, 1165.
7. Edwards, "Native American Poverty during the Great Recession."
8. Prucha, *The Great Father*, 5.
9. Daws, *Shoal of Time*, 275.
10. Case and Voluck, *Alaska Natives and American Laws*, 6.
11. Nies, *Native American History*, 203.
12. Ibid., 209.
13. Prucha, *American Indian Treaties*, 4.
14. *Johnson & Graham's Lessee v. McIntosh*, 21 U.S. 543 (1823).
15. Prucha, *Documents of United States Indian Policy*, 35–36.
16. Ibid., 39.
17. Barnes, *The Historical Atlas of Native Americans*, 268.
18. Edwards, "Native American Poverty during the Great Recession."
19. Prucha, *Documents of United States Indian Policy*, 57.
20. Prucha, *The Great Father*, 315–318.
21. Ibid., 737–738.
22. Pevar, *The Rights of Indians and Tribes*, 8–9.
23. Edwards, "Native American Poverty during the Great Recession."
24. Pevar, *The Rights of Indians and Tribes*, 10.
25. Prucha, *The Great Father*, 1191.
26. Anderson, *Sovereign Nations or Reservations?*, 5.
27. Edwards, "Tribal Government Responses to Poverty."
28. Miller, *Reservation Capitalism*, 39.
29. Edwards, "Tribal Government Responses to Poverty."
30. Colt, "Financial Performance of Native Regional Corporations."
31. Unless noted otherwise, the summary information that follows is drawn mainly from Brooks, "The Alaska Land Transfer Acceleration Act"; and Edwards, "Native American Poverty during the Great Recession" and "Tribal Government Responses to Poverty."
32. Colt, "Financial Performance of Native Regional Corporations."
33. Statewide Library Electronic Doorway, "FAQ Alaska."
34. Anders, "Social and Economic Consequences of Federal Indian Policy."
35. Colt, "Financial Performance of Native Regional Corporations."
36. Pevar, *The Rights of Indians and Tribes*, 301.
37. Colt, "Financial Performance of Native Regional Corporations."
38. Ibid.
39. Jones, "Alaska Native Claims Settlement Act of 1971 (Public Law 92–203)."
40. Statewide Library Electronic Doorway, "FAQ Alaska."
41. Harvard Project on American Indian Economic Development, *The State of the Native Nations*, 101.
42. Pevar, *The Rights of Indians and Tribes*, 302.
43. Atkinson, "The Alaska National Interest Lands Conservation Act."
44. Wolfe, "Subsistence in Alaska."
45. Ibid.

46. Atkinson, "The Alaska National Interest Lands Conservation Act."
47. Ibid.
48. Coates, *The Trans-Alaska Pipeline Controversy*, 308.
49. Edwards and Natarajan, "ANCSA and ANILCA."
50. LaFleur and Grabell, "Alaska Native Corporations Annual Reports."
51. Getches, Wilkinson, and Williams, *Cases and Materials on Federal Indian Law*, 899.
52. Daws, *Shoal of Time*, 264–270.
53. Ibid., 391.
54. Getches, Wilkinson, and Williams, *Cases and Materials on Federal Indian Law*, 920.
55. Ibid., 922–923.
56. Edwards, "Native American Poverty during the Great Recession."
57. Getches, Wilkinson, and Williams, *Cases and Materials on Federal Indian Law*, 920–921.
58. Calloway, *The Western Abenakis of Vermont*, 119–120.
59. Haviland and Power, *The Original Vermonters*, 205–242.
60. Ibid., 244–246.
61. Calloway, *The Western Abenakis of Vermont*, 250.
62. Wiseman, *The Voice of the Dawn*, 179.
63. Vermont Statutes and Codes, "Recognition of Abenaki People."
64. Vermont Land Trust, "Nulhegan Abenaki Attain First Tribal Forestland in More than 200 Years."

Bibliography

Anders, Gary C. "Social and Economic Consequences of Federal Indian Policy: A Case Study of the Alaska Natives." *Economic Development and Cultural Change* 37 (1989): 285–303.

Anderson, Terry L. *Sovereign Nations or Reservations? An Economic History of Native Americans.* San Francisco: Pacific Research Institute for Public Policy, 1995.

Atkinson, Karen J. "The Alaska National Interest Lands Conservation Act: Striking the Balance in Favor of 'Customary and Traditional' Subsistence Uses by Alaska Natives." *Natural Resources Journal* 27 (1987): 421–440.

Barnes, Ian. *The Historical Atlas of Native Americans.* New York: Chartwell, 2009.

Brooks, Nathan. "The Alaska Land Transfer Acceleration Act: Background and Summary." Congressional Research Service Report for Congress, RL32734. Washington, DC: Congressional Research Service, Library of Congress, 2005.

Calloway, Colin G. *The Western Abenakis of Vermont, 1600–1800.* Norman: University of Oklahoma Press, 1990.

Case, David S., and David A. Voluck. *Alaska Natives and American Laws.* 2nd edition. Fairbanks: University of Alaska Press, 2002.

Coates, Peter A. *The Trans-Alaska Pipeline Controversy: Technology, Conservation, and the Frontier*. Anchorage: University of Alaska Press, 1993.

Colt, Steve. "Alaska Natives and the 'New Harpoon': Economic Performance of the ANCSA Regional Corporations." Working paper. Anchorage: Institute of Social and Economic Research, 2001.

———. "Financial Performance of Native Regional Corporations." Cited in Gigi Berardi, "Natural Resource Policy, Unforgiving Geographies, and Persistent Poverty in Alaska Native Villages." *Natural Resources Journal* 38 (1998): 85–108.

Cooter, Robert, and Thomas Ulen. *Law and Economics*. 5th ed. Boston: Pearson/Addison-Wesley, 2008.

Daws, Gavan. *Shoal of Time: A History of the Hawaiian Islands*. Honolulu: University of Hawaii Press, 1974.

Edwards, Wayne. "Native American Poverty during the Great Recession." In *The New Faces of American Poverty: A Reference Guide to the Great Recession*, edited by Lindsey Hanson and Timothy Essenberg, 286–297. Santa Barbara, CA: ABC-CLIO, 2013.

———. "Tribal Government Responses to Poverty." In *The New Faces of American Poverty: A Reference Guide to the Great Recession*, edited by Lindsey Hanson and Timothy Essenberg, 560–569. Santa Barbara, CA: ABC-CLIO, 2013.

Edwards, Wayne, and Tara Natarajan. "ANCSA and ANILCA: Capabilities Failure?" *Native Studies Review* 17 (2008): 69–97.

Federal Register. Volume 75, Number 190. Notices: Page 60810–60814. Accessed June 30, 2010 at http://www.artnatam.com/tribes.html.

Getches, David H., Charles F. Wilkinson, and Robert A. Williams, Jr. *Cases and Materials on Federal Indian Law*. 5th ed. St. Paul, MN: Thomson West, 2005.

Harvard Project on American Indian Economic Development. *The State of the Native Nations: Conditions Under U. S. Policies of Self-Determination*. New York: Oxford University Press, 2008.

Haviland, William A., and Marjory W. Power. *The Original Vermonters*. Hanover: University Press of New England, 1994.

Jones, Richard S. "Alaska Native Claims Settlement Act of 1971 (Public Law 92–203): History and Analysis Together with Subsequent Amendments." Report No. 81–127 GOV, a revision of CRS Report No. 72–209 GGR, originally prepared May 22, 1972. Document downloaded from the Institute of Social and Economic Research website, University of Alaska Anchorage, December 15, 2006.

LaFleur, Jennifer, and Michael Grabell. "Alaska Native Corporations Annual Reports." Last modified December 15, 2010. Accessed December 18, 2012, http://projects.propublica.org/tables/alaska-native-corporations-annual-reports.

Miller, Robert J. *Reservation Capitalism: Economic Development in Indian Country*. Lincoln: University of Nebraska Press, 2013.

Nies, Judith. *Native American History*. New York: Ballantine Books, 1996.

Norris, Tina, Paula L. Vines, and Elizabeth M. Hoeffel. "The American Indian and Alaska Native Population: 2012." 2010 Census Briefs, Document C2010BR-10. Washington, DC: United States Census Bureau, 2012.

Pevar, Stephen L. *The Rights of Indians and Tribes.* 3rd ed. New York: New York University Press, 2004.

Prucha, Francis Paul. *American Indian Treaties: The History of a Political Anomaly.* Berkeley, CA: University of California Press, 1994.

———. *Documents of United States Indian Policy.* 3rd edition. Lincoln, NE: University of Nebraska Press, 2000.

———. *The Great Father: The United States Government and the American Indians.* Lincoln: University of Nebraska Press, 1984.

Statewide Library Electronic Doorway. "FAQ Alaska—Frequently Asked Questions About Alaska: Alaska Native Claims Settlement Act." Downloaded June 16, 2005, from http://sled.alaska.edu/akfaq/akancsa.html.

Vermont Land Trust. "Nulhegan Abenaki Attain First Tribal Forestland in More than 200 Years," press release, December 18, 2012.

Vermont Statutes and Codes. "Recognition of Abenaki People." Downloaded July 14, 2014, from http://statutes.laws.com/vermont/title-01/chapter-23/853.

Wiseman, Frederick Matthew. *The Voice of the Dawn: An Autohistory of the Abenaki Nation.* Hanover: University Press of New England, 2001.

Wolfe, Robert J. "Subsistence in Alaska: A Year 2000 Update." Report issued by the Division of Subsistence, Alaska Department of Fish and Game, Juneau, Alaska, 2000.

Chapter 10

Punitive (and) Pain-and-Suffering Damages in Brazil

Osny da Silva Filho

Pain-and-suffering damages have become one of the cornerstones of the modern regulation of liability. The functions they should perform, however, have been controversial since their explicit recognition in the seventeenth and eighteenth centuries. Once completely set aside from the exemplary, vindictive, or punitory damages of the early English law,[1] compensations for pain and suffering slowly got closer (again) to punitive roles, both in theory and in practice.[2]

It has been no different outside common law countries.[3] Over the past decades, it has been practically unanimous among Brazilian scholars that pain-and-suffering damages (in Portuguese, *danos morais*) have basically two aims: its primary purpose is to provide reparation for losses, but they also serve to punish wrongdoers or prevent accidents.[4] In other words, its awards would function at the same time as a compensatory and punitive or preventive measure. This understanding, synthetized in the notion of *danos morais punitivos*—literally, punitive pain-and-suffering damages—has spread quickly over Brazilian courts and is now well-established in the country's contemporary case law.[5]

On the other hand, among the few who criticize the punitive dimension of pain-and-suffering damages, a rather radical orientation seems to predominate: not only do these authors reject the punitive function of pain-and-suffering, but they also try to completely eliminate the idea of punishment from Brazilian tort law.[6] The argument here goes with the restriction of the courts' ruling to the reparation of actual and certain damages, in a strictly *compensatory* (and from an Aristotelian point of view, *commutative*) understanding of civil liability. This understanding is legitimized by the idea of the so-called full reparation, that is, the idea that civil liability satisfactorily fulfills its tasks once the losses and injuries are completely compensated and nothing more required from it.[7]

Between the punitive pain-and-suffering damages hybridism and the radical expunction of all punishments, this chapter explores the limits and possibilities of a third way: an alternative doctrine based on the distinction between *danos morais* and *punições civis*. The former is a strictly compensatory award for some nonpecuniary damages.[8] The latter is a micro-transplant—albeit a fairly modified one—of the Anglo-American punitive damages.[9]

My starting point is the Brazilian courts' ruling regarding the so-called undue credit reports (*negativação indevida*), which nowadays constitute the largest source of nonpecuniary damages caused to consumers in Brazil. The perceptions of those involved in its adjudication, gathered among lawyers and members of the São Paulo Court of Appeals, will be used in the first part of the text as a reference to discuss two myths whose deconstruction reinforces the need of an autonomous structure for the practice of the punitive function in the discipline of torts. My purpose in the first part of this chapter is not to implicitly defend judicial intuitionism, still less, at the other extreme, to dogmatically delegitimize the perceptions gathered in the court. My aim is to establish the basis for a *transparent* doctrine, that is, a doctrine aligned with the reasons for action of those involved in the adjudicatory procedure.[10]

The legal viability of punitive damages in civil law countries, and specifically in Brazil, is the subject of the second part of the chapter. Here, I deal specifically with some obstacles posed to punishment-based notions in private law, as well as some particularities of the punitive damages regulation and its actual application. Starting from the current perception of judges and their clerks regarding the cases of undue credit reports, I shall speak in favor of a prospective model of application of punitive damages, that is, a model whose guidelines will not be restricted to losses detected or retrospectively estimated by courts. Furthermore, this model offers a solution to the problem of unjust enrichment of the victims (an enrichment characterized by the victim receiving damages that do not correspond to the losses effectively suffered), an argument brought up by the majority of jurists who are against the application of punitive damages in Brazil.

The Boom of the Undue Credit Report Cases

An undue credit report (UCR) is the name given to an abusive or mistaken negative record of an individual's past borrowing and repaying in a credit-reporting agency database. In Brazil, these databases are known by a metonymy with the names of the bureaus or agencies that keep them, such as Serviço de Proteção ao Crédito (SPC) and Serasa Experian. Several reasons can be listed for choosing UCR as the ideal starting point for this chapter, including the treatment that the subject is being given in practice and its recurrence in Brazilian courts.

From a formal point of view, consumers with bad credit ratings (in Portuguese, *negativadas* or *negativados*) suffer restrictions in the credit market and, in the case of identity theft, may suffer civil lawsuits for debts they did not contract, or even undue criminal persecutions. Informally, these people are subject to discrimination in their workplaces, vexatious situations in stores, direct or indirect offenses to their honor and reputation, and even instability in their family structure.[11] In face of these formal and informal losses, Brazilian case law was settled to allow compensation over pecuniary losses (*indenização*) as well as over unduly reported consumers' nonpecuniary losses (in this case, *compensação*). A few years ago, the Superior Court of Justice (Superior Tribunal de Justiça or STJ) allowed for pain-and-suffering damages compensability *in re ipsa* (being sufficient to demonstrate the occurrence of the wrongdoing), ruling out the demand for *probationes diabolicae* (evidence almost impossible to produce) over it.[12] Initially regarded with mistrust, then with excitement, and finally with a mixture of contempt and lack of control, pain-and-suffering damages have thus become inseparable from UCR cases.

Articles about the adverse effects of UCR have become increasingly popular in newspapers, whether these effects are real, like the fact that credit is becoming even more expensive,[13] or illusory, like the creation of a "pain-and-suffering damages industry." Internet websites gather hundreds of complaints from unduly reported individuals, sometimes contributing to consumer's rights defense, and sometimes merely exposing empty complains. In the beginning of 2012, a gang that claimed pain-and-suffering damages on behalf of credit reported individuals was torn apart by the Rio de Janeiro Federal Police, and the news was promptly spread by mass media. Are these worries justified?

Between 2010 and 2011, a group of researchers led by Flávia Portella Püschel conducted broad research about pain-and-suffering damages adjudication in Brazil under the project *Pensando o direito* (Thinking about law), funded by the Brazilian Ministry of Justice. More than a thousand judicial decisions of the Federal, State, and Labor Courts were analyzed by Püschel's group. The results were published in the report *A quantificação do dano moral no Brasil: justiça, segurança e eficiência* (Quantifying pain-and-suffering damages in Brazil: justice, predictability and efficiency). The research's aim was to outline the actual dimension of the certainty or predictability stemming from an alleged volatility in the pain-and-suffering damages awards ruled by Brazilian courts (figure 10.1).[14]

One of the most noteworthy data raised in the Püschel group's report indicates how many cases involving UCR (and, to a lesser degree, phantom debt collections) there were in proportion to the total amount of cases that dealt with pain-and-suffering damages. The largest source of pain-and-suffering damages in the State Justice (considering almost every federated state) are definitely UCR (51 percent). The same happens in the Federal Justice (49 percent). These data are even more alarming due to the fact that they refer only to matters taken to the Courts of Appeals. Many companies, common litigants (in Marc Galanter's famous words, "repeat players"), may be strategically deciding not to appeal against some of their convictions, selecting only the cases in which they are more likely to succeed.[15]

When we focus on the São Paulo Court of Justice, it is impressive to see not only the large number of cases involving UCR, but also the increase in these cases over the past years. Between 2010 and 2011, the number of cases taken to this court has almost doubled, going from scarcely less than 7,000 to over 12,000.[16] What we are seeing here is a boom of the number of cases of UCR in São Paulo—a proliferation that, it is reasonable to believe, does not belong to a phenomenon neither geographically nor temporally confined.

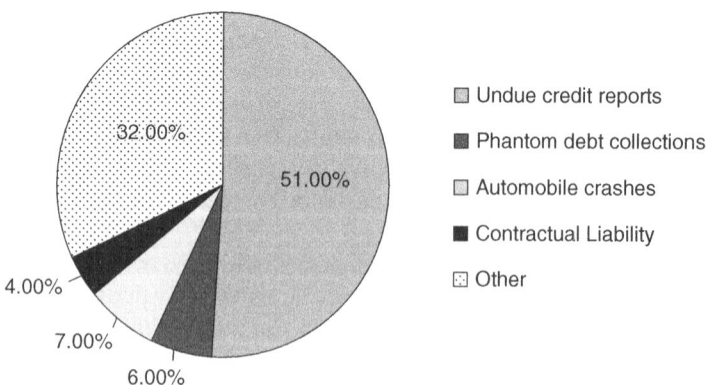

Figure 10.1   Cases involving pain-and-suffering damages in Brazil's State Courts of Appeals.

How Do Judges and Lawyers Think?

If the only problem caused by the increasing number of UCR cases was the amount of time it consumes from judges and clerks, the solution would be simple: either to hire more judges and clerks, and in so doing increasing the "supply" of jurisdiction, or by ruling the cases after grouping them, exploiting economies of scale.[17] Nonetheless, the UCR's boom is actually a symptom of much deeper problems that cannot be settled by growing the adjudication structure. These problems demand the establishment of a new adjudication pattern, a different way of thinking about these cases—an alternative doctrine.

Next, I will show the results of a qualitative empirical research conducted in the São Paulo Court of Appeals between March and June of 2012 and confront the results with two different lines of thinking, those of judges and their clerks (that do not necessarily possess a law degree) and those of the companies' lawyers. More than being simple common sense—and common sense is undoubtedly relevant when what is at stake is the interest of common people—these opinions have proven to be a significant indication of practical wisdom, the virtue that Aristotle called *phronēsis*, something that should not be confused with either knowledge (as if the only task of a judge were to assert how things in the world really are) or art (because to decide is more than to simply write a decision).[18]

An inquiry made on the judicial treatment of UCR was conducted with 36 officials of the São Paulo Court of Appeals: 6 judges, 16 clerks, and 14 technicians (a sort of clerk that does not necessarily have a law degree). Albeit a quite small group compared to the totality of officials that deal with cases of this sort (São Paulo Court of Appeals is the largest court in the world), the homogeneity of their answers suggests, at least for our modest purposes, that this sample suffices. All interviewees think the awards are excessively high. Twenty-three of them (including 2 judges) claim that reducing the "punitive" compensations would be a good solution. Thirteen (only 1 of them a judge) believe the compensations should be eliminated (some said the compensations should be either reduced or eliminated) (figure 10.2).

The first and most significant remark from the survey concerns the awards involved in the convictions. All of the participants believe the compensations offered to the victims of UCR to be excessively high. The second most common remark concerns the perceived need to reduce these awards. Reducing the compensations would certainly discourage those who seek the Court of Appeals expecting to gain

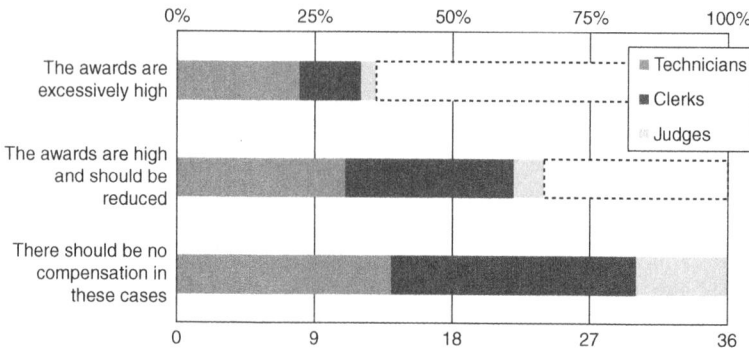

Figure 10.2 São Paulo Court of Appeals' judges, clerks and technician's opinions about UCR cases.

"easy money." On the other hand, the consequential reduced number of such cases would allow judges and their assistants "more time to deal with the matters of actual importance, such as family law," as one of them put it. Last, some of them suggested that compensations due to UCR cases should be put to an end. According to these officials, this act would be followed by the immediate elimination of "frivolous litigations," and in time would produce more satisfying results than the mere reduction of compensation awards.[19]

Those who suggested reducing the awards remarked that this solution could indirectly benefit the bureaus in charge of credit reports. To avoid this effect, they propose that when the compensation awards are reduced, a state's counterpart should be created in order to monitor illegal conduct. Though a reasonable proposal, its actualization would face many political difficulties, its maintenance costs would be high, and it would be overly dependent on state action. Two clerks and one judge suggested a solution quite similar to the one I shall defend in this chapter (for the sake of its transparency): that the difference between the pain-and-suffering damages award and a sufficiently deterrent punishment should be allocated to third parties other than the victim of credit reporting. All three of them, however, state that such solution would require a legislative intervention.

Three lawyers working for companies liable for UCR were interviewed.[20] Two of them are partners in a law firm; the third is the leader in the law department from a big enterprise. The latter has worked on roughly 2,500 cases of UCR; the former two together have tended to roughly 500 cases on the subject, involving five different defendants. Thus, they all sponsor defendants involved in virtually identical cases (the aforementioned "repeat players") that litigate over time against different plaintiffs—and who only sporadically go to the Courts (and are hence referred to as "one shooters" by Galanter).[21]

Since about 40 percent of all cases seemed to involve some sort of identity theft, the lawyers claimed that the companies should be considered the "true victims."[22] They all regarded UCR demands to be "unwanted costs" to the companies they defend. Pragmatically, they maintained that two measures could be taken to reduce these costs: strengthening bureaucracy for contracting (for instance, demanding certifications of signature or proof of income) or investing in technology (for instance, developing software capable of comparing handwritings). One of them had yet another suggestion: a controlling network of information between selling companies, enabling them to check occasional disparities between customers' registrations.[23]

The company lawyer made some interesting remarks. In his experience, approximately 60 percent of all cases end in an agreement between the parties. When the case is taken to court, the decision hardly ever favors the defendant: nine out of ten are ruled in favor of the plaintiffs. From the company's point of view, UCR poses not only a risk of legal fees and charges—though that is definitely the most relevant factor, with costs approximately 20 million reais (about 10 million dollars) for the first half of 2012—but may also lead to less obvious losses. For instance, in 2011, a CEO was charged with disobedience (Criminal Code, art. 330). The deputy in charge of the case commanded that the unduly reported consumer's registration be produced, but it had been lost among company's files; this led to the CEO's indictment. In another case explained by the interviewed lawyer, a newspaper article suggested that the company was involved in criminal practices, which caused an immediate and significant decrease in its stocks' value of nearly 10 percent.

But the conversations went beyond anecdotal cases. When legal reasoning is concerned, the lawyers shared the belief that guilt plays an important role in the measurement of compensations. All of them noted that "imperceptible" identity thefts (derived, for instance, from slightly different signatures) usually lead to lower awards. One of them stipulated that awards granted in cases in which the identity theft is obvious are in average 50 percent superior to awards granted in cases in which the identity theft goes unnoticed. Under this perception, the interviewees defended the argument—which is technically wrong, as I shall explain momentarily—that strict liability, usually described as a regimen in which "guilt is irrelevant," would be unsuited to cases of UCR, in which guilt supposedly plays an indisputable role.

It is worth mentioning the lawyers' reasonableness (despite, of course, this somewhat impressionist approach). None of them claimed that pain-and-suffering damages awards due to UCR are abusive or technically undue. None of them proposed the awards should be drastically reduced. None of them mentioned the infamous "pain-and-suffering damages industry." On the contrary, when asked about the number of cases in which the consumer would profit from the company's mistakes, they unanimously answered that these are an exception. A pain-and-suffering damages industry may exist, of course, but the UCR cases would not be its raw material.[24]

Two Myths and the First Signs of an Alternative Doctrine

Two main premises sustain the aforementioned proposals for reducing (or even eliminating) compensation awards. The first maintains that there exists a "pain-and-suffering damages industry" in Brazil, that is, several stimuli to those who, knowingly without legal grounds, seek high compensations for inexistent or insignificant nonpecuniary damages. The second premise is that consumers regard nonpecuniary damages stemming from UCR cases as a positive or beneficial eventuality, something that, albeit intrinsically negative, "is worth the trouble," a true "stroke of good luck." In this case, the premises are codependent: due to the "pain-and-suffering damages industry," arguably ever more unduly reported individuals would be gaining compensation awards incompatible to their actual losses, encouraging a positive understanding of something that should be regarded as a negative occurrence. At the same time, itchy-palm consumers, eager for allegedly handsome awards, would be multiplying demands, resulting in the explosion of disproportionate compensation awards. Is it really so?

In Brazil, the notion that compensation awards granted by the courts are excessively high is fairly common. This is largely due to selective importing of yellow press news on pathological condemnation in the United States, which results in the belief in the existence of a "pain-and-suffering damages industry."[25] The data gathered by Püschel and her team, however, show that pain-and-suffering damages awards granted by Brazilian courts are systematically low. In the Courts of Appeals, 41 percent of the victims were granted less than R$5,000; only 9 percent were granted awards of R$25,000 or more; and as few as 2 percent of wrongdoers were condemned to pay more than R$100,000. The researchers pointed out that "one must conclude that the absence of legal criteria to calculate the pain-and-suffering damages awards has not led to the dreaded situation of condemnations worth millions in compensation awards."[26] In other words, there is no sign of the infamous "industry."

Furthermore, the perceived need to fight the supposed pain-and-suffering damages industry is incompatible even with the punitive function attributed to pain-and-suffering damages. As Püschel and her team noticed, "Unlike what is commonly believed, the criticism that could be directed against courts of appeal is that the awards granted are excessively low, particularly if their aim is to punish as well as compensate, which is a well-accepted aspect of pain-and-suffering damages in courts."[27] This means that discourses legitimizing punishments actually work the other way around, in fact limiting them. This paradox is not restricted to UCR cases, and currently pervades the entire field of tort law.

The inquiry made in the São Paulo Court of Appeals corroborates the conclusions of Püschel's group. Indeed, there seems to be a contradiction between acknowledging that tort law should include punitive mechanisms and affirming that compensation awards are excessively high. This paradox is the result of a lack of theoretic distinction between pain-and-suffering damages and punitive damages, concepts mingled by Brazilian doctrine and case law. Judges and clerks are right to believe the awards should be reduced in some cases, but that would only be advisable if they were typified as being exclusively compensation.

Could it be that granting huge awards to some individuals turns litigation into a welcome event for their victims? In 2010, a judge from the São Paulo Court of Appeals claimed that "mass media publishes news on millionaire awards granted by judges both in and outside the country to alleged pain-and-suffering damages cases, which leads people to believe they might gain significant awards over events that, far from configuring pain-and-suffering damages, are little more than upsets."[28] This could be the case, but when it comes to UCR cases, one should evaluate this claim more carefully. First, the "pain-and-suffering damages industry" is, as mentioned, an exaggerated idea. Second, UCR's victims do not go to courts expecting only to gain a handsome award, which may well be quite reasonable if proportionate to the actual dimension of nonpecuniary losses suffered by them; their main motivation is to "clean their names," that is, to recover their good credit history. Ordinarily, the complaint in an undue credit report case involves at least two claims. One, the removal or undoing of the registration reporting the nonexistent, overdue, or alien debt; two, compensation for occasional harms done to the victim's assets, personality, family situation, reputation, psychological integrity, and so forth.[29]

Let us imagine a scenario in which UCR would not be compensated with pain-and-suffering damages awards, as some of the interviewees have suggested. Would it disengage greedy consumers from litigating? Taking into account the aforementioned claim to remove or undo the registration regarding the nonexistent, overdue, or alien debt, it would not. But let us assume, for the sake of argument, that it might. In this case, the consumers' names would remain in the report, engorging the demand for a "credit reports market"—a market fed by promises of "quick and easy money" in "24 hours" with "no proof of income needed" and "without consulting SPC or Serasa," as a well-known Brazilian company advertises.

It is true that reducing the awards makes sense in specific cases. To do so, however, it is mandatory to separate compensatory and punitive functions of liability, granting the latter its own structure, taking into account what judges actually do when deciding UCR cases (and they think they are doing). In the next section, I'll discuss this further.

The Distinction between Punitive and Pain-and-Suffering Damages

Punitive Damages: Reasons and Restrictions

Punitive damages (and related mechanisms like what I have been calling *punições civis*) are a matter of private law in general and tort law in particular. I would like to start by discussing two different lines of thought related to these two fields. The first concerns the decriminalization of private law; the second, the incompatibility between punishment and strict liability.

Those who reject the applicability of mechanisms like punitive damages in Brazil frequently argue that the idea of punishment is incompatible with private law regulation. Anderson Schreiber, for instance, maintains that admitting punitive damages would be a violation to the dichotomy between civil law and criminal law, going against the "foundations of the Brazilian legal system."[30] This argument is supposed to have a constitutional basis: it claims that, without a *specific legislative authorization*, applying the punishments would go against Article 5, XXXIX in the Constitution, according to which "there is no crime without a previous law that defines it, nor punishment without statutory grounds."

Nevertheless, this disposition is explicitly and unmistakably restricted to *crimes*, which are a *species* of illegal practice, not its very *genus*. The discussion is not about separating civil law punishments from criminal law punishments, nor even private law punishments from public law punishments.[31] The point is to distinguish a continence relationship (crimes are species of illegal practices) from a false equivalence relationship (crimes are the only sort of illegal practice). Article 5, XXXIX in the Constitution is on the species (punishments for crimes) not on the genus (punishments for illegal practices in general).

Another argument against the application of punitive damages in Brazil cites Article 5°, LVII, also in the Constitution, according to which "nobody shall be considered guilty before the establishment of a criminal *res judicata*" (or judgment). This reference is erroneous as well. There are no strict boundaries between the contents of criminal and civil (or common) law. If there ever was some truth to such strict distinction, nowadays it is nothing more than a propaedeutic resource. Current criminal law deals with matters traditionally regarded as civil; and civil law with traditionally criminal matters. Besides, restricting punishments to criminal courts would not be compatible with the application of a series of mechanisms inherent to civil law, from penalty clauses to the exclusion of homicidal heirs from the victim's will.[32]

In Brazil, punitive damages are frequently claimed to be incompatible with strict liability. At least three arguments are cited to corroborate this claim. First, unlike negligence, in which the level of fault may be used to proportionately reduce compensation awards (according to the Brazilian Civil Code, article 944), strict liability inexorably promotes full reparation, forbidding any condemnation to supplementary awards (in order to avoid overdeterrence).[33] Second, applying punitive damages requires a particularly severe harm, and the liability for this could not, by definition, be considered under the regime of strict liability.[34] The third argument, a broader one, is that punitive damages are incompatible with the private (and consequently tort) law scopes. This final argument has already been refuted in the earlier section. Now I shall examine the others.

Let's start with the argument of full reparation. It is true that strict liability theoretically provides full compensation for injuries and losses; however, that is not the point with punitive damages. These awards' aim is to prevent wrongdoings, censured not only because of the dimension of the losses they cause. Even if punitive damages awards were granted directly to the victims, these awards still could not be strictly considered compensatory (even though they might be regarded as such in practice, as it happens in punitive pain-and-suffering damages). It is true that the undue application of punitive damages may imply overdeterrence. However, this can also happen due to disproportional pain-and-suffering damages, or may not be achieved even in the presence of costly punishments.

The second argument relates the irrelevance of fault in the field of strict liability to the requirement of the same fault in the field of punitive damages. The problem, here, is mixing the two functions that fault has in the field of civil liability.[35] By saying that someone is guilty of some harm under strict liability, we mean simply that this harm's occurence can be attributed to someone. Little does it matter whether the agent intended to do it or not. In this case, guilt is the consequence of the liability's ascription.[36] On the other hand, when we say a punishment should be reduced for lack of willful misconduct or gross negligence, the issue ceases to be about ascription and becomes a matter of calculating the sanction. In this case, the aim is to modulate the consequences of wrongdoings from how censurable they are. Once the ascription is given, one must evaluate the appropriate punishment according to the wrongdoer's conduct.

Regulating punições civis in Brazil

Every translation involves a choice among several communicative possibilities. This holds true not only to literature, but also to the transplant—the micro-transplant, to use Graziadei's precise expression—of legal doctrines and concepts.[37] That is why Montesquieu noted, even in the eighteenth century, that only by chance would the same civil law rules produce the same results in different societies.[38] The term *punições civis* means more than a mere translation from punitive damages to Brazilian doctrine, even if the American concept is its basis. This requires a clearer outline of its discipline, especially of the aspects in which it differs from its northern congener.

There would seem to be no place in Brazil for a culture as profoundly libertarian—that is, a culture that holds freedom as the most important device for promoting equality—as the one that defines a significant portion of the political spectrum in the United States.[39] In spite of that, over the past few years the law of torts has proven to be propitious for consolidating a point of view closely related to the libertarian culture, in which the punitive function of tort awards should be accomplished by estimating a "total damage," thus eliminating all other kinds of sanctions not based on the idea of retrospectively repairing an undue harm.[40]

There are reasons particular to Brazil that lead to such an understanding. By the end of the 1980s, the well-known lawyer and professor

Orlando Gomes identified a shift of focus in Brazilian doctrine, drifting away from wrongdoings toward victims' repair, a phenomenon he called "conceptual twist."[41] This phenomenon was reinforced by the promulgation of the Consumer Defense Code (1990) and the new Civil Code (2002), both of which regulated several strict liability hypotheses, and established the framework for the consolidation of the idea (rhetorically transformed in a principle) of *full reparation*, which is nowadays an inherent part of Brazilian forensic vocabulary and is considered a path toward an "effective solidarity" and the long-awaited "constitutionalization of private law."

This point of view has quickly become, so to speak, "official." The 46th statement of the *I Jornada de Direito Civil do Conselho da Justiça Federal* (a traditional seminar organized by Brazil's Federal Justice Council), which took place on September 2002, states that "the possibility of reducing the awards' sum due to the agent's guilt, established in the [aforementioned] art. 944, par. un. in the Brazilian Civil Code, should be interpreted restrictively, because it represents an exception to the principle of the damages' full reparation." In this scenario, regulating wrongdoings would be seen as a "crusade against the illicit,"[42] and the division between damages and wrongdoings would be described, rather curiously, as an "artificial and historical fragmentation between the victim's right and the wrongdoer's duty."[43]

Unlike what one might believe, however—in a classic example of the paradox of unintended consequences—the discourse on full reparation did not lead to a more effective prevention against wrongdoings. On the contrary, it started to restrict condemnations to more singular and punctual losses, losses that do not always correspond to the benefits gained from the wrongdoer. In this scenario, the punitive function of civil liability has become a hostage to pain-and-suffering damages.

From a procedural perspective, the most obvious difference between *punições civis* and punitive damages concerns those who define the awards. In the United States and in England, it is up to a jury to determine the sum of awards granted as punishment. The members of the juries are selected in a process similar to the one adopted in Brazil, and receive some instructions from the judge before deliberating in secret over the punitive damages' award. The whole process aggravates a series of behavioral susceptibilities, especially those that lead to an increase in the compensation awards' sum.[44] This problem incidentally contributes to the historical perception that American courts do not have much control over the application of punitive damages.[45]

A second difference concerns the destination of the *punições civis*. In the American system, the punitive damages' recipient is generally the victim. In Brazil, even though the *punições civis* would be regarded as a distribution mechanism, it could not be denied that granting the victims the full amount might have caused significant distributive distortions. In any case, to preserve the due legal process and obey the "congruence rule," avoiding decisions that are *ultra* or *extra petita* (articles 128 and 460 from the Brazilian Civil Process Code), it is required that the awards be very clearly and specifically stipulated (some exceptions apply in the case of pain-and-suffering damages). In the end, it is a compromise between the plaintiffs' interests and the defendants' pecuniary security.

Correcting Distributive Distortions

The most common argument in Brazilian courts against the use of mechanisms related to punitive damages (or, more frequently, against the punitive function of pain-and-suffering damages) is the unjust enrichment these awards could bring the victims. It is argued that, if a "deterrence function" of liability can be employed as a healthy means of regulating conducts, it could also lead to pathological unduly pecuniary transmissions.[46]

An implicit assumption in this assessment is that tort law grounds are exclusively *corrective* or *commutative*.[47] This idea is not new: correcting unbalanced exchanges (whether voluntary or involuntary) should be a primary concern in private law according to the late Scholastics. In effect, the configuration of private justice is one of the most debated subjects in the works of law scholars like Domingo de Soto (1494–1560), Luis de Molina (1535–1600), and Leonard Lessius (1564–1623), who applied Aristotle's ethics (mainly through Aquinas's readings) to the Roman jurisprudence, establishing the grounds of the modern private law in general and modern law of torts in particular.[48] Here, I want to relate this assumption to the regulation of the field of unjust enrichment in Brazil.[49]

First, it is necessary to distinguish unjust enrichment as an autonomous institution, regulated in article 884 of the 2002 Civil Code,[50] from the value or principle related to the justification of pecuniary gains in general.[51] When contrasting punitive damages to unjust enrichment, what is at stake is not the institution regulated by the Civil Code, but rather the principle that forbids unjust pecuniary gains (even the causal ones). However, as the decision mentioned in the beginning of this section shows, courts are confusing these two meanings, using indiscriminately systematic and restricted justifications to deny "distributive surpluses" to the victims.

Few authors have been able so far to overcome the narrowness of the commutative understating. It is not to be forgotten that there is nothing wrong with the idea of commutative or corrective justice; the point is rather to recognize the development of structures that requires the local prevalence of distributive reasoning where commutative reasoning used to suffice. The late University of São Paulo professor Antônio Junqueira de Azevedo was the first to propose an alternative to this traditional understanding in Brazil. While dealing with what he called "social damages," Junqueira observed that the notion of punishment required further reflection, and that even awards that did not correspond to the victim's perceived damages could, according to some criteria, be granted to them, "because," as he would say, "the victim is the one that actually worked to gain the compensation. The worker earns the paycheck."[52]

This is not an absurd proposition, yet it becomes riskier as the consequences of wrongdoings become less obvious. In cases of lucrative illegality, for instance, notably those very likely to go unnoticed, offering the total sum of the punishment to the individual plaintiffs could result in a significant distributive distortion. The same goes for micro-losses (injuries or losses, generally slight, caused to a large number of victims) and exceptionally severe harms (like human rights violations). If there is indeed value in granting the author an award superior to what her or his losses are worth, it is definitely trickier to explain offering extremely high awards to a single person while depriving those who did not go to the courts.[53] In Brazil, some authors have come up with solutions that, despite sometimes lacking a clear distinction between compensations and deterrence of wrongdoing, would allow for the correction of distributive distortions caused by granting the full amount of punishment awards to victims.[54]

Article 883 of the Civil Code reads that "those who have given anything to obtain an illicit, immoral or legally prohibited end" shall have no right to the recovery of undue payments (*repetitio indebiti*). Following this, in the sole paragraph of the same article, it is stated that "what was given shall be reverted in favor of a local charity establishment, to be decided by the judge." Applying this statement to the discipline of punitive damages by analogy poses obvious advantages— the most interesting of which is reducing the distortions caused by a "winner takes all" model—but it also faces significant obstacles. Even though it does not seem entirely wrong to assume that the wrongdoer subject to the *punições* might be regarded as one of those who give something to achieve an "illicit, immoral or law-forbidden end," one cannot deny that this interpretation requires a controversial use of the article.

Fortunately, this is not the only way to avoid the distributive distortions potentially brought by *punições civis*. It is possible to think of an alternative solution that is also immediately enforceable, with the advantage of being free from any controversial stretch of meaning or analogy. It involves a set of federal statutory provisions that authorize the deliverance of the difference between punishments and compensations to the Common Rights Defense Fund, a public account established under the Ministry of Justice to compensate for damages caused to the environment, the cultural heritage, the economic order, and other common and collective interests.[55] The advantage this solution brings is the congruence between the fund's scope, destined to repairing damages caused by consumers due to violation of collective interest, and the collective nature (ex post) of punitive damages, whose aim is to conform wrongdoers to socially adequate (or less inappropriate) conduct.

Conclusion

In his *Manual de zoología fantástica* (Handbook of fantastic zoology), written in 1957 and then republished in expanded form in 1967 as *El libro de los seres imaginarios* (The book of imaginary beings), Jorge Luis Borges describes the "heavy amphisbaena," a kind of "two-headed" serpent that lives in the Antilles and that in some regions in America is called "double walker." In Greek, Borges tells us, *amphisbaena* appropriately means "what goes in two directions." Like Borges's beast, punitive pain-and-suffering damages also go in two ways: they aim to compensate as well as to ground punishments. Nowadays, they represent the most common criterion used by Brazilian courts in deciding on UCR cases; hence, it is the paradigmatic model of dealing with nonpecuniary losses in Brazil.

In this context, controversies involving exceptionally severe harms, microlosses, or lucrative illegality—of which UCR cases are the most significant example—reveal a profound deadlock. Either a punitive nature is attributed to pain-and-suffering damages awards (as the majority of Brazilian scholars and judges suggest) or all traces of punishment are eliminated from the law of torts (as defended by a few isolated scholars, ever more rare). In the first case, the pain-and-suffering damages would be subject to limitations alien to their nature by taking the wrongdoing as the parameter for measuring awards, instead of the harm actually inflicted; in the second case, punishments would simply vanish. In both cases, the adjudication of liability would be subject to an exclusively commutative and retrospective account, as if the world we had before any injury or loss was the best possible world.

The aim of this chapter was to demonstrate that, besides these two positions, there is a third, transparent, and prospective way, one that is already suggested by some prudent judges and clerks (though without the legal grounds I seek to offer in this chapter), and which seems to be the only way actually able to promote the defense of Brazilian consumers against financial abuses. All the caution is understandable: the idea of autonomous *punições civis* still lacks doctrinaire support. Here I argued that these references may come from the American punitive damages but should not stop there. Brazilian *punições civis* require a peculiar normative framework, adapted to the country's legal culture and to its officials understanding of law. Without it, different aims would continue to go indiscriminately side-by-side in decisions whose compensatory mechanisms are justified on punitive grounds.

In the end, it comes down to granting structural autonomy to an already recognized punitive function of liability: a function that furtively entered Brazilian courts and is still shyly applied, but whose results have been the opposite of what judges expected. This is the beginning of a long path toward a better tort law, and this journey requires continued empirical criticism and doctrinaire experimentation. The boom in UCR cases suggests its first step cannot wait.[56]

Notes

1. See O'Connell and Carpenter, "Payment for Pain and Suffering through History," 413: "In 1851, a New York trial court judge specifically rejected the defense argument that recovery for pain and suffering was tantamount to punitive damages, and that recovery for pain and suffering, like punitive damages, should be restricted to cases involving intentional wrongdoing. The court stated that recovery for pain and suffering was compensatory, like damages for loss of time and money, and treated compensation for pain and suffering as a settled issue."

2. Chapman and Trebilcock, "Punitive Damages," 768–769.

3. In the European context, see Jansen and Rademacher, "Punitive Damages in Germany," 77–78 (reporting the confusion between *Schmerzengeld* and a poorly defined notion *punitive damages* that persists in German case law), as well as the similar reports on France, Hungary, Italy, Scandinavia, and Spain in the same book.

4. For example, Amaral, *Direito Civil: Introdução*, 544; Silva, *O dano moral e a sua reparação civil*, 177; and Freitas Filho and Lima,

"Indenização por dano extrapatrimonial com função punitiva no direito do consumidor."

5. Paradigmatic cases are STJ, AgRg/Ag 1259457/RJ (13.04.2010); and REsp 487.749/RS (19.08.2003). For further references, see REsp 355.392/RJ (26.03.2002); and REsp 663.196/PR (14.12.2004). This does not mean, however, that the allegedly punitive condemnations are being sufficiently deterrent, as discussed in Fortes, "The Phenomenon of Lucrative Illegality."

6. For example, Theodoro Júnior, *Dano moral*, 59–62; Zavascki, *Processo coletivo*, 40–41; and Schreiber, *Novos paradigmas*, 203–204.

7. On this compensatory paradigm, see Villey, "Esquisse historique," 45–58 (discussing the origins of the word "liable"); and Ricoeur, "Concept de responsabilité," 48–52 (developing a conceptual history of the word "liability"); a monographic presentation of the matter may be found in Brazilian Superior Court of Justice's judge Sanseverino's book, *Princípio da reparação integral*.

8. Even though pain-and-suffering damages are not this chapter's primary concern, it is worth mentioning that here they are not to be understood as a natural result of a loss or injury, but rather as the legal assessment of their nonpecuniary consequences. *To suffer* pain-and-suffering damages (as Brazilian jurists frequently say) shall thus mean to suffer a loss or injury whose effects may be legally qualified as pain-and-suffering. Likewise, *to demand* pain-and-suffering damages does not mean to claim for direct reparation after a loss or injury, but to claim for a sum that corresponds to the pecuniary transposition of nonpecuniary losses. The loss or injury is one thing; their consequences, another; and another yet is their compensation. Pain-and-suffering, therefore, shall not be the loss or injury, nor the award granted for it, but the damages that bond them. On that, see Marino, "Perdas e danos," 654–657; and Azevedo, "Cadastros de restrição ao crédito," 291–292.

9. The main point of reference here is Polinsky and Shavell, "Punitive Damages," 954: "Punitive damages should be set at a level such that the expected damages of defendants equal the harm they have caused, for then their damage payments will, in an average sense, equal the harm...We also discussed a deterrence rationale for punitive damages that is not based on the possibility of escaping liability: that punitive damages may be needed to offset the socially illicit utility that individuals obtain from committing malicious acts. This rationale, as we noted, does not apply to firms."

10. See Smith, *Contract Theory*, 24–32. I do not believe that transparency should always be measured by judge's reasons for action. In situations that do not involve opposing or conflicting interests, transparency may be founded on the reasons for contractual or regulatory action.

11. Take, for example, TJ-SP, Apelação 7.031.795–4/Bauru (19.10.2006), a case in which the author alleges to have lost his job *and his wife* due

to the report. On this, see Lopucki, "Human Identification Theory and the Identity Theft Problem," 89 (reporting that identity theft is one of the fastest growing economic crimes in the United States, and that in the beginning of the twenty-first century, there were still no effective defenses against this phenomenon in the American consumer's credit system).

12. Rather adversely, however, this reasonable orientation led to a significant and at times undue enlargement of pain-and-suffering damages hypotheses. See recently (and reporting older precedents) STJ, AgRg/REsp 957.880/SP (06.03.2012). Besides, the simple lack of communication regarding the credit report is enough to ground pain-and-suffering damages. The statutory basis, in this case, is the art. 43, §2°, of the Brazilian Consumer Protection Code. Cf. STJ, REsp 992.168/RS (11.12.2007), as well as the Súmula 359 of STJ.

13. Even here the causal relation is not that clear. See the related discussion among Arida, Bacha, and Lara-Resende, "Credit, Interest, and Jurisdictional Uncertainty"; Ferrão and Ribeiro, "Os Juízes Brasileiros Favorecem a Parte Mais Fraca?"; and Falcão, Schuartz, and Arguelhes, "Jurisdição, incerteza e Estado de Direito."

14. Püschell et al., "Resultados do levantamento jurisprudencial," 30. There is an interesting literature about the relationship (or the boundaries) between the notions of certainty and predictability, but this goes beyond the scope of this chapter. For a bird's eye view, see Falcão, Schuartz, and Arguelhes, "Jurisdição, incerteza e Estado de Direito."

15. Galanter, "Why the 'Haves' Come Out Ahead" (strategically selected cases may eventually form a favorable case law).

16. Further details on this data are discussed in a broader version of this study, Silva Filho, *Danos morais e punições civis.*

17. It is also worth mentioning that without an adequate procedural routine, such economies of scale could make the decisions subject to deeply undesirable heuristics (as described in Kahneman, *Thinking Fast and Slow*, 43–44). For a specific application, see Sunstein, Schkade, and Kahneman, "Do People Want Optimal Deterrence?"

18. Aristotle, *Nicomachean Ethics*, book VI.

19. The expression "frivolous litigation" was coined by Moraes, "Punitive Damages em Sistemas Civilistas," 76.

20. The interviews were conducted in March 2012 and were purposely informal and methodologically open and unstructured. Albeit less rigorous, this option allows for gathering a broader and unexpected range of data, appropriate to the research's incipiency at the time. This idea was taken from Fontana and Frey, "The Interview," 645–646.

21. Galanter, "Why the 'Haves' Come Out Ahead," 97–107.

22. From January to September 2012, Serasa Experian uncovered 1.56 million attempts to identity theft involving RGs e CPFs, a third of which involved contracts for mobile telephone services. See http://folha.com/no1182808.

23. This could, however, result in severe violation to consumers' privacy. According to the interviewee, the entries would refer exclusively to the consumer's pecuniary rights (in Portuguese, *direitos patrimoniais*) without any assumptions regarding his or her personality. Nevertheless, the matter is more complex than that. Whereas it is known that the consumer's pecuniary situation does indeed involve—and in this case, this is paramount—his or her privacy, it is also true that injuries against the pecuniary rights may lead to nonpecuniary losses. See Falzea, "Fatto di sentimento," 461.

24. We must consider the possibility that their openness might have been affected by my own position: an interview aiming to evaluate, from an academic point of view, the opinion of individuals who face victims of UCR would certainly mitigate their words.

25. For example, Tepedino, "O Futuro da Responsabilidade Civil," 407 (warning against the risks of a "collapse of the system, a violence for economic activity and a stimulus to pecuniary engorgement").

26. Püschell et al., "Resultados do levantamento jurisprudencial," 67–69. The results obtained in the Courts of Appeals were also observed in the Federal and Labor Courts.

27. Ibid., 69.

28. TJ-SP, Ap. 994.05.100903–0/São Paulo (04.20.2010).

29. Sometimes the petition contains three claims; the third is a declaration of the debt's nonexistence or expiration is also claimed for. If not, the name could theoretically be reported once again.

30. Schreiber, "Arbitramento do dano moral no Código Civil," 14; for a similar argument, Theodoro Júnior, *Dano moral*, 62. In contrast, see Dias, *Da responsabilidade civil* I, 11–14.

31. As indicated, for instance, in Serpa, *Indenização Punitiva*, 218–219.

32. A matter of statutory regulation in civil law countries (e.g., Brazilian Civil Code, art. 1.418, I), this hypothesis was famously discussed in the United States in the case *Riggs v. Palmer*, 115 N.Y. 506 (1889). Much later, Dworkin applied the reasoning developed in this decision to his argument for legal principles in his "The Model of Rules."

33. Levy, *Responsabilidade civil*, 117.

34. See Martins-Costa and Pargendler, "Usos e abusos da função punitiva," 24.

35. On this, see Calixto, *A culpa na responsabilidade civil*, 299.

36. See Hart, "The Ascription of Responsibility and Rights."

37. Graziadei, "Legal Transplants," 704–710. See also Sacco, "Legal Formants"; and Mattei, *Comparative Law and Economics*, 223.

38. Montesquieu, *De l'esprit des lois*, 26–30.

39. For an overview on this scenario, see Kymlicka, *Contemporary Political Philosophy*, 102–165. For the roots of Brazilian political culture, see Carvalho, *A construção da ordem* (for the Imperial period); and Faoro, *Os donos do poder* (tracing the root of the Republican bureaucratic structure to the Colonial period).

40. In this case, an estimation of losses effectively caused would be the *only* criterion in defining the adequate punishments, including the cases that were not taken to the courts. Thus, for instance, if the odds of noticing $100,000 worth of damage were 25percent, the condemnation should involve $400,000 (sum equivalent to the "full reparation" in case all cases were noticed). The responsibility cannot exceed effectively and actually occurred damages (though approximately calculated), except, according to some authors, in cases of unmistakable malice of the agent responsible for the dangerous activity. See Polinsky and Shavell, "Punitive Damages," 875–876.

41. Gomes, "Tendências modernas," 296; for the American context, see Galanter, "Punishment," 764.

42. Theodoro Júnior, *Dano moral*, 62.

43. Schreiber, *Novos paradigmas*, 185.

44. Viscusi, "Do Judges Do Better?," 186–210 (showing that *punitive damages* awards granted by members of a jury tend to be significantly higher than the average individually suggested sums prior to collective deliberation).

45. An exemplary case of reasonable common sense is reported in Silva, *O dano moral e a sua reparação*, 158. Many empirical studies on the application of *punitive damages* can be found in Sunstein et al, *Punitive Damages*.

46. STJ, REsp 401.358/PB (05.03.2009): "The unrestricted application of 'punitive damages' regulatory obstacle lies in the national legal system that, since before to the enactment of the 2002 Civil Code, forbade unjust enrichment as a principle of law, and then started prescribing it explicitly, more specifically, in art. 884 of the 2002 Civil Code." More recently, this argument was referred to in AgRg/Ag 850273/BA (03.08.2010).

47. It is true that granting unjustified awards to low-income victims may be regarded as a means of redistribution; here, however, I will restrict this notion to awards larger than the compensational amount (despite the difficulties in its assessment, especially when it comes to pain-and-suffering damages equivalents). The main points of reference here are Weinrib, *The Idea of Private Law*; and Gordley, *Foundations of Private Law*.

48. Gordley, *Foundations of Private Law*, 4–5; and "Tort Law in the Aristotelian Tradition," 131–158.

49. Strictly speaking, it is hard to talk about unjust enrichment as a field (of private law) in Brazil. Indeed, even in United States this characterization was born controversial: the first treaty on the subject would be published 50 years after the American Law Institute's *Restatement of Restitution* in Palmer, *The Law of Restitution* (1978), in four volumes; but see Dawson, "Restitution without Enrichment," 564 (suggesting that the field is a patchwork construction, whose parts are linked only by name).

50. Michelon, *Direito restituitório*, 178 (let us not forget that this case brings a positive advance that was already being contemplated by previous jurisprudence).
51. The word "principle," in this case, is closely related to the idea of *intelligibility criterion* or *common grounds* than to some sort of judicial norm. On the same subject, see Gordley, *Foundations of Private Law*, 7–14.
52. Azevedo, "Por uma nova categoria de dano na responsabilidade civil: o dano social," 217.
53. It is no coincidence that in the United States some scholars maintained that the image of a *private attorney general* would have resulted in some kind of "public contamination" for the field of punitive damages, masking its true (and reasonable) motivations inside private law (as seen in Zipursky, "Palsgraf, Punitive Damages, and Preemption").
54. For example, Melo, "Ainda sobre a função punitiva da reparação dos danos morais," 86.
55. I discuss the statutory details of this proposal in Silva Filho, *Danos morais e punições civis*.
56. Mark D. White, Bruno M. Salama, Sérgio Mendes Filho, and Pedro H. Butelli provided valuable criticism of earlier drafts.

Bibliography

Amaral, Francisco. *Direito Civil: Introdução*. 6th ed. Rio de Janeiro: Renovar, 2008.

Arida, Pérsio, Edmar Lisboa Bacha, and André Lara-Resende. "Credit, Interest, and Jurisdictional Uncertainty: Conjectures on the Case of Brazil." In *Inflation Targeting, Debt, and Brazilian Experience. 1999 to 2003*, edited by Francesco Giavazzi, Ilan Goldfajn, and Santiago Herrera, 265–293. Cambridge, MA: MIT Press, 2005.

Aristotle. *Nicomachean Ethics*. Trans. W. D. Ross. 350 BCE. Available at the Internet Classics Archvie, http://classics.mit.edu/Aristotle/nicomachaen.html.

Azevedo, Antônio Junqueira de. "Cadastros de restrição ao crédito. Conceito de dano moral" (2000). In *Estudos e Pareceres de Direito Privado*, 289–299. São Paulo: Saraiva, 2004.

———. "Por uma nova categoria de dano na responsabilidade civil: o dano social." *Revista Trimestral de Direito Civil* 19 (2004): 211–218.

Calixto, Marcelo Junqueira. *A culpa na responsabilidade civil: estrutura e função*. Rio de Janeiro: Renovar, 2008.

Carvalho, José Murilo de. *A construção da ordem: a elite política imperial*. Rio de Janeiro: Campus, 1980.

Chapman, Bruce, and Michael Trebilcock. "Punitive Damages: Divergence in Search of a Rationale." *Alabama Law Review* 40 (1989): 741–829.

Coelho, Francisco Manuel Pereira. *O enriquecimento e o dano*. Coimbra: Almedina, 1999.

Dawson, John P. "Restitution without Enrichment." *Boston University Law Review* 61 (1981): 563–622.

Dias, José de Aguiar. *Da responsabilidade civil*. Vol. I. Rio de Janeiro: Forense, 1944.

Dworkin, Ronald. "The Model of Rules." *University of Chicago Law Review* 35 (1967): 14–46.

Falcão, Joaquim, Luís Fernando Schuartz, and Diego Werneck Arguelhes. "Jurisdição, incerteza e Estado de Direito." *Revista de Direito Administrativo* 243 (2006): 79–112.

Falzea, Angelo. "Fatto di sentimento." In *Ricerche di teoria generale del diritto e di dogmatica giuridica: Dogmatica giuridica*. Vol. II., 435–450. Milano: Giuffrè, 1997.

Faoro, Raymundo. *Os donos do poder* (1958). 3rd ed. São Paulo: Globo, 2001.

Ferrão, Brisa Lopes de Mello, and Ivan César Ribeiro. "Os Juízes Brasileiros Favorecem a Parte Mais Fraca?" *Revista de Direito Administrativo* 244 (2007): 53–82.

Fontana, Andrea, and James H. Frey. "The Interview: From Structured Questions to Negotiated Text." In *Handbook of Qualitative Research*, edited by Norman K. Denzin and Yvonna S. Lincoln, 645–672. 2nd ed. London: Sage, 2000.

Fortes, Pedro Rubin Borges. "The Phenomenon of Lucrative Illegality: Understanding Why Brazilian Companies Constantly Break the Law." Working paper, 2012. Avaliable at http://www.law.harvard.edu/news/spotlight/ils/events/fortes-final.pdf.

Freitas Filho, Roberto, and Thalita Moraes Lima. "Indenização por dano extrapatrimonial com função punitiva no direito do consumidor." *Revista de Direito do Consumidor* 87 (2013): 93–122.

Galanter, Marc. "Punishment, Civil Style. Punishment Outside the Criminal Law in the Contemporary United States." *Israel Law Review* 25 (1991): 759–778.

———. "Why the 'Haves' Come Out Ahead: Speculations on the Limits of Legal Change." *Law and Society Review* 9 (1974): 95–151.

Gallo, Paolo. *L'arricchimento senza causa*. Padova: Cedam, 1990.

Gomes, Orlando. *"Tendências modernas na teoria da responsabilidade civil."* In José Roberto Pacheco Di Francesco. *Estudos em homenagem ao Professor Silvio Rodrigues*, 291–302. São Paulo: Saraiva, 1989.

Gordley, James. *Foundations of Private Law: Property, Tort, Contract, Unjust Enrichment*. Oxford: Oxford University Press, 2006.

———. "Tort Law in the Aristotelian Tradition." In *Philosophical Foundations of Tort Law*, edited by David G. Owen, 131–158. Oxford: Oxford University Press, 1995.

Graziadei, Michele. "Legal Transplants and the Frontiers of Legal Knowledge." *Theoretical Inquiries in Law* 10 (2009): 693–713.

Hart, H. L. A. "The Ascription of Responsibility and Rights." *Proceedings of the Aristotelian Society* 49 (1949): 171–194.

Jansen, Nils, and Lukas Rademacher. "Punitive Damages in Germany." In *Punitive Damages: Common Law and Civil Law Perspectives*, edited by Helmut Koziol and Vanessa Wilcox,75–86. Vienna: Springer, 2009.

Kahneman, Daniel. *Thinking Fast and Slow.* New York: Ferrar, Straus and Giroux, 2011.

Kymlicka, Will. *Contemporary Political Philosophy: An Introduction.* 2nd ed. Oxford: Oxford University Press, 2002.

Levy, Daniel de Andrade. *Responsabilidade civil: de um direito dos danos a um direito das condutas lesivas.* São Paulo: Atlas, 2012.

Lopucki, Lynn M. "Human Identification Theory and the Identity Theft Problem." *Texas Law Review* 80 (2001): 89–136.

Marino, Francisco Paulo De Crescenzo. "Perdas e danos." In *Obrigações*, edited by Renan Lotufo and Giovanni Ettore Nanni, 653–685. São Paulo: Atlas, 2011.

Martins-Costa, Judith Hofmeister, and, Mariana Souza Pargendler. "Usos e abusos da função punitiva (punitive damages e o Direito brasileiro)." *Revista Cej* 28 (2005): 15–32.

Mattei, Ugo. *Comparative Law and Economics.* Ann Arbor, MI: University of Michigan Press, 1997.

Melo, Diogo Leonardo Machado de. "Ainda sobre a função punitiva da reparação dos danos morais (e a destinação de parte da indenização para entidades de fins sociais—art. 883, parágrafo único do Código Civil)." *Revista de Direito Privado* 26 (2006): 105–145.

Michelon Jr., Cláudio. *Direito restituitório: enriquecimento sem causa. Pagamento indevido. Gestão de negócios.* São Paulo: Revista dos Tribunais, 2007.

Montesquieu, Charles-Louis de. *De l'esprit des lois.* Vol. 1. Paris: Gallimard, 1995 [1748].

Moraes, Maria Celina Bodin de. "Punitive damages em sistemas civilistas: problemas e perspectivas." *Revista trimestral de direito civil* 18 (2004): 45–78.

O'Connell, Jeffrey, and Keith Carpenter. "Payment for Pain and Suffering through History." *Insurance Counsel Journal* 50 (1983): 411–417.

Palmer, George E. *The Law of Restitution.* 4 vols. Boston: Little, Brown, and Co., 1978.

Polinsky, A. Mitchell, and Steven Shavell. "Punitive Damages: An Economic Analysis." *Harvard Law Review* 111 (1998): 869–962.

Püschel, Flávia Portella, et al. "Resultados do levantamento jurisprudencial." In *A quantificação do Dano Moral no Brasil* (2011): 30–99. Avaliable at http://portal.mj.gov.br/main.asp?View={329D6EB2-8AB0-4606-B054-4CAD3C53EE73}.

Ricoeur, Paul. "Concept de responsabilité: essai d'analyse sémantique." In *Le juste*, 41–70. Paris: Esprit, 1995.

Sacco, Rodolfo. *L'arrichimento ottenuto mediante fatto ingiusto.* Torino: Utet, 1959.

———. "Legal Formants: A Dynamic Approach to Comparative Law." *American Journal of Comparative Law* 39 (1991): 1–34.

Sanseverino, Paulo de Tarso Vieira. *Princípio da reparação integral*. São Paulo: Saraiva, 2010.

Schreiber, Anderson. "Arbitramento do dano moral no Código Civil." *Revista Trimestral de Direito Civil* 12 (2003): 3–24.

———. *Novos paradigmas da responsabilidade civil: da erosão dos filtros da reparação à diluição dos danos* (2007). 2ª ed. São Paulo: Atlas, 2009.

Serpa, Pedro Ricardo e. *Indenização Punitiva*. Dissertação de mestrado apresentada à Faculdade de Direito da Universidade de São Paulo, 2011.

Silva, Wilson de Melo da. *O dano moral e a sua reparação* (1955). 2nd ed. Rio de Janeiro: Forense, 1963.

Silva Filho, Osny da. *Danos morais e punições civis: direito, economia e justiça*. Trabalho de conclusão de curso apresentado à Faculdade de Direito da Universidade de São Paulo, 2012.

Smith, Stephen A. *Contract Theory*. Oxford: Oxford University Press, 2004.

Sunstein, Cass R., et al. *Punitive Damages: How Juries Decide*. Chicago: University of Chicago Press, 2002.

Sunstein, Cass R., David Schkade, and Daniel Kahneman. "Do People Want Optimal Deterrence?" *Journal of Legal Studies* 29 (2000): 237–250.

Tepedino, Gustavo. "O Futuro da Responsabilidade Civil." In *Temas de Direito Civil*. Vol. III. Rio de Janeiro: Renovar, 2009.

Theodoro Júnior, Humberto. *Dano moral* (1998). 4th ed. São Paulo: Juarez de Oliveira, 2001.

Villey, Michel. "Esquisse historique sur le mot 'responsable.'" *Archives de philosophie du droit* 22 (1977): 45–58.

Viscusi, W. Kip. "Do Judges Do Better?" In *Punitive Damages: How Juries Decide*, edited by Cass R. Sunstein et al., 286–209. Chicago: University of Chicago Press, 2002.

Weinrib, Ernest J. *The Idea of Private Law*. Cambridge, MA: Harvard University Press, 1995.

Zavascki, Teori Albino. *Processo coletivo: tutela de direitos coletivos e tutela coletiva de direitos* (2006). 4th ed. São Paulo: Revista dos Tribunais, 2009.

Zipursky, Benjamin C. "Palsgraf, Punitive Damages, and Preemption." *Harvard Law Review* 125 (2012): 1757–1797.

Index

Lightning Source UK Ltd.
Milton Keynes UK
UKOW06n2333100315

247628UK00005B/62/P